Praise for Divorce, Simply Stated[1]

SAREZKY SKILLFULLY MAPS THE GEOGRAPHY OF DIVORCE... *Sarezky also displays sensitivity to the emotional devastation caused by the process.* ALWAYS, HE SUGGESTS AVENUES TO MINIMIZE THE HURT. ... WRITTEN IN CLEAR, EASILY UNDERSTANDABLE LANGUAGE, THIS BOOK IS A HIGHLY VALUABLE RESOURCE *for anyone facing the many challenges of divorce.*
Booklist (reprint from BlueInk Review)

"FROM THE KIND OF DIVORCE LAWYER ANYONE WOULD WANT: funny, kind, laser-focused, nonjudgmental, and extremely informative . . . . THE BOOK STANDS OUT FOR ITS CALM, DELIBERATE, AND WINNING TONE, WHICH FEELS BOTH REASSURING AND NURTURING."
Foreword Clarion Reviews

"LARRY SAREZKY HAS WRITTEN SIMPLY THE BEST BOOK OF ITS KIND. Clear, convincing, comprehensive, and straight-forward. A must read for anyone thinking about divorce."
Arthur Balbirer, Esq.; past president
American Academy of Matrimonial Lawyers

"THIS BOOK IS A MASTERPIECE! Only Larry Sarezky could have written a book that contains all the divorce essentials plus priceless strategies for success and savings that you won't find anywhere else. And it's all delivered with caring and soul. If you don't think so, check out the illustrations by Larry's granddaughter designed to remind divorcing parents to attend to their children's needs."
Joanie Winberg, CEO
National Association of Divorce for Women and Children

"LARRY SAREZKY'S WORK IN THE FIELD OF FAMILY LAW IS AWE-INSPIRING! Larry's critically acclaimed film about the realities of child custody battles titled Talk to Strangers *literally brought tears to my eyes. I expected nothing less from this book and he didn't disappoint me. Whether you are divorcing, dissolving a non-marital relationship involving children, attempting to modify post-judgment issues from one of those situations, and whether you intend on representing yourself or working with professionals, this book is a must-read."*
Mark Baer, Esq.
co-author, *Putting Kids First in Divorce*

---

1. The *BlueInk Review* is for the 2nd edition; all others relate to the 1st edition.

"HANDS DOWN, THIS IS THE BEST BOOK OUT THERE when it comes to learning about the divorce process. Larry Sarezky condenses over 35 years of experience as a family law attorney into practical, easy to read advice. . . . IF THERE'S ONLY ONE BOOK TO READ AS YOU PREPARE FOR DIVORCE, THIS IS IT!"
Shawn Leamon, MBA; Certified Divorce Financial Analyst, and Host, Divorce and Your Money podcast series

"If you're divorcing, you must read Larry Sarezky's Divorce, Simply Stated. The nuggets in the chapter on 'Divorce Pearls and Perils' alone will save you thousands of dollars—and your sanity! DIVORCE, SIMPLY STATED *DELIVERS NOT ONLY DIVORCE BASICS BUT A DIVORCE INSIDER'S TIPS AND STRATEGIES YOU CAN ONLY GET FROM LARRY. We know from his Telly Award-winning child custody film,* Talk to Strangers, *that Larry is uniquely devoted to helping parents and children in their hours of greatest need."*
Terry McNiff, Esq.
Author, *Picture Your Divorce to See the Right Decisions*

*"*DIVORCE, SIMPLY STATED *IS THE BOOK TO READ IF YOU'RE LOOKING FOR A CLEAR, WONDERFULLY READABLE EXPLANATION FROM A VETERAN DIVORCE LAWYER WHO CARES! Sarezky provides valuable insight about how the divorce process works - and how you can make it work for you. And he does it with humor and compassion!"*
Rosalind Sedacca, CCT; Divorce & Parenting Coach
Founder, Child-Centered Divorce Network

"Larry represented me in a divorce and again in post-judgment proceedings. As a lawyer myself, I was tremendously impressed with his formidable cross-examination and other legal skills. But what I valued most of all was that Larry always had time to listen and calm me in anxious moments. Anyone reading Divorce, Simply Stated *will be incredibly fortunate to get that same blend of knowledge, wisdom and compassion!"*
Jamie G.
Fairfield County, CT

"I don't know how my young children and I would have survived my divorce without Larry's talent, guidance, and humor while at the same time teaching me much needed life skills. It is exciting to know that Larry will be giving others the benefit of all of that in his new book, Divorce, Simply Stated!*"*
Helen B.
Fairfield County, CT

This Is Not Your Parents' Divorce Book!

*D*ivorce, Simply Stated will empower you to take control of your divorce by maximizing results, reducing costs, and staying in balance during this turbulent time in your life.

With a rare blend of wisdom, wit, and sensitivity, Larry Sarezky explains the mechanics of divorce; principles of divorce law and finance; how to find, afford, and work with the right divorce professionals; how to care for yourself and your children during divorce; and how to avoid the dysfunctional conflict that is encouraged in traditional divorces.

But there's much more to this remarkably frank book. In it, you will learn to recognize dangerous divorce myths, avoid divorce's most common mistakes, take advantage of divorce tax opportunities, and save money by sidestepping rarely discussed attorney billing practices.

Divorce, Simply Stated offers a uniquely refreshing approach to navigating divorce—a 10-year-old illustrator to keep your focus on your children; stress-reducing quizzes that make you laugh while you learn; a golden retriever named "Chuck" to guide you through the divorce thicket; and an array of skills to help you cope, organize, relax, and even sleep better.

Perhaps the most unique feature of *Divorce, Simply Stated* is the compassion with which its author shares 35 years of accumulated wisdom to help you overcome divorce's miseries, unravel its mysteries, and emerge better able to meet the future head-on.

About the Author

Larry Sarezky is one-of-a-kind; an accomplished divorce lawyer who uses award-winning creative skills to improve the lot of divorcing spouses and their children.

A practicing attorney for 35 years, Larry has represented clients from the ranks of Fortune 500 CEOs, Major League Baseball Hall of Famers, and Oscar, Grammy, and Emmy Award winners. During that time, Larry developed an approach to divorce designed to maximize results while minimizing financial and emotional costs. Larry has now made that approach available to the public in his award-winning Amazon #1 best-seller, *Divorce, Simply Stated* which is now in its second, expanded edition.

Throughout his career, Larry has focused on the care and protection of children of divorce. Acting on that concern, Larry wrote and directed the Telly Award-winning short film, *Talk to Strangers,* and wrote its companion guide to help both parents and professionals prevent the harm to children caused by unnecessary child-related litigation. The highly acclaimed film, which is being co-distributed by the American Academy of Matrimonial Lawyers, is currently in use for that purpose throughout the United States and abroad.

Larry has sought to improve the divorce experience in many other ways as well. In 2002, while serving as Chair of the Connecticut Bar Association's Family Law Section, he designed a program to provide divorcing spouses pro bono representation by young lawyers mentored by seasoned matrimonial attorneys. The next year, Connecticut Supreme Court Justice Peter Zarella enlisted Larry's help to secure confidentiality for divorcing spouses' financial affidavits, distributing one of Larry's legal commentaries to each of the state's family judges.

Larry's articles on divorce have appeared in *The Huffington Post,* divorcedmoms.com, ezinearticles.com, and numerous other online venues as well as in professional and consumer publications. Larry has spoken on divorce issues to judges, lawyers, mental health professionals, and consumers throughout the U.S., and has presented *Talk to Strangers* at national meetings of the American Academy of Matrimonial Lawyers, the American Psychoanalytic Association, and the Association of Family and Conciliation Courts. Larry is a member of The American Bar Association, The Association for Conflict Resolution, and The Association of Family and Conciliation Courts.

DIVORCE, SIMPLY STATED,

How to Achieve More, Worry Less, and Save Money in Your Divorce

LARRY SAREZKY, ESQ.

Illustrations by Laila Sarezky

Divorce, Simply Stated, 2nd Edition
How to Achieve More, Worry Less, and Save Money in Your Divorce
21st Century Divorce Books
A division of When We Were Nine Productions, LLC
180 Inwood Road
Fairfield, CT 06825
http://www.21stCenturyDivorceBooks.com

Illustrations by Laila Sarezky
Graphics by Ethan Sarezky
Cover design by Lewis Agrell: lagrell@commspeed.net

Library of Congress Control Number: 2018901566

Names: Sarezky, Larry, author.

Title: Divorce, simply stated : how to achieve more, worry less, and save money in your divorce / Larry Sarezky.

Description: Second edition. | Fairfield, CT : 21st Century Divorce Books, [2019] | Includes bibliographical references.

Identifiers: ISBN: 978-9963809-5-9 | LCCN: 2018901566

Subjects: LCSH: Divorce--Law and legislation--United States. | Divorce suits--United States. | Divorce settlements--United States. | Divorce mediation--United States. | No-fault divorce--United States. | Matrimonial actions--United States. | Alimony--United States. | Custody of children--United States. | Child support--Law and legislation--United States. | Equitable distribution of marital property--United States. | Divorce--United States--Costs. | Divorce--Taxation--United States. | Trials (Divorce)--United States. | BISAC: FAMILY & RELATIONSHIPS / Divorce & Separation.

A catalog record of this publication is available through the Library of Congress.

Printed in the United States of America

10 9 8 7 6 5 4 3 2 1

To Chuck ...

For staying by my side for as long as he could while I worked on this book, taking me outside to play catch when I needed a break, and being so wonderfully, immutably in the moment.

Chuck 9/12/03 — 1/16/14

This book has website support!
Visit www.DivorceSimplyStated.com for
free supplements, updates and additional
divorce resources.

Acknowledgments

My thanks to all those who gave so generously of their time to help me navigate this book through vast and uncharted seas: Clara Batista, Gabriella Cascante, Attorney Jamie Gerard, Brenda Grover, Attorney Deb Grover, Mike Klassen, Attorney Rick Kurshner, Rita Mockler, Sharon Mulligan, Shawn Munday, Amy Rizzo, Ethan Sarezky, and Attorney David Urubshurow.

And special thanks to Attorney Mark Baer for making this book better; to Roz Sedacca, Rick Lite and Amy Collins for their kindness and skill in moving the project forward; to my friends Diana Cicero and Attorney Kirk Bennett for their sage advice and assistance; to my teachers Kittisaro and Thanissara for their boundless wisdom; and to my wife Sheryl who no doubt considered seeking a divorce on the grounds of intolerably endless book editing.

Important Notice to Readers of This Book

LIMITATION OF LIABILITY AND DISCLAIMER OF WARRANTY

The law and its interpretation, procedure, and customs regarding divorce and other aspects of family law issues differ significantly among the jurisdictions within the United States and between the United States and other nations. Law, procedure, and customs mentioned in this book apply differently to different facts and may have changed since this writing. Divorce-related and other laws, procedures and customs referenced in this book are intended only as examples of variations among United States jurisdictions.

This book is intended to provide general information regarding the subjects covered within it. It is made available to readers on the express condition, and with the understanding that the author is not rendering legal, accounting, financial, or counseling services. The author, publisher, contributors, and endorsers are not responsible for nor shall be liable for damages arising from, and make no representations regarding the accuracy or completeness of material contained in this book nor appearing at divorcesimplystated.com, witnesstutor.com, 21stcenturydivorce.com, divorceresourcessite.com, childcustodyfilm.com, larrysarezky.com, or linked websites; or the accuracy or completeness of material or the quality of products mentioned at those or other websites or in other resources referenced in this book. The author and publisher expressly disclaim all warranties regarding the accuracy or completeness of such material or the quality or fitness of such products, including but not limited to warranty of fitness for a particular purpose. No warranties shall be deemed to be extended, offered, or created by any material promoting or supplementing this book.

No portion of this book should be considered advice regarding the reader's situation or pending family case, or to be substituted for advice and counsel from an experienced matrimonial attorney licensed by the relevant jurisdiction, or other qualified financial, tax, and mental health professionals. It is the reader's responsibility to seek such advice when necessary.

Summary of Contents

Contents

Getting the Most Out of This Book

Why I Worry About Your Divorce

During 35 years as a lawyer and mediator, I've seen too many people achieve too little in their divorces, while spending and suffering far too much. I don't want that to happen to you, and I wrote this book so that it won't.

A lot can go wrong during divorce, to be sure. Some folks damage their prospects right off the bat by choosing the wrong lawyer, the wrong kind of divorce (yes, you have a choice!), or the wrong divorce goals. Others make poor decisions based on emotion rather than logic. Still others, overwhelmed by anxiety or cost, abandon their goals too early and easily.

And there are even more mistakes that are made much too often. Parents with solvable child-related disputes endanger their children's emotional health by choosing court battles over cooperative problem solving. Self-represented spouses, and even those with attorneys, hurt themselves in court with poorly prepared paperwork and testimony that damages their cases.

This book shows you how to avoid those kinds of mistakes with methods I've used for my clients over the last 35 years.

But you'll learn much more than how to avoid mistakes. The material in the pages that follow will prepare you to reach your goals at the least financial and emotional cost to you and your children.

For example, you'll learn how mediation works. Then you'll find out how to maximize your mediation outcome by finding a qualified mediator, formulating a mediation game plan, and being able to stick to that plan.

What's In This Book?

You will find two types of information in this book:
1. The legal rules and financial principles that decide family court cases
2. Strategies and tips for using those rules and principles to reach your goals

Some of that material cannot be found in any other book of this kind, because despite its title, this is not a dumbed-down divorce how-to. To the contrary, the "simply" in *Divorce, Simply Stated* refers not to the type of matters covered, but how they're explained. I would be cheating you, the reader, if I left out material just because it might be difficult. But don't worry! Even if—despite my best efforts—you don't fully understand something you read, you will have been alerted to an area where you may need the resources provided in Chapter 18 and elsewhere to get help.

For example, let's say you feel you're entitled to a share of your spouse's pension. You don't necessarily need to know how to value the pension or even which of the kinds of pensions discussed in Chapter 13, it is. It's enough to know that there *are* different kinds of pensions, and that many require an expert to value them and prepare documentation to ensure that you get your fair share.

In short, I've tried to cover the range of divorce issues you're most likely to encounter. Again, you don't need to master all of that. Just knowing that a topic might be relevant to your case will enable you to ask the right questions and get the help you need. And that alone will put you way ahead of the pack!

What's in a List?

You'll need to use your time, money, and energy efficiently to achieve your divorce goals. That begins with the learning process in this book. To help you learn efficiently about divorce, I make frequent use of lists to convey information. Much as a straight line is the shortest distance between two points, lists deliver the most information in the fewest words. That's efficient—or put another way—that's *Divorce, Simply Stated.*

More specifically, the lists in this book will help you:
- Select and work efficiently with skilled divorce professionals
- Decide if mediation or other alternative dispute resolution (ADR) methods are right for you
- Choose realistic divorce goals by getting an idea of the range of likely outcomes in your case
- Increase your chances to achieve your goals by becoming an effective advocate for yourself
- Learn the details of how divorce works in your state
- Enhance the value of your divorce outcome by, for example,
    - Taking full advantage of tax breaks and other divorce "break-upportunities"
    - Identifying hidden costs that can erode the value of property you receive in your settlement
    - Discovering your spouse's undisclosed income
    - Avoiding excessive legal fees by
        - Discovering the "bargain table" of quality divorce lawyers
        - Paying lawyers only for services you need
        - Using non-lawyers who charge substantially less than lawyers
        - Becoming your own paralegal

And if you doubted the efficiency of lists to convey information, consider how much is contained in the one you just read.

Some of the lists you'll see summarize typical state laws regarding child support guidelines, spousal support formulas, "marital property" definitions, grandparents' rights, and numerous other divorce and custody case issues. The lists do not contain the laws of every state. Instead, they illustrate common approaches to issues that arise frequently in family court cases. That information will enable you to identify what more you need to learn about your state's laws.

To help you get any state-specific information that you might need (and to access your state's court forms), you'll have the following tools:
- Links found in Chapter 18 in the section called "Resources For Federal and State Family Law, and For Making Sound Divorce Decisions"

• Appendix 6, a page index of each mention of specific state laws

Notwithstanding these tools, I will remind you periodically—including right now—that your best source of information regarding your state's law is an experienced local matrimonial lawyer.

What's So Funny About Divorce? (Nothing.)

Q. What's so funny about divorce?

A. Nothing.

So what's with the jokes and silly dog photos sprinkled through the chapters, and dopey (yet instructive) quizzes at the end of them?

The silliness in this book is meant to give you a break from the bleakness of divorce, and ... despite my best efforts ... the boredom you might feel while reading about it.

The occasional dopiness is not meant to make light of what you're going through. Quite the opposite; it's there in recognition of how miserable divorce can be and the importance of getting some relief from it.

Laughter may not always be the best medicine, but psychoneuro-immunological research suggests that it does reduce stress, and can even boost the immune system![1] And hardly anyone questions that research—at least not out loud—since hardly anyone can pronounce "psychoneuroimmunological."

I've used humor over the years to assist struggling clients to get through rough patches, to keep things in perspective for my clients (and myself), and even to navigate settlement negotiations through choppy seas. Still, I understand that the humor in this book may not work for you. So I've tagged it with one of these smiling faces, so that if you're not in the mood, you can just skip it:

---

1. *Alternative Therapies in Health and Medicine 2003 Mar-Apr; 9(2): 38-45.*

In case you're wondering, that dog is Chuck, my loyal companion while I wrote this book.[2] You'll see some more photos of Chuck from time to time, also intended to give you a healthy . . . Chuckle.

Chuck's Selfie

Whether or not you feel like chuckling during this very unfunny phase of your life, use the silly stuff as a reminder that you need breaks from your divorce. Catch a movie, go on a hike, drop in on a meditation group, YouTube some Too Cute pet clips, binge-watch last season's Grey's Anatomy—whatever it takes for you to get the relaxation you need to stay in balance.

You owe that to yourself—and to your kids.

Speaking of Your Children . . .

The well-being of my clients' children has always been a priority for me in my law practice, and it remains so in this book. In that spirit, I'll be reminding you from time to time to stay focused on your kids. Children need not be harmed by divorce—conscientious, mindful parents can prevent that.[3]

You might feel that you don't need me to remind you to look after your children. And you might be right. But I've seen the most well intentioned divorcing parents become preoccupied with their own concerns, and lose sight of what's best for the young ones around them.

Laila's selfie portrait

With that in mind, I've illustrated this book with pictures drawn in school by my then 9-year-old granddaughter Laila—a gentle soul offering you gentle reminders of what matters most.

---

2. Sadly, Chuck passed away while this book was being completed. There might be a better dog somewhere out there, but you couldn't prove it by me.

3. From time to time I will refer to *Talk to Strangers*, a short film I made to discourage parents from subjecting their children to custody and access battles. Visit www.ChildCustodyFilm.com to preview the film and its companion parents' guide, and to stream or buy the DVD.

Break-Upportunities

After you've completed your divorce journey, you may realize how much you've learned along the way about matters besides divorce—things like personal finance, parenting, handling conflict and other adversity ... and about yourself.

Though it might be difficult to imagine while you're in the thick of it, divorce can provide extraordinary opportunities for learning and personal growth. Over the years, I've enjoyed watching people acquire insights, knowledge, and skills that served them well during their divorces and long afterward.

It's my sincerest hope that this book helps you become one of those people.

Finally, if you visit www.DivorceSimplyStated.com for the free updates and supplements available there, use the "Contact Us" page to email me and let me know how you're doing, how this book helped you, or how you think it might be improved for those who use it after you. I'd love to hear from you!

I sincerely wish you all the best of luck.

Larry Sarezky
Fairfield, CT

CHAPTER 1

Ending a Dysfunctional Marriage With a Functional Divorce

"I am not afraid of storms for I am learning how to sail my ship."

— Louisa May Alcott

The Functional Divorce

In this chapter we begin gathering the tools necessary to end a dysfunctional marriage with a "functional divorce." A functional divorce achieves reasonable goals at the least financial and emotional cost to you and your children. That game requires two willing players (you and your spouse) who will:

- Agree upon ground rules to communicate productively, and protect your children from the harmful impact of a high-conflict divorce[1]
- Formulate reasonable goals
- Share all necessary information and documents necessary for a fair and efficient resolution of all issues

What you read in this and the chapters that follow will help you accomplish a functional divorce by:

- Making your children's needs a priority
- Helping you find affordable divorce professionals who meet your needs
- Showing how to use lawyers creatively to get more for less
- Showing how to save money using the tax code
- Showing how settlement agreement language and seemingly small adjustments can protect you and maximize your divorce results
- Showing you how to reach a fair agreement that both spouses will want to uphold
- Providing you with resources to find

---

1. See Chapter 10.

ᵒ Additional information about your state's divorce laws
ᵒ Local lawyers and other professionals
- Reducing your and your children's stress by
  ᵒ Demystifying divorce
  ᵒ Enabling you to handle whatever arises during your divorce

Deciding When to File

The decision to "file for divorce" is a momentous and emotionally challenging one. As if that weren't difficult enough, deciding when to file involves a number of considerations, namely:
- Whether you are emotionally prepared to proceed and have identified a therapist or divorce coach who you (and your children) can see if necessary
- Whether reasonable attempts to save the marriage have been exhausted
- Whether you have decided between a "court-based" or alternative dispute resolution divorce
- Whether you have chosen, or at least consulted, a lawyer or mediator
- Whether you have begun the document gathering and other work described in this chapter
- Whether you have reached out to other professionals you may need, such as divorce coaches and divorce financial analysts

Filing Now

If the answer to all of the above is "yes" and you still haven't filed, you may simply be procrastinating. That's certainly understandable given the magnitude of the decision you are making. However, delay might not serve your interests. Below are some reasons you might not want to wait:
- Filing protects you by activating automatic court orders prohibiting your STBX (soon-to-be-ex) . . . and you . . . from taking unilateral action regarding finances or your children
- If you wait to file and do not finalize your divorce until 2019, you won't be able to use alimony to save taxes
- Filing begins resolution of conflict that is stressful for you and your children
- Filing starts the clock ticking toward the beginning of the rest of your life

Filing Later

On the other hand, there may be reasons to put off filing, such as:

It's not uncommon to be on the fence about filing for divorce.

- You want to wait in order to delay the beginning of the 3-year post-divorce period during which federal law ("ERISA") guarantees availability of health insurance comparable to your current coverage through your spouse's employment.
- Your marriage is nearing the 10-year mark and you wish to preserve your rights to Social Security retirement benefits based on your spouse's income (rather than yours). You can become entitled to those benefits if:
  - ○ You claim benefits after a marriage of at least 10 years
  - ○ You claim benefits at least 2 years after that 10-year marriage
  - ○ You and your former spouse are both over 62
  - ○ You are not remarried at the time you apply for benefits
  - ○ You are not already receiving Social Security benefits
- Your marriage is nearing the 10-year mark throughout which time your spouse has been in military service and you want to preserve your rights to military retirement pay and to receive enforcement assistance through the Department of Defense under The Uniformed Services Former Spouses Protection Act (USFSPA). [2]
- Your marriage is nearing the 20-year mark throughout which time your spouse has been on active duty and remains in the military, entitling you to full USFSPA benefits.[3]
- You want to still be married on the last day of the year in order to preserve your right to file a joint tax return.

Alternatives to Divorce

There are two ways for spouses to resolve support, property, and child-related matters without filing for an "absolute divorce":

---

2. The Uniformed Services Former Spouses' Protection Act (USFSPA), 10 U.S.C. 1408 et seq.

3. *Ibid.*

- Filing for a "Legal Separation." If you are hesitant to initiate a divorce action, consult an attorney about commencing a "legal separation" or "limited divorce" action that will resolve all issues just as a divorce or "dissolution of marriage" case does. In most states, these cases can be easily converted to a divorce, so you don't have to start over if you decide you want a divorce. Also, if your STBX wishes to file for divorce by way of a "counterclaim" or "cross-complaint," the case will then proceed as a divorce action.
- Signing a "Prenuptial" or "Postnuptial" Agreement. These marital agreements settle support, property, and children's issues much in the same way that a divorce settlement agreement does. The differences are that:
  - Because there are no orders from a court, spouses seeking to enforce such agreements will not be able to initiate contempt of court proceedings that divorced individuals use for expedited access to the courts. Instead, enforcement would require a new lawsuit to enforce the agreement just like any other contract. And that could take several years.
  - If spouses later decide to incorporate a marital agreement into a divorce decree, a court usually must find that the agreement:
    - Was fair at the time it was signed
    - Remains fair under the circumstances existing at the time it is presented to the court for incorporation into a dissolution decree

See Chapter 12 for more on pre- and post-nuptial agreements.

States with statutes or case law (court decisions) that have been interpreted to approve marital agreements are: Alabama, Alaska, Arkansas, California, Colorado, Connecticut, Delaware, Florida, Georgia, Idaho, Illinois, Indiana, Kansas, Kentucky, Louisiana, Maryland, Massachusetts, Minnesota, Mississippi, Missouri, Montana, Nebraska, Nevada and New York.

Residence Requirements

One good reason not to file for divorce is that you can't. Nearly every state requires that one of the parties reside in the state for a minimum period before divorce proceedings may be commenced or judgment is entered. Those requirements are as follows:

- 12 months: Connecticut, Iowa, Maryland, Massachusetts, Nebraska, New Hampshire, New Jersey, New York, Rhode Island, South Carolina, West Virginia
- 6 months: Alabama, California, Delaware, District of Columbia, Florida, Georgia, Hawaii, Indiana, Kentucky, Louisiana, Maine, Michigan, Minnesota, Mississippi, New Mexico, North Carolina, North Dakota, Ohio, Oklahoma, Oregon, Pennsylvania, Tennessee, Texas, Vermont, Virginia, Wisconsin
- 3 months: Arizona, Colorado, Illinois, Missouri, Montana, Utah
- 2 months: Arkansas, Kansas, Wyoming
- 6 weeks: Idaho, Nevada
- No statutory requirement: Alaska, South Dakota, Washington

Some states also require a couple to be separated before filing for divorce. For example, Maryland and New Jersey require separation periods of 12 and 6 months respectively before filing. Such periods are not to be confused with "cooling off" periods that many states require after a divorce is filed. In those states, a divorce can't be obtained until after a specified period.

For example:

- California—6 months
- Connecticut—3 months
- Michigan—2 months
- Rhode Island—5 months
- Texas—2 months
- Vermont—3 months

Quickie Divorces

States such as California and Connecticut offer expedited or "summary divorces" for short-term marriages with no children, very limited assets, and where neither spouse owns real estate.

Parenting During Divorce

A functional divorce in families with children must begin with those children. Decisions regarding them must be governed by the children's—not your—best interests. Your conduct should be guided by the children's well-being, not your parental "rights."

More on Divorce Parenting

In Chapter 10 you'll find pointers on parenting during divorce, including:
- Do's and Don'ts of Divorce Parenting
- Do's and Don'ts of Breaking the News to the Kids
- Questions Your Children May Ask About Your Divorce

The 10 Steps to a Functional Divorce

Functional divorces require planning. Each of the following 10 steps to a functional divorce is discussed in more detail below.

- Obtaining Professional Advice
- Protecting Yourself with Automatic Restraining Orders
- Protecting Yourself Financially and from Violent Confrontations
- Thinking About Your Divorce Goals
- Locating Key Documents
- Beginning to Plan for the Future
- Creating a Paper Trail to Success
- Educating Yourself About Divorce in Your State
- Caring for Your Children
- Caring for Yourself

Obtaining Professional Advice

Even if you don't feel that you can afford an attorney or other divorce professional, try to consult with one or more of the following anyway. If you can only meet with one, choose a lawyer who is experienced in both traditional divorce and alternative dispute resolution (ADR), which is discussed in Chapter 5.

- Divorce Lawyers: An hour and a half or so with a local divorce lawyer can be hugely informative. It might also help eliminate those 3:00 AM anxiety attacks. Download from www.divorcesimplystated.com the Initial Consultation Checklist (ICC) and Statutory Criteria Summary (SCS) that appear in Appendices 1 and 2 to this book. You can make your initial consultation much more productive by bringing a filled-out SCS with you, and selecting a few questions from the ICC to ask. Always ask the lawyer about the benefits of ADR.

- Mediators and Collaborative Divorce Lawyers: ADR should always be considered for a more efficient and less stressful divorce.
- Certified Divorce Financial Analysts (CDFAs) and Certified Financial Divorce Practitioners (CFDPs): CDFA/CFDPs provide financial advice for less than lawyers charge. They can help with organizing finances, preparing disclosure statements, understanding tax and retirement plan issues, and projecting the impact of settlement alternatives. As discussed in Chapters 3 and 6, you may save even more by having some of this work done before hiring a lawyer.
- Mental Health Professionals: Consider checking in with a therapist both for your benefit and the benefit of those around you. If you notice any behavioral changes in your children such as declining grades or changes in eating or sleeping patterns, consider counseling for them.
- Certified Divorce Coaches (CDCs): Although not a substitute for an attorney, mediator, CDFA, or CFDP, a CDC can help you:
  - Manage emotions
  - Communicate goals
  - Maximize your attorney/client relationship
  - Transition to post-divorce life
- Forensic and Other Experts: Generally, the decision to retain an expert comes later, with the advice of your lawyer. However, you should be aware of the following experts who are sometimes needed in divorce cases:

A consultation with a divorce professional can help relieve some of the anxiety that keeps you up at night.

  - Actuaries used primarily to value defined benefit pensions
  - Accountants to explain (or analyze) tax returns and "financials" of a self-employed spouse's business
  - Business appraisers to
    - Calculate the value of a business interest
    - Calculate the actual compensation a spouse receives from a business

    ○ Personal property appraisers to establish values for antiques,
       artwork, collectibles, or technical equipment
    ○ Real estate appraisers
    ○ Vocational experts and forensic accountants to determine earn-
       ings potential that courts can impute to voluntarily unemployed
       or under-employed spouses
    ○ Forensic psychologists and other mental health professionals
       to evaluate fitness of parents (and sometimes grandparents and
       other third parties) in child custody and access cases
    ○ Computer forensic experts to recover and analyze data that has
       been deleted or otherwise lost from electronic devices

Why Is There So Much Bad Advice Out There?

The good news is there is a wealth of advice available about divorce.

The bad news is there is a wealth of advice available about divorce.

You'll hear a lot about divorce from well-meaning friends, family, and members of divorce support groups. And you'll look at blogs, articles, and unnerving official-looking websites. Information from all of those sources is often misleading because it is offered:
- With no knowledge of the facts of your case
- With no knowledge or little understanding of the relevant laws in your state
- By friends and family members who care dearly about you and whose advice is biased as a result
- By folks who will care dearly about you (briefly) after you buy their products or services, help promote their causes, or "like," "follow," or listen to them grouse about their own divorce experiences

In this Chapter and in Chapters 2–4, we will address the "bad advice problem" by:
- Clearing up common misconceptions about divorce (Chapter 2)
- Sharing basic truths about divorce (Chapter 3)
- Helping you find a competent, affordable lawyer who knows how to apply your state's law to the facts of your case (Chapter 4)

In deciding whether to accept a particular piece of advice, ask yourself if:
- The advice is designed more to make you feel better than to help you achieve your goals
- The advice is consistent with principles that are important to you, such as
  - Protecting your children from your conflict with your spouse
  - The desire for fairness
- There are other options that
  - Are less stressful to you and your children
  - Move you more efficiently (and less expensively) toward your goals

Protecting Yourself With Automatic Restraining Orders

In most states, "restraining" or "injunctive" orders take effect automatically upon the filing of a divorce or legal separation case. These orders are designed to prevent either party from:
- Gaining advantage over the other
- Taking action that alters finances
- Taking action that alters children's living circumstances

In situations where one spouse might try to hide money, transfer property, or act irresponsibly regarding the children, automatic orders are a good reason to file for divorce sooner rather than later. These orders typically prohibit:
- Selling, transferring, concealing, wasting, dissipating or encumbering (e.g., borrowing against) marital property
- Failing to maintain, modifying, changing beneficiaries, or assigning life, health, disability, homeowners, or automobile insurance policies
- Spending or incurring debt except in payment of ordinary and normal expenses and attorneys' fees related to the divorce
- Relocating children, except if they are at risk, without written permission of the other parent
- Harassment of the other party
- Destroying, hiding, or spoiling potential evidence including electronically stored material

Some spouses use the period before a divorce is filed to buy big-ticket items, squander or hide cash and other property, or run up debt. Depending upon the severity of the situation, you may need—with a lawyer's advice—to take drastic steps to protect yourself from such conduct, by:

- Freezing or closing joint credit card accounts and home equity credit lines
- Placing in an account in your name
    - 50% of joint bank accounts
    - 50% of available home equity line credit
- Preserving (or improving) your credit rating by arranging with your STBX to pay bills on time
- Triggering automatic restraining orders by commencing a divorce or legal separation action
- Filing a motion for temporary support and contribution to attorneys' fees
- Placing in a safe place items with substantial monetary or nostalgic value

Protecting Yourself From Violence

If you have been the victim of violence in the past or feel that your spouse may become violent, call 911 at the very first sign that you may be in danger. But before things get to that point, protect yourself as follows:

- Inquire at your local courthouse about protective or "restraining" orders that can keep your spouse away from you. Note that under federal law, one who is the subject of a domestic violence protective order cannot possess a firearm while the order is in effect.[4] If you seek a protective order against a gun owner, bring this issue to the court's attention.
- Reach out to additional resources such as:
    - Your local domestic abuse hotline for information regarding local facilities and resources available to violence victims
    - National Domestic Coalition against Domestic Violence State Coalition list for local resources, at https://ncadv.org/state-coalitions.
    - The National Domestic Violence Hotline at www.thehotline.org

---

4. U.S. Code sec. 922(g)(8). Protective orders should never be sought frivolously as they can have lasting emotional impact on children, and can affect job prospects, etc. of those subject to them.

- If you feel violence may be imminent and you cannot move elsewhere:
    ○ Keep your cell phone with you at all times.
    ○ Keep a spare car key concealed with you or near your car.
    ○ Establish a code word for texting or calling family members, trusted friends, or co-workers that will prompt them to call for help.
    ○ Secure your computer with a code.
    ○ Choose a room in your home with outside access if possible, for you (and your children) to go in a threatening situation.
    ○ Store with a trusted friend or family member items such as:
        ▪ Jewelry and other valuables
        ▪ Important documents
        ▪ Evidence of past abuse
    ○ Keep key items such as credit cards and your social security card in a safe place that you can access quickly in an emergency.
    ○ Arrange with a friend to take you (and your children) in.

Thinking About Your Divorce Goals

It's not too soon to think about what you want to get out of your divorce … besides getting out of your marriage. Below is a list of matters commonly resolved in divorce cases. The "Big Three,"—child-related issues, support, and property distribution—will be covered in subsequent chapters. So don't freak out because you don't know what everything means. That's what the rest of this book is for.

Many of the issues listed will not apply to your case. And there are likely to be some minor details of your case that don't appear on the list. Don't worry about that now. Just scan the list and as you continue to learn about divorce, return to these pages and use them as a checklist to make sure you've "covered all the bases." You can download and print the list at www.DivorceSimplyStated.com.

Child-Related Issues

- Legal Custody (decision-making regarding children)
- Joint vs. Sole Custody
    ○ Major decisions
        ▪ General health and well-being
        ▪ Education

- Religious training
  - Day-to-day decisions
  - Whether either parent has the sole right to make specific decisions
- Physical Custody
  - Joint vs. Sole Custody/Primary Residence
- Parenting Plan Schedules
  - School year weekend and midweek time
  - School year vacations
  - Holidays and three-day weekends
  - Summer vacation
  - Special days: Mother's and Father's Days, parents' birthdays, children's birthdays, traditional family gatherings
  - Access to and communication with children
  - Transportation of children to and from the parents' homes
- Relocation of custodial parent with children
  - Notice requirements
  - Prohibition of move without written agreement or court order
  - Defining geographical area within which agreement or court order is not required
- Other Considerations
  - Nurturing parental relationship with both parents
  - Communications with and about children
  - Transportation
  - Significant Others
    - Grandparents and other third-party access
    - Appropriate role of subsequent spouses

Support Issues

- Spousal Support
  - Amount
    - Flat periodic payments
    - Support as a percentage of obligor's (the spouse paying support) income
    - "Base" (minimum) flat amount plus percentage of income exceeding a certain amount
    - Alimony (tax deductible spousal support until 2019)
      - Tax considerations and I.R.C. recapture risks

- Unallocated alimony and support (single tax deductible payment that includes both child and spousal support)
- Support "floors" (an agreed-upon minimum amount of support)
- Income "caps" or "ceilings" on the amount of the obligor's income that will be subject to spousal support
- "Safe harbors": Income increases that cannot trigger, or be considered in, post-judgment modification proceedings such as, for example
  - New income of a spouse who is reentering the workforce
  - Anticipated increase in obligor's income already factored into agreed-upon alimony[5] amount
- Health insurance—COBRA rights to equivalent coverage for 3 years (at additional cost)
- Duration of spousal support
  - Transitional ("rehabilitative") and compensatory spousal support
  - Permanent spousal support
  - Statutory rights to modification due to changes in circumstances, unless limited or prohibited by parties' agreement
  - Nominal alimony ($1 per year) that allows the court to modify if there is a substantial change of circumstances in the future
  - "Wedding Gift": Spousal support payoff or continuing alimony after remarriage in rare circumstances such as when recipient's remarriage is anticipated
- Modification upon substantial change in circumstances
  - Limits on modification
  - Termination, modification, or suspension upon cohabitation by recipient
- Child support
  - Child Support Guidelines mandated in every state
    - Deviation criteria for orders outside of the Guidelines
    - Per child amount that allows for automatic reduction upon older children attaining majority; vs. Single amount for several children that may require renegotiation

---

5. From time to time in this book, the term "alimony" may be used interchangeably with "spousal support" or "maintenance," as state statutes use all three. Alimony under federal law means spousal support that qualified prior to 2019 for special tax treatment. See Chapters 9 and 12

- ° Duration
- ° Modification upon substantial change in circumstances
- ° "Extras" (e.g. camp, extracurricular expenses, etc.)
- ° Private school/college obligations
  - ▪ Funding plans (e.g. 529 education accounts)
- ° Allocation of responsibility for children's health insurance
- Life insurance on "obligor's" life to insure spousal and child support
  - ° Allocation of benefits between children and spouse
  - ° Designation of personal representative to receive life insurance proceeds for minor children
  - ° Reductions of required coverage over time as the amount of remaining support obligation declines

Property Issues

- Property Distribution
  - ° Identification and valuation of "marital property" that can be distributed by the court
  - ° Identification and valuation of separate or "non-marital" property
    - ▪ Date of acquisition (before or after marriage)
    - ▪ Nature of property (e.g., inheritance, gift, etc.)
    - ▪ "Transmutation" of non-marital property to "marital property" e.g., through comingling of funds or augmentation of an asset's value with joint funds or other contributions
  - ° Occupancy of the family home after the divorce
    - ▪ Ownership
      - ▪ Legal effect of divorce on joint ownership and rights of survivorship
      - ▪ Transfer of interest in real estate in return for a mortgage note and mortgage deed that "secures" the transferring spouse's claim to a percentage of the proceeds of the property
    - ▪ Allocation of responsibility for pre-sale "fix-up" expenses, necessary repairs and capital improvements
    - ▪ Mechanisms to resolve disputes
    - ▪ Buy-out provisions
  - ° Valuation, vesting, and tax issues regarding pensions and other pre-tax assets such as 401(k) plan, IRAs, stock options, and stock plans

- ○ Personal property
  - ▪ Personal effects
  - ▪ Valuables (e.g. antiques, artwork, and collectibles)
  - ▪ The rest of the stuff
- ○ Valuation of spouse's business
  - ▪ Whether minority or marketability discounts apply
  - ▪ Whether valuation would "double dip" spousal support
  - ▪ Whether a business's "Good will" should be valued
- ○ Trusts
  - ▪ Established by spouse for benefit of children or third parties
  - ▪ Established for others for benefit of a spouse
- ○ Life insurance surrender value
- ○ Frequent flyer rewards points
- ○ Digital assets such as
  - ▪ Websites
  - ▪ Domain names
- ○ Allocation of debt between the parties
  - ▪ Credit cards, credit lines, etc.
  - ▪ Indemnification of other spouse by the spouse who's responsible for a debt

Miscellaneous Issues

- Taxes

Don't sacrifice long-term needs to scratch a momentary itch.

  - ○ Allocation of exemptions and child tax credits between parents
  - ○ Entitlement to refunds: obligations for payment regarding past and future joint returns
  - ○ Entitlement to deductions (e.g. mortgage interest, property tax, and charitable contributions)
- Professional fees
  - ○ Contribution by one spouse to attorneys' fees of other spouse
  - ○ Allocation of other professional fees

A Sample Goals Statement

Writing a Goals Statement can help you prioritize your needs. Use the following as an example.[6]

- Shield the kids from our conflict
- Divide our time with the kids in a practical way that doesn't cause them hardship
- Decide if the kids might benefit from counseling
- Alimony thru summer after J.'s high school graduation
- Split cost of kids' extra-curriculars, camp, tutoring, religious training, 60% STBX and 40% me
- We each contribute to college tuition and room and board according to our abilities at the time
- Divide property 50/50, except I get my USB account (including inherited money)
- We each pay our own credit cards and divide the joint Visa evenly
- Give court "continuing jurisdiction" to resolve disputes re sale of the house after the divorce
- Split 50/50 necessary house repairs and roof work if necessary
- Determine off-the-books cash receipts in STBX's business—need expert?
- If there's an IRS audit, protect me from deficiencies resulting from STBX's business
- Protection for me if STBX files for bankruptcy
- Prevent any new home equity line borrowing
- Life insurance to insure support
- Provide for kids' health insurance & non-covered medical expenses.

Deciding on Your Divorce Goals

Once you have familiarized yourself with the issues requiring resolution in your case (and have learned more about them), you can decide how you'd like to resolve them. When that time comes, use the following approach to formulate your goals, together with the detailed material on negotiation in Chapter 14:

- Think long term: Consider what will matter to you 3, 5, and 10 years from now, rather than focusing only upon immediate cash flow or other current problems.
- Consult with an attorney: Even if you plan to represent yourself or use alternative dispute resolution (ADR) methods such as mediation, consult a divorce lawyer for assistance in formulating goals

---

6. Note: Items in this Goals Statement are examples only, and may not apply to your case.

that are realistic in light of your circumstances and your state's laws. Straying too far from the likely range of outcomes can prolong or doom attempts to negotiate settlement. Discuss with the attorney whether the following common outcomes are likely in your case, and whether you might be able to do better:

- ○ Roughly equal division of marital property in long-term first marriages or "principal" marriages that produced children
- ○ Restoration of pre-marriage financial positions in short-term marriages (equitable distribution states)[7]
- ○ Duration of spousal support consistent with your state's law and customs
- ○ Child support per your state's Child Support Guidelines

• Prioritize your goals: You are highly unlikely to achieve all of your goals, so decide which are the most essential, and which can be "horse-traded" or abandoned if necessary during settlement negotiation.

• ⚠ Emphasize needs over positions: For example, if you wish to maximize your time with your children whose primary residence will be with your STBX, you might decide to demand "joint custody." Joint custody is a "position." Your "interest" is to have as much time with your children as possible. Focus on the latter and avoid problematic labels like "joint custody."

• Familiarize yourself with legal terms: Learn some "Lawglish" words like "permanent alimony" and "marital property" so that you ...
- ○ Understand the legal advice you receive
- ○ Don't take positions based on a misunderstanding of legal terms
- ○ Don't misunderstand your STBX's positions

Locating Key Documents

Documents have a habit of disappearing once talk about divorce begins. To avoid that, locate and

Gather vital paperwork without delay!

---

7. The differences between equitable distribution states and community property states are discussed in Chapter 13.

copy important paperwork ASAP. As you gather documents, keep the following in mind:

- Your tax preparer will have some of what you need. But if you don't want to alert your STBX, try initially to locate the documents yourself.
- If you cannot locate, for example, old stock account statements, see if you can find the last 3 year-end statements, and be on the lookout for the next statement.
- If you or your spouse uses Quicken, Moneydance, or other personal finance software, print or transfer on to flash drives current summary reports and year-end reports for the last 3 years.

The section of Chapter 7 called "Where to find financial documents and information" shows how to access the following: [8]

- Deeds, mortgages, and other documents relating to real estate
- Information regarding military pay and allowances such as Basic Allowance for Subsistence (BAS) and Basic Allowance for Housing (BAH)
- Estimates of your Social Security retirement, disability, and survivors benefits
- Your filed federal income tax returns
- Wills, trusts, accountings, inventories, etc. relating to pending and closed estates
- Your bank and credit card records
- Local real estate prices
- Loan applications
- Retirement plan information
- Life, homeowners, valuable items, and umbrella insurance policies

Financial Documents You May Need

The following documents are typically needed during divorce:
- Personal and business tax returns for at least 2 years
- Most recent and year-end pay stubs for at least 2 years
- Bank/brokerage statements
- Check registers
- Employment agreements

---

8. For e-book readers, some references in this book will be to chapters or sections rather than pages.

- Buy/sell agreements, partnership agreements, etc. regarding any business entity in which you or your STBX own a significant interest or actively participates
- Financial statements for businesses you or your STBX own/operate
- Regarding retirement, pension, and other deferred compensation plans such as stock ownership and option plans from current or prior employment . . .
    - ○ Most recent, and year end statements for the last 2 or 3 years
    - ○ Plan summaries (available from the employer's Human Resources or Personnel Office)
- Major credit card account statements including annual online summaries
- Loan applications
- "Closing statements" regarding purchase and sale of real estate
- Powers of attorney
- Appraisals of
    - ○ Real estate
    - ○ Businesses
    - ○ Particularly valuable "personal property" such as collectibles, antiques, and artwork
- Your tax preparer's "cost basis" calculations regarding your home and other real estate
- The deed to your home, or other document such as a mortgage deed, which contains a legal description
- Year-end statements for "529 plans," UTMA/UGMA accounts, and any other accounts maintained for the benefit of your children
- Life insurance policy summary pages ("dec. sheets")
- Health insurance policy summaries
- Homeowner's, renter's, and personal property policies including schedules of covered personal property
- Safe deposit box inventories
- Trust agreements for
    - ○ Trusts that you or your STBX have established
    - ○ Irrevocable trusts set up by others in which you have a legal interest (in states where such trusts may be marital property)[9]
- Resumes

---

9. See Chapter 12.

Non-Financial Documents

In some cases, significant non-financial issues are in dispute, such as:

- Child-related matters including custody; allocation of parenting time; access to children by parents, grandparents, or other "third parties;" handling of children's special needs; and disputes regarding decision-making concerning, for example, religious training, private school, extracurricular activities, therapy, etc.
- Reasons for the breakdown of the marriage in states where those reasons can impact financial orders

If such matters are disputed in your case, the following documents may become important:

- Phone records
- Emails, letters, and transcriptions of texts, electronic communications, and posts
- Print and digital photos and other images
- Children's schoolwork (including younger children's artwork)
- Children's medical records
- Parents' medical records relevant to custodial fitness
- Calendars, schedules, and other documents used by the primary caregiver
- Police records where there has been domestic violence or criminal behavior that bears on custodial fitness

---

Scan and Organize Documents

Consider investing in a scanner to digitize and organize key documents. This can be especially helpful if your lawyer's staff routinely scans such documents. You can recoup the price of the scanner and more with the paralegal time charges you save by doing it yourself.

If your time is limited, you can scan key portions of certain documents. For example:

- Insurance policy declaration ("dec.") sheets that summarize the policy on a single page
- The key parts of personal income tax returns, namely
    - The summary on the first 2 pages
    - Schedule "A" (itemized deductions)
    - Schedule "B" (Interest/Dividend Income)
    - (If applicable) Schedule "C" (Business Profit/Loss)

Beginning to Plan For the Future

It's never too soon to plan for your divorce afterlife. Facing a suddenly uncertain future can be frightening, to say the least. The other side of that coin is the empowerment that comes from taking control of your life. Focus on empowerment as follows:

- Dust off and update your job skills. Start with computer courses offered by local libraries, colleges, and other organizations.
- Begin strengthening your credit rating. Use a credit card in your name only, to build a credit history independent of your STBX. If you don't have your own credit card, apply for one.
- Health insurance provided through your STBX's employment will be available to you for 3 years following the divorce. But the cost might be substantial. Visit your state's Affordable Care Act online exchange or the federal site at http://www.healthcare.gov/ to view alternatives.
- Begin assessing your post-divorce financial needs and changes in spending habits that might become necessary.
- Discuss with an estate lawyer the changes to your will that the divorce will require.

Creating a Paper Trail to Success

I can't remember all the court hearings in which I've wished my client had kept better records. But I do recall the cases in which my client's documentation helped achieve great results. Start creating a paper trail to success with the following:

- Keep a record of how you use your ATM withdrawals.
- If you anticipate receiving child support, hold on to receipts that document your children's expenses—it's nearly always more than you think.
- If issues arise regarding time with the children, keep a log of each parent's time.
- Communicate with your spouse by email to
  - ° Create a record of significant events
  - ° Preserve requests you've made or your responses to those of your STBX
  - ° Confirm any agreements reached

Educating Yourself About Divorce

Universal Divorce Principles

No two states' divorce laws are completely the same. But the law on some matters is the same or very similar:
- Matters governed by federal law (the law is the same in every state)
- Matters covered by "uniform acts" (the law is the same or similar in states that have adopted a particular uniform act or some form of it)

Below are examples of divorce-related federal laws and uniform acts. They and others are discussed in Chapters 9 and 10.
- Federal law governs divorce issues including
    - Divorce tax breaks such as
        - Alimony (pre-2019)
        - Tax exempt property transfers[10]
        - Special rules relating to sales of primary residences
        - Assignments of children's tax exemptions (pre-2018) and credits
    - Protecting children and spouses in interstate and international cases[11]
    - Dividing pensions
- Most states have adopted versions of the following uniform acts.[12]
    - The Uniform Interstate Family Support Act (UIFSA), adopted in all states
    - The Uniform Child Custody Jurisdiction and Enforcement Act (UCCJEA), adopted in every state except Massachusetts, which uses its predecessor, The Uniform Child Custody Jurisdiction Act (UCCJA)

Basic Family Law Principles[13]

In addition to federal laws and uniform acts, the following basic divorce principles apply to varying degrees in most jurisdictions:
- Children's issues: Decisions concerning children are based on the "best interests of the child."

---

10. See Chapter 9.
11. See Chapter 10.
12. See Chapter 10.
13. Each of these basic principles will be covered in later chapters.

- Property distribution: Except in short marriages, "marital property" is often divided approximately evenly. However, the definition and handling of marital property varies substantially from state to state, and in particular between "community property" and "equitable distribution" states. (See Chapter 13.)
- Child support: In every state, child support is calculated according to that state's Child Support Guidelines formula. (A Guidelines booklet should be available on your state's court system or bar association website. See page 23 regarding how to access the Guidelines booklet and related information.)
- Judges' discretion: Judges in most states have broad discretion in deciding family case issues, especially . . .
- Non-financial orders regarding children's matters
  ○ Financial orders in equitable distribution states
- Making your own agreement: Settlement agreement provisions that differ from what a judge might customarily order will usually be acceptable to the court nevertheless, as long as they
  ○ Are knowingly and voluntarily agreed to
  ○ Don't violate state or federal law or policy
  ○ Aren't clearly unfair under the circumstances
  ○ Don't put spouses, especially custodial parents, at financial risk

---

Types of Case Law

Decisions by a state's highest appellate court are binding upon trial judges. Decisions by lower appellate courts are binding if the state's highest court has not ruled on an issue. Principles established or refined in a decision by a trial judge, and decisions from other states are known as "persuasive authority" that does not bind other courts in the state.

Note that the names of the appellate courts vary from state to state. Most states' highest courts are called "supreme courts." However, in New York, the Supreme Court is the lowest or "trial court," where trials and other hearings are conducted. Go figure.

Where State Divorce Law Comes From

There are two kinds of state laws:
- "Statutory law" (including uniform acts) passed by state legislatures
- "Case law" established by state appellate court judges

State laws can differ regarding
- Legal principles
- The factors judges use in applying legal principles

Here are some examples of significant differences among state laws that will be discussed in later chapters:
- Children's issues: Your state may have "legal presumptions"—for example, a "presumption" that places the burden of proof on a parent who opposes joint custody of the children.
- Property distribution: Most but not all states define "marital property" to exclude inheritances, gifts, and property owned by one of the spouses prior to the marriage.
- Child support: States differ as to what "deviation criteria" judges can use to award child support that differs from the amount calculated under the Guidelines.

Learning About Divorce in Your State

It's important for you to learn the basics of how divorce works in your state. However, be wary of blogs about divorce law written by:
- Non-lawyers writing about strictly legal issues
- Lawyers or others outside your state

Your state's judicial division or bar association websites are excellent resources regarding divorce law and procedure in your state. To access them, search either of the following:
- Your state's court system (or judicial "branch" or "department") website
- The American Bar Association's directory of state and local bar associations: http://shop.americanbar.org/ebus/ABAGroups /DivisionforBarServices/BarAssociationDirectories /StateLocalBarAssociations.aspx

Then, to obtain information on a judicial branch or bar association site, follow this type of path:[14]
Select a topic such as
- "For the public"
  - "Public resources"
  - "Online help center"

---

14. If selecting your state doesn't work, search "[your state] judicial department" or "[your state] bar association" and proceed from there in the same manner as described above.

- ○ "Self-Help"
- ○ "FAQs"

Then, select a topic such as
- • "Family Law" or "Family Matters"
- • "Divorce"
- • "Alimony" or "Spousal Support"
- • "Child Support"

If the above doesn't get you where you need to go, look for one of the following:
- • A link to the state bar's Family Law Section
- • A link to a Lawyer Referral Service
- • An index of publications, videos, etc.

Divorce Procedure: The Steps to Your Divorce

In addition to "substantive" law on divorce issues like support and property division, each state (and some counties) have their own procedural law and rules. As with substantive law, there are many similarities among the states regarding how most court-based divorce cases proceed, which is generally as follows:

- • Preparation of initial pleading and related documents (available on your court system website) including:
  - ○ "Complaint" or "Petition" for dissolution of marriage or legal separation[15]
  - ○ Summons
  - ○ Notice of automatic injunctive orders that prohibit unilateral action regarding finances or the children
  - ○ Temporary or *pendente lite* (Latin for "pending the litigation") motions for court action ("relief") that is needed immediately, such as motions for temporary support or custody, award of attorney's fees, or motions for exclusive possession of the marital residence
  - ○ Notice of *lis pendens* or other documents to be served and recorded on the land records in the municipality or county in which real estate is owned by both or one of the spouses, in order to
    - ▪ Prevent your STBX from transferring the property
    - ▪ Give your divorce claims priority over subsequent creditors

---

15. Some states allow filing of a less formal "letter of complaint."

- Filing with the Court: In some jurisdictions, "service of process" (see below) occurs before filing. In others, the papers are filed and then served. If you are self-represented, make sure that both service of process and filing—no matter in which order they occur—are completed by the applicable deadlines. Assistant clerks at the courthouse can help you with that.
- Service of process: A sheriff, marshal, or other legally authorized person "serves" (usually by handing the papers to the defendant) the following documents signed by the plaintiff or counsel.
  ○ The Complaint or Petition for dissolution of marriage.
  ○ A Summons commanding the defendant to appear in court or respond to the Complaint by a certain date. Note that a requirement to appear in court can generally be satisfied by filing a court form called an "Appearance." Court personnel can assist you with this.
  ○ Where necessary, the additional documents mentioned above.

  Note that in amicable situations in some states, service can be pre-arranged between the process server and the defendant. Also, in some jurisdictions the defendant's lawyer can agree to accept service on behalf of his client.

- Preparation of a financial disclosure statement: (also known as a "financial affidavit" and by other similar names).[16] As discussed in Chapter 8, divorcing parties disclose their financial circumstances on forms that summarize income, expenses, assets, and liabilities. The expense section can be time-consuming to prepare so you should begin working on it as soon as you decide to divorce. The disclosure statement is so important that Chapter 8 is dedicated to it.
- "Cooling off" period: During this period that lasts as long as 90 days in some states, the case cannot proceed to judgment. Nevertheless, much can be accomplished during cooling off periods, including
  ○ Preparation and exchange of the parties' financial disclosure statements
  ○ "Discovery" (see below)
  ○ Interim agreements

---

16. See Chapter 8 for more on financial disclosure statements.

- o In the absence of agreement on pressing issues, hearings on *pendente lite* motions for custody, support, attorney's fees, exclusive possession of marital home, etc.
  - o Settlement negotiation
- Status or other Court Conferences: Depending upon state procedure, these conferences may occur during the cooling off period. At a status conference, the court can refer certain issues to ADR, order custody evaluations, or enlist the assistance of parenting coordinators and discovery referees. Subsequent status conferences with a judge or clerk serve to monitor case progress and can include resolution of disputes regarding discovery and other matters.
- Discovery: The process by which information, documents, and other material is exchanged between parties to a lawsuit. Discovery in divorce cases consists primarily of the exchange of financial information and documents, though in cases where custody or responsibility for the breakdown of the marriage is at issue, other types of information and documents can be relevant as well. The most frequently used discovery procedures are . . .
  - o Interrogatories: Written questions directed to a party to a lawsuit. Unless objections are filed or the parties agree to an extension of time, interrogatories must be answered in writing under oath within a specified period of time such as 30 days. The major drawback of interrogatories, as compared with depositions (see below), is that follow-up questions cannot be asked. States like Illinois and Florida use standardized interrogatories. Litigants can ask additional questions only by court order.

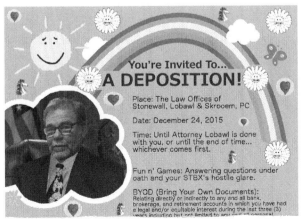

Study the material in Chapter 15 to turn your deposition into a party for you, not for this guy.

- ° Document Requests: The most frequently used discovery tool, document requests are governed by the same rules as interrogatories. Note that document requests apply to electronically stored documents.
- ° Depositions: Proceedings in the office of the examining lawyer who questions a witness (usually the opposing party) under oath. A court stenographer records the deposition. The expense of two lawyers plus a transcript makes the deposition the most expensive discovery tool. But depositions allow the lawyer to pursue a line of questioning until an answer is obtained. Sending out interrogatories and document requests beforehand can reduce deposition time by eliminating the need to ask already answered questions.
- ° Requests For Admissions: The least-often-used discovery tool consisting of a list of statements that the responding party must either admit or deny under oath.
- Pretrial (settlement) Conference: An informal proceeding conducted by a judge ("judicial pretrial") or by a pair of court-appointed matrimonial attorneys sometimes called "special masters." The parties submit financial disclosure statements and often "proposed orders" as well. Counsel and self-represented parties speak briefly in support of the financial and other orders they seek. The pre-trier(s) then recommend how the case should be settled.
- Uncontested hearing: If you have settled your case, a judgment or decree dissolving your marriage is entered after a brief hearing at which the allegations in the Complaint are proved, usually by the plaintiff's testimony (see details below). The judge then reviews the parties' settlement agreement for clarity and fairness in light of the financial circumstances reflected on the financial disclosure statements.
- Trial: If all attempts to settle the case have failed, evidence including the parties' testimony is presented to the court for adjudication.

What to Expect at Your Uncontested Hearing

If your divorce case settles, as the overwhelming majority of cases do, you will probably be required to attend a final or "uncontested" hearing. Uncontested hearings typically last 15 or 20 minutes. In my state of Connecticut, for example, a judge does the following at an uncontested hearing:

- Receives documentation from the parties including

- º A financial disclosure statement ("financial affidavit") from each party
- º Signed counterpart of the settlement agreement
- º Judgment of Divorce
- º Dissolution of Marriage Report containing statistical information for the State Health Dept.
- º Where applicable,
    - Advisement of rights form informing support recipients of their right to obtain a wage withholding order by which the obligor's employer deducts the amount of support from the obligor's paycheck and sends it directly to the court or support recipient
    - Calculation of child support on a Child Support Guidelines worksheet
    - Affidavit regarding custody of children
    - Certificate of Completion of Parenting Education Program
- If the defendant is not present, establishes that he/she has been served and has notice of the hearing
- Takes testimony (usually from the plaintiff) to "prove up" the allegations in the Complaint or Petition for dissolution of marriage, including
    - º The parties' state of residence
    - º The date and place of marriage
    - º Names and ages of children of the marriage
    - º That the marriage has broken down irretrievably
    - º That neither party is receiving public assistance
- Reviews each party's financial affidavit
- Where applicable, reviews the Child Support Guidelines worksheet
- Reviews the settlement agreement and asks questions if necessary to enable the judge to find that the agreement is fair under all the circumstances
- Inquires regarding provision for post-majority educational support (if not covered by the settlement agreement)
- "Canvasses" the parties; i.e., asks each spouse questions such as
    - º Have you entered into the Separation Agreement freely, voluntarily, and without duress?
    - º Has anyone made any promises that are not contained in the Agreement to induce you to enter into it?
    - º Do you fully understand the Agreement?

- º Do you feel that the Agreement is fair under all the circumstances?
- º [If applicable:] Do you understand that by waiving your right to receive spousal support now, you cannot come back to court and claim spousal support in the future?
- Makes findings on the record that
  - º The parties have satisfied the state's residency requirements
  - º The parties have established legal entitlement to a dissolution of marriage
  - º The parties' settlement or "separation agreement" is fair and reasonable under all the circumstances
  - º The parties have made suitable provisions for the higher education of their children, or have deferred that decision as permitted under state law
- Restores birth names if requested
- Enters a judgment of dissolution of the marriage and incorporates the separation agreement into the judgment, thus making its terms orders of the court enforceable by the court's contempt power

Caring For Your Children

Many of my clients have worried about how their children will fare during and after their divorce. Certainly not all children are damaged by divorce. How they do depends mostly on how the adults act. For children to emerge from divorce in good shape, the parents must:
- Manage their conflict and shield their children from it
- Educate themselves about the basics of child development and shepherding children through divorce
- Agree when and what to tell the children about the divorce (with the help of a therapist or divorce coach if necessary)
- Work cooperatively to quickly resolve all divorce issues
- Stay aware of, and attend to their children's needs

On the other hand children in divorcing families (or intact families for that matter) are at high risk for emotional harm when:
- Parental conflict is intense
- The conflict is witnessed by the children
- The children are the focus of the conflict, as is the case in custody and access battles

Chapter 10 covers methods to build cooperative parenting arrangements that avoid subjecting children to prolonged, bitter divorces. In addition, tips for divorce parenting are provided there, including:

- Do's and don'ts of breaking the news to your children
- Questions your children may ask about your divorce
- Telltale signs of distress in children
- Divorce parenting "no-no's"
- Using family therapists and divorce coaches for advice and support

Caring For Yourself

The stress of divorce can pose challenges to your health and well-being. At the same time, you'll need to be at your best to maximize your divorce results and to support your children. That will take the following, as discussed in more detail in Chapter 17:

- Practice relaxation techniques like meditation
- Maintain an exercise schedule
- Keep hydrated and eat regular healthy meals
- Check in with a counselor, therapist or divorce coach
- Avoid isolation
- Get sufficient sleep
- Take free advice for what it's worth
- Have some fun once in a while!

Yes, there IS a quiz! Test what you have (or haven't) learned.

1. The difference between a statute and case law is:
   A. Statutes break when they fall off pedestals.
   B. Case law, like anything that comes by the case, is cheaper.
   C. Case law is for those who don't care for potato salad.
   D. Statutes are laws passed by state legislatures or Congress, while case law
      derives from reported decisions by judges.

**2. See if you can pronounce out loud, and then unscramble these key
   phrases from this chapter!**
   olgas mettanest
   fatunnolic ridovec
   scetenutdotn hragien
   dilch poputrs snideluige

CHAPTER 2

Divorce Fact-Checking

"It ain't what you don't know that gets you into trouble. It's what you know for sure that just ain't so."

— Mark Twain

Separating the Wheat From the Cow Chips

This chapter contains basic facts about divorce that you probably didn't know. You may also find out here that some of what you thought you knew about divorce, is wrong.

At the end of the chapter, after you've seen why many popular beliefs about divorce are myths, you'll find some vital truths that should serve you well. Included—perhaps most importantly—among those truths is: *This Too Shall Pass.*

Divorce BS and Semi-BS

We'll start with the myths. Many folks believe the following statements to be entirely accurate, though none of them are.

"'No-fault divorce' means that family law judges cannot take into consideration the reason a marriage broke down."

FALSE. No-fault divorce means that a spouse is entitled to a divorce without misconduct by the other spouse. Nonetheless, in a number of states the reason for the breakdown of the marriage remains one of the factors a judge can consider when making financial orders. Judges are most likely to take notice when a spouse's conduct is "egregious," such as an extramarital affair that
- Puts the children at risk
- Is flaunted in a way that humiliates the other spouse

- Involves diverting money to a paramour
- Involves other wrongdoing such as concealing or wasting assets

"In community property states, everything gets split 50/50."

FALSE. In community property states, property acquired prior to the marriage or received by inheritance or gift, is separate or "non-marital property," which remains with its owner. Although the remaining marital property is typically divided evenly, extraordinary circumstances can sometimes alter the 50/50 split, even of marital property (see Chapter 12.)

Where No-Fault Divorce REALLY Began

 California is considered to have begun the era of "easy divorce" with its 1969 "no-fault" divorce law. But 100 years earlier, divorce may have been even easier to get in Mississippi, where being an idiot at the time of marriage was a ground for divorce. Which, a cynic might say, would have made divorce available to just about all of us!!

"In equitable distribution states, everything gets split 50/50."

FALSE. "Equitable distribution" means a fair division of property. That's not necessarily the same as an equal division. Judges in equitable distribution states have the discretion to apply some or all of a number of factors in making financial orders. In addition, many equitable distribution states treat inheritances and property acquired prior to the marriage as separate property that may not be distributed in divorce.

"I don't need a lawyer to figure out child support because any dope can look it up on a Child Support Guidelines chart."

FALSE. It helps if that dope is a lawyer, because it isn't quite that simple. "Deviation criteria" can render Guidelines inapplicable. A spouse's real income on which support is based can be hotly disputed—especially a self-employed spouse's income. Even accurate numbers entered in the wrong spots on Guideline worksheets can create "garbage in, garbage out."

"If I give up my ownership interest in my home, I'm no longer responsible for the mortgage."

FALSE. Such a transfer does not get you off the hook for the mortgage. The same applies to car loans and other "secured debts."

"Child and spousal support obligations can be avoided by filing for bankruptcy."

FALSE. Neither is "discharged" in bankruptcy. To preserve other support-related obligations against discharge, support recipients' lawyers sometimes classify as "support" obligations such as contribution to
- The support recipient's health insurance premiums
- The support recipient's attorneys' fees.

"My spouse and I can save on legal fees by having one lawyer represent both of us."

FALSE. Lawyers can only represent one spouse in a divorce. The other spouse is self-represented.

"'Legal separation' is living apart from your spouse pursuant to a written agreement."

FALSE. A legal separation is a lawsuit or "action" like a divorce or "dissolution of marriage" action. It is the same as a divorce in that all financial and child-related issues are resolved, and an enforceable judgment is entered incorporating the spouses' agreement or a judge's decision. The difference between legal separation and divorce is that legally separated individuals may not remarry.

If you live in Colorado or North Dakota, "marital agreements" entered into during marriage are governed by The Uniform Premarital and Marital Agreements Act (UPMAA). Other states that have not adopted UPMAA nevertheless honor such agreements in certain circumstances. These agreements resemble what people often think of as "legal separation."

"My spouse is not entitled to any of my pension."

FALSE. The federal statute known as "ERISA" contains exceptions to the general rule that protects pensions from claims by creditors and other third parties. One of those exceptions permits distribution of pension benefits as part of a divorce settlement pursuant to a court order known as a qualified domestic relations order or "QDRO" (pronounced "Kwah-dro").

"When my older child is 18, I can cut my child support payment by half."

HALF FALSE. We'll give this one a "Half False" because the result depends upon the language in your order or agreement. If your provision requires, for example, child support of $500 per month for your 2 children (as opposed to "$250 per child" or "$250 each") the obligor (payer) cannot automatically reduce the payment by half when the older child reaches majority. An order modifying the original one would be required, and whether the reduction would be a full 50% would depend upon the financial circumstances at the time modification is sought.

On the other hand, a provision requiring child support of "$250 per month per child" does permit the obligor to eliminate child support for a child when state law no longer requires it.

"'Joint custody' means that parents divide evenly their time with the children."

MOSTLY FALSE. This is true in Louisiana, Georgia, and Arizona. In most states, however, a joint custody order can specify anything from a 50/50 division of child-time to the often-used arrangement of primary residence with one parent and every Wednesday evening and alternating weekends with the other.

Note that the term "custody" can be confusing because it can refer to either
- "Legal custody," meaning decision-making, and/or
- "Physical custody," meaning where, when and with which parent the children will reside and spend time. (See Chapter 10.)

"Children benefit when parents 'insulate' them from the divorce."

HALF TRUE. There is a difference between shielding children from the antagonisms of divorce and insulating them from it altogether. It is impossible to "insulate" children from their parents' divorce. And even if insulation were possible, children don't need or want it. Parents who feel they are helping their children by refusing to discuss the divorce, may instead be raising the children's anxiety levels by depriving them of necessary information.[1]

"Children have the resilience to bounce back from child-related litigation."

HALF TRUE. Many children are resilient, but certainly not all of them. And high conflict divorces pose challenges to even the most resilient child.

Studies of children who experience high-conflict between their parents, show high incidences of emotional disorder. That experience is particularly damaging in custody battles that place children squarely on the battlefield.

Seanan Michael Ellis ("Nicky Sherwood") in Talk to Strangers. Photo by Kitryn Ellis

"If the adults act appropriately during custody litigation, the children will be fine."

MOSTLY UNTRUE. Some experts feel that custody battles place children unnecessarily at risk except in situations that require court intervention such as those involving abuse, neglect, or untreated mental illness and substance abuse. Child-related litigation can take a toll on children even where parents are not overly antagonistic. And even proper conduct by parents and professionals doesn't guarantee that children will emerge unscathed. Custody litigation is a war, and children are its prisoners.

"The custody evaluation process is designed to protect children and is implemented by professionals acting on the children's behalf."

HALF TRUE. While the professionals generally do try to protect children, the process is not designed for that purpose. It is designed to gather information for the court. This unavoidably requires intrusion into children's lives and privacy.

Neither court services personnel, attorneys for minor children (AMC), guardians *ad litem* (GAL), parenting coordinators nor mental health

---

1. The child-related myths discussed here are exposed in the author's Telly award-winning short dramatic film *Talk to Strangers*. Visit www.childcustodyfilm.com.

professionals can protect children from the intrusions, humiliations, and untenable situations that are unavoidable in contested custody cases.

"Judges protect children during custody battles."

HALF TRUE. Judges protect children when they can. However, judges don't supervise the custody evaluation process that precedes a trial. By the time a judge hears a custody case, that process has been completed and children may have been humiliated, compromised, and frightened along the way.

"Lawyers are not allowed to testify in court."

MOSTLY TRUE. As a rule, only witnesses are permitted to testify in court. However, there are 2 instances in which lawyers can be said to testify.

- Lawyers appointed as guardians *ad litem* of children in custody cases may be questioned about what custody arrangement or parenting plan they feel is in a child's best interests and why. The role of lawyers acting as GALs in such situations is similar to that of an expert witness.
- Skilled lawyers use "leading questions" to in effect testify when they cross-examine a witness. Leading questions
  ○ Contain the cross-examiner's conclusions or versions of facts
  ○ Can be answered "yes" or "no"

Cross-examiners typically press witnesses to either agree or disagree with the facts or conclusions in the question by answering it either "yes" or "no." When a witness agrees with those facts or conclusions, the cross-examiner's words have become the witness's testimony. For example:

Attorney Stonewall: So, you sold your jewelry and placed the proceeds in a bank account that you failed to tell your spouse about, correct?

The Witness: I wasn't trying to hide ...

Attorney Stonewall: Can you answer that question "yes" or "no?"

The Witness: Yes.

In Chapter 13, you will learn how to handle leading questions and other aggressive cross-examination techniques.

Divorce BT (Basic Truths)

Here are some important truths about divorce that are often overlooked:

- Being organized won't guarantee that your divorce will proceed efficiently; but being disorganized pretty much guarantees that it won't.
- Asking your lawyer questions throughout the process is critical to maximizing your results.
- Your divorce will give you the opportunity to be a hero to your children by placing their interests above your conflict with your STBX, and by sparing them as much of that conflict as possible.
- Your divorce should also give you the "break-upportunities" to learn or improve important life skills such as
  - Parenting
  - Communicating effectively in pressure situations
  - budgeting and managing personal finance
- The vast majority of divorce cases are settled. Your case is much more likely to be settled if you
  - Think in terms of your "interests" rather than "positions"
  - Take the high road by avoiding petty disputes
  - Work hard at cooperative parenting
  - Avoid the dozen biggest divorce mistakes listed at the end of Chapter 3
- "This too shall pass": Keep your spirits up with the knowledge that
  - Your divorce will end
  - You can emerge from it better able to meet life's challenges

Yes, there IS a quiz! Test what you have (or haven't) learned.

1. This Chapter is mainly about:
   A. Mark Twain's cow chips
   B. How to pronounce "QDRO"
   C. How many lawyers it takes to spell "QDRO"
   D. Distinguishing divorce facts from myths

2. Pronounce out loud (if you dare) and then unscramble the following key phrases from this chapter!
   tooverpieca gipennart
   yimcunotm yetrpop
   diagnaur da mitel
   quebaltie tutsinidibor

CHAPTER 3

Divorce Pearls and Perils: Secrets of Saving Money and Avoiding Mistakes

"Keep your gaze on the bandaged place. That's where the light enters you."

— Rumi

There won't be rainbows at the end of your divorce, and probably not any pots of gold. But along the way, there will be some golden opportunities to save money and maximize your divorce results.

In this chapter you'll learn how to take advantage of those opportunities . . . and how to avoid screwing it all up.

Find the Quality Lawyer Bargain Table!

It's true! There is a bargain table out there of quality divorce lawyers who:
- Have practiced principally or exclusively in the field of family law for at least the last 5 years
- Have been trained at either
  ○ A small "boutique" matrimonial law firm that specializes in family cases, or
  ○ The matrimonial department of a larger law firm
- Are still firm associates and thus charge substantially less than the firm's partners
- Combine
  ○ Youthful energy
  ○ A caring relationship with clients
  ○ Mentorship by some of the better family lawyers in the area
  ○ Their own family law experience, which exceeds that of many general practitioners who have been members of the bar for far longer

In Chapter 4 we'll discuss how to find these Bargain Babies!

When More Can Be Less: Learn About "Effective Billing Rates"

Q. When is a 3-minute call to a lawyer who charges $300/hr., more expensive than the same call to a $400/hr. attorney?

A. When Attorney $300 charges in increments of 2/10 of an hour ($60 for 3 minutes) and Attorney $400 charges in 1/10 hr. increments ($40 for 3 minutes). See Chapter 4 to learn how to cope with incremental billing.

Discover the Secret Fount of Family Law Knowledge

Here's how to find lawyers who know your state's family law as well as anyone:
* On your state bar association's website, find "Sections and Committees"
* Select The Family Law Section or similarly named committee
* Find the meeting minutes and locate the names of lawyers who regularly present "recent developments," OR
* Call the office of one of the Section officers and ask for the names of the Family Law Section members who present programs on recent developments in the law.[1]

Learn the Witness's Magic Word

Witnesses can stop a cross-examining attorney in his tracks with a single word: "speculation." For example: "I would just be speculating if I answered that question." Judges don't allow speculation because it has no "probative value." See Chapter 15.

---

1. If you feel compelled to give a reason for your call, tell the staff person that you are researching an article on Cross-Frontier Surrogacy Issues under the Hague Abduction Convention. That should shut up any of the firm's lawyers who might want you to sign up as a client!

Save Attorneys' Fees With Good Timing

You can save some money by delaying hiring a lawyer for a short period of time while you:

- File for divorce yourself using forms available on your state's court system website
- Consult a certified divorce planner or certified divorce financial analyst to
  - Help you organize your financial paperwork
  - Help you prepare your financial disclosure statement
  - Discuss with you other divorce-related issues such as pensions, pre-2019 alimony deductions, etc.
- Consult a certified divorce coach, if necessary, regarding organizing for divorce and dealing with non-financial issues

Note that this approach is advisable only in the following circumstances:

- You have consulted with a matrimonial attorney who has advised you that there are no pressing matters that require immediate legal representation such as *pendente lite* (temporary) support or custody issues
- You and your children are not at risk of harm
- You have very little funds available for attorneys' fees
- There are experienced CDPs or CDFAs in your area
- You understand that divorce coaches, unlike attorneys, can be required to disclose clients' oral and written communications

Finally, note that there is a related option called "unbundled," "discrete task," or "consulting attorney" representation. In an unbundled representation arrangement, you hire a lawyer to handle only certain parts of your case. Unbundled pros and cons are discussed in Chapter 4.

Settle Your Case Quicker and Cheaper

Fifty years ago, a song called "What the World Needs Now Is Love" assured us that love was the only thing the world needed more of.

Not to nitpick, but love isn't the only thing the world has too little of. These days, it seems there's an increasingly short supply of empathy as well. And lack of empathy can be a serious hindrance to settling your case, whether you choose ADR or a court-based divorce.

Spouses who use empathy to understand and identify with each other's emotions and attitudes have a decided advantage in settling their cases. Borrowing from another lyric, if you can "walk a mile in your (spouse's) shoes," you're likely to arrive at "yes" that much faster, easier and cheaper. Try to experience emotions and attitudes such as anxiety or entitlement that your spouse may have regarding certain issues. The resulting insights can be of tremendous assistance to you during settlement negotiation.

Staying True to Yourself; Random Acts of Kindness

> You will not be punished for your anger.
> You will be punished by your anger."
> — The Buddha

It's all too easy during divorce to let anger and anxiety "get the best of you." But that can only hurt you, your children, and your chances for a functional divorce that resolves issues fairly and efficiently, and allows ex-partners to move forward with dignity toward a new, happy life.

Besides hindering your ability to achieve your divorce goals, giving in to the divorce furies can leave you feeling out of balance and can even affect your health. You have the responsibility to try to protect your children and your financial future. But try not to let those efforts obscure principles that guide your life.

It won't always be easy. At times, adherence to the Golden Rule, the Buddhist concept of metta ("loving kindness"), or a similar creed may seem impossible or senseless. One great way to reconnect with the "best of you" in those tougher moments is through "random acts of kindness." It's amazing how helping out another, even ever so briefly, can help put things back in perspective and get you feeling better about yourself.

Try it! What have you got to lose?

Mess Makes Stress

As noted in Chapter 2, being organized won't guarantee a functional divorce; but a lack of organization usually assures that it won't be. Divorce requires you to get a grip on your finances. Use that as a "break-upportunity" to get organized and thus become more efficient and less stressed during your divorce and afterward by:

- Managing your time more efficiently with electronic To-Be-Done lists linked to smart-phone calendars with reminder alerts
- Using personal finance software such as Quicken, Personal Capital or MoneyDance
- Handling paperwork more efficiently with "one-touch" and other management techniques
- Organizing correspondence, bills, and account statements with a system of color-coded folders
- Keeping that stress-inducing cluttered desktop clear!

Your Lawyer's Secret Weapon: You

In a foreign world of lawyers and judges, you can claim expertise on at least one subject: your spouse. Your knowledge of your spouse can be key in developing an effective negotiation strategy and, if necessary, helping your lawyer prepare for depositions and contested hearings. (See Chapter 7.)

But don't wait for your lawyer to ask you for this information. Schedule a meeting so that you can share it before negotiation sessions or court proceedings. Tell your lawyer what you know about your spouse's communication style, motivations, vulnerabilities and even body language clues. You can be a terrific resource for your lawyer, but only if you are proactive in telling what you know.

"Yes, Virginia, There Are Bad Lawyers Out There."

In Chapter 4, you'll learn why the best sources of divorce lawyer recommendations can be their colleagues and other professionals. A lawyer's clients are also on the list of referral sources. But you'll be cautioned that clients' perceptions of their lawyer's competence are sometimes distorted.

However, that doesn't mean clients' opinions aren't valuable. On the contrary, they are indispensable for things about which a lawyer's colleagues may know very little. For example, information about a lawyer's billing practices and responsiveness can be key factors in your decision whether to retain that lawyer.

You'll want to avoid "divorce mills"—firms that handle a high volume of divorces, and bill out big chunks of attorney and paralegal time for clerical tasks that clients can do themselves like document scanning, copying, organizing, analyzing, and review.[2] You can become stuck with a firm like that, especially late in your case when it's

- Too close to a trial date to find a new lawyer willing to take over, and/or
- Too expensive to start from scratch with a new lawyer

You can learn another piece of key information about a lawyer by asking former clients: "How is your relationship with your co-parent?" If it's poor, ask, "to what extent do you feel your lawyer contributed to that?"

Clients' perceptions of their lawyers can be skewed for a variety of reasons. Some want to blame their lawyers for what went wrong in their divorce. Others feel the need to brag about how smart they were to have picked the best barrister out there. But don't hire a lawyer until you've spoken with at least one current or former client about the lawyer's billing practices and how the attorney/client relationship worked for the client.

Divorce Math: Making Sure the Numbers Add Up

Sometimes property settlements are tweaked or "adjusted" for money or other property a spouse has already received. Be sure to analyze such adjustments carefully to make sure that what appears to be fair … really is.

For example, let's say that your car died while your divorce was pending. You and your spouse agree that you can take $3,000 from a joint bank account to use as a down payment on a new car. Eventually, you agree on a settlement that evenly divides your joint bank accounts. However, your spouse's lawyer argues that your spouse should get an extra $3,000 in order to balance out the $3,000 you already received. Sounds reasonable, right?

But it isn't!

Since you are dividing your cash 50/50, half of the $3,000 you received would have been yours anyway. So, your spouse is not entitled to an extra $3,000 but to half of that, or $1,500.

The best way to understand and test the accuracy of divorce calculations is to plug in actual numbers. In our example, let's assume that before you got the $3,000, the joint bank accounts totaled $80,000. Had you divided the $80,000 at that time, you and your spouse each would have received $40,000 (50% of $80,000). However, because you already received $3,000,

---

2. See Chapter 7 to learn how to "Be Your Own Paralegal."

50% of the $77,000 remaining in the accounts is $38,500 or $1,500 less than $40,000, not $3,000 less.

To double-check that answer, look at your side of the property division ledger. If you add the $3,000 you received for the car payment to the $37,000 you are getting now (the $38,500 that equals half the $77,000 balance less the $1,500 going to your spouse to offset the money you got for the car), the total is the $40,000, which is what you would have gotten had you not bought the car.

Now splash some cold water on your face before your head explodes.

Handling Spouses with Personality Disorders

Divorcing someone with borderline personality disorder or narcissistic personality disorder can be especially challenging. Both personality types are likely to exhibit rage during divorce.

Narcissists in particular often react furiously when confronted with divorce. Many try to use the court's adversarial system as a vehicle for abusive conduct toward spouses who no longer tolerate their behavior. Principal breadwinners may threaten to quit working to avoid paying support. Even parents who have been detached from their children may threaten a custody battle.

There are no perfect answers here, but the following should help you pre-pare for extreme behavior from your spouse and guide you in handling it better:

- Get yourself centered. Seek counseling to reinforce your feelings of self-worth. This will help counter a narcissistic spouse's attempts to demean and control you. A therapist can also help you learn to ignore gratuitous slights and insults, and stop you from unrealistic attempts to appease or change his/her behavior.
- Draw boundaries. Agree with your lawyer on a plan to establish firm rules and boundaries for your spouse. One way to do that is by obtaining *pendente lite* (temporary) support orders at the beginning of your case. Your lawyer must also be prepared to disprove any false claims about you that your spouse makes, to keep them from obscuring the facts of your case.
- Get everything in writing. Make sure that any agreements or "stipulations" reached during the divorce contain enough detail

to avoid your spouse "gaming the system." Ask the court to enter orders in accordance with any major agreements so that they can be quickly enforced.

- Work with a therapist. Consider meeting with your spouse and his/her therapist to devise a plan to help you both get through the divorce.

- Don't rule out mediation. This is especially important regarding children's issues, which should be resolved outside the courthouse whenever possible. If you're thinking, "my spouse is too crazy to listen to a mediator," keep the following in mind:
    ○ Not everyone who displays characteristics of a personality disorder actually suffers from one.
    ○ The severity of personality disorders varies, so even some people who do suffer from one may be able to act reasonably on some issues.
    ○ It might be possible to find a mediator who commands enough respect from your spouse to be effective. (See Chapter 5.)

For additional information, see Chapter 10 regarding handling difficult spouses in child-related matters. Also use the resources provided in Chapter 18 under the heading "Dealing with Domestic Violence and Impaired Spouses."

Think Globally—Dig Locally

Q. What do divorce and sustainable agriculture have in common?

A. Both require digging around locally.

Books like this one explain prevailing legal and financial principles and offer strategies for using those principles. No book, however, can cover every county courthouse's rules and customs. So it's extremely important that you talk to a local divorce lawyer about:

- How it's done here: This includes local "standing orders" covering filing deadlines, etc., requirements relating to written submissions to the court and rules for preparing and marking exhibits, etc. in advance of court proceedings. In addition, local customs, such as limits on the length of trials can hamper spouses trying to prove complex matters like the value and/or earnings of a business.

- Judges' tendencies: You can learn about local judges' inclinations, including whether any are considered "pro-wife" or "pro-husband," and whether particular lawyers tend to be successful with particular judges. Particular judges' habits are worth knowing as well. For example, a judge I knew (and thought the world of) often adjourned court at 4:30 rather than 5:00 to catch a less crowded train home.

Making Your Spouse's Bankruptcy Work for You

A spouse's threatened or actual bankruptcy during or after divorce is usually considered bad news. But if you are a support recipient, it may not be.

First, spousal and child support obligations are not discharged (wiped out) by bankruptcy. They remain in full force and effect.

Second, spouses saddled with payments of credit card debt and other obligations typically struggle to fulfill support obligations. Thus, an "obligor" whose credit card and other debts are discharged may be better able to fulfill support obligations . . . or even capable of paying more!

Create Cost of Living Increases for Your Support Payments

In most places, child and spousal support do not include cost of living adjustments (COLAs) to keep up with inflation.

If you are a support recipient it will be difficult, if not impossible, for you to negotiate them in those jurisdictions. But don't despair. (Never despair!) You may be able to negotiate support with a built-in COLA that doesn't look like one.

Here's how. Let's say you'll be staying in your home for a period after the divorce and receiving spousal support during at least some of that time. Propose dividing the spousal support into a payment to you plus contributions to house expenses such as capital improvements, major repairs, property taxes[3], etc. The effect of such direct payments is that they automatically increase as the expense does. Thus you're receiving the equivalent of a COLA—and often more—without calling it that.

---

3. Consult your tax advisor first, however, to make sure the loss of the property tax deduction doesn't hurt you more than the "COLA" helps.

It can be even easier to build a COLA into child support. Many agreements provide for a base payment of child support plus a contribution (often 50%) to other expenses such as extracurriculars. As those expenses increase, the obligor's contribution will also. Similarly, a percentage contribution to children's health-related expenses that are not covered by insurance ("unreimbursed healthcare expenses") will increase as those expenses do.

Divvying Up Your ... Advisors

You and your spouse will spend a fair amount of time during your divorce dividing things. Cash, personal property, responsibility for debts and parenting obligations all get divvied up. While you're at it, consider divvying up some ... people.

If you and your spouse have been equally involved with your accountant, financial advisor, estate lawyer, insurance agent and other professionals, you may both wish to continue using them. However, consider "divvying up" the advisors; i.e., deciding which of them will continue to advise which of you.

Often, one spouse is primarily responsible for dealing with family advisors. That can result in close relationships between that spouse and the advisors that the other spouse doesn't share. If your spouse has been the one dealing with the professionals, you should decide whether to continue using them during and after the divorce, or whether you should find new ones. If you're considering switching, do it before or at least early on in the divorce so that you have expert advice available throughout the process keyed to your needs—not your spouse's.

You may feel that your divorce to-do list is long enough without adding a search for new professionals. But having a professional with undivided loyalties to consult during your divorce is worth the trouble.

A Dozen of Divorce's Biggest Perils

Now let's look at what not to do in your divorce. A functional divorce includes not only taking the right steps but also avoiding the following serious mistakes:

- Placing your goals ahead of your children's interests: When your goals clash with what's best for your kids, the kids come first.
- Choosing the wrong divorce method: If both you and your STBX wish to achieve a fair result more quickly and at less expense, you would be foolish not to consider alternative dispute resolution (ADR), which is discussed in Chapter 5. Conversely, if your spouse is "out for blood" and not open to ADR, choosing a lawyer who is not an experienced litigator could be a costly error.
- Not using a lawyer even though you can afford to: Failure to at least consult with a lawyer at the beginning of your divorce reduces your chances for a successful outcome. In the chapters that follow, you will learn methods to limit attorneys' fees such as ADR and "unbundled representation" that don't require eliminating lawyers altogether.
- Failing to investigate your self-employed spouse's "real earnings": See Chapter 8 on analyzing disclosure statements.
- Trading property in your settlement that is not subject to tax, for property that is taxable, such as:
  - Retirement assets that are taxed upon withdrawal (and subject to a 10% penalty for early withdrawal if unrelated to the divorce)
  - Stocks with low cost bases, subject to capital gains tax upon sale
  - Depreciated rental real estate, subject to capital gains tax upon sale
- Telling your lawyer only part of the story: Facts you neglect to share with your lawyer have a habit of popping up at the worst possible times … like during depositions and court hearings.
- Driving yourself nuts with advice from sources other than qualified professionals: Accept helpful emotional support, not legal advice, from friends and family members. As a matter of common sense, you should avoid divorce advice from non-divorce professionals. But

even emotional support can have a downside, which is why I use the phrase "helpful emotional support." Your friends and family are likely to "take your side" during divorce. That loyalty may well comfort you. But if coupled with animosity toward your spouse, it can increase and prolong the conflict between you. And that can delay or even prevent resolution of the legal, financial and emotional divorce issues that will allow you and your children to begin moving on with your lives. Finally, be wary of divorce websites and blogs that misstate or overgeneralize legal concepts that might not apply to your case in the first place.

- Adhering to rigid "positions" rather than identifying what you need and how best to get it.
- Failing to put together a reasonable set of goals: Even if you mediate or represent yourself, you should obtain legal advice to ensure that your goals are sensible and achievable. Don't fight for a house that you can't carry, or demand a parenting schedule that you can't live up to.
- Allowing emotion to cloud your judgment: Understand the difference between "emotional divorce" and the "legal divorce" process that requires you to understand and deal with legal and financial matters as dispassionately as possible.[4] Don't try to resolve the issues in your divorce if you are in early stages of grief that can hinder your ability to think clearly and make decisions thoughtfully. There's too much at stake to allow anxiety or other emotions to affect those decisions, or to cause you to sacrifice important long-term needs for lesser, short-term ones.
- "Giving in": If you think you might become intimidated by your spouse or exhausted by the divorce process, choose a strong advocate or proactive mediator who will not permit strong-arm tactics or fatigue to dictate results.
- Failing to educate yourself about divorce: Your state's judicial department and/or bar association websites will have material regarding divorce in your state. Check out also the resources listed in Chapter 18.

---

4. Visit http://www.divorcemag.com/articles/the-grief-progression to learn more about "emotional divorce."

Yes, there IS a quiz! Test what you have (or haven't) learned.

1. This chapter is mainly about:
   A. Ponce de Leon and The Fountain of Youthful Lawyers
   B. Finding your spouse's pot of gold
   C. The penalty for early withdrawal that you wish someone had told you about before you got married
   D. Saving money during divorce and avoiding common divorce mistakes

2. The legal term "*pendente lite*" is Latin for:
   A. "Cheap necklace"
   B. An ornament for your Pendente Holiday Tree
   C. The beer of choice among court clerks and Latin teachers
   D. "Pending the litigation," a term used to designate requests and court orders entered on a temporary basis in family court cases

CHAPTER 4

Choosing the Right Divorce Lawyer For You

"Experience is the name everyone gives to their mistakes."

— Oscar Wilde

Your Two Most Important Divorce Decisions

The list of your most important divorce decisions is a short one:
- How do you choose between a traditional ("court-based") divorce and an alternative dispute resolution (ADR) divorce?
- How do you choose the right (and affordable) lawyer?

We'll cover lawyer affordability later in the chapter. For now, let's assume that you're hiring a lawyer to handle your court-based case; one that proceeds through the court system in the traditional manner. We'll also look at cases in which a lawyer handles part of your court-based case under an "unbundled representation" arrangement (see below).

The two key decisions above are related. There are some skills that all lawyers need. But "court-based" and ADR lawyers require different skill subsets. Thus, your choice of a lawyer will depend on whether your divorce will be court-based or ADR.

In Chapter 5, we'll discuss the significant advantages of ADR and the skills that mediators and other ADR practitioners must have. (If you're uncertain about what type of divorce you want, see Chapter 5.) In this chapter, we'll cover qualifications that all lawyers should have plus those that are of particular importance for court-based lawyers

> ### *The Ideal Credentials Bundle*
> Chances are your case does not require the best divorce lawyer around. Unless your circumstances are unusually complex, there may be many family lawyers in your area who can handle your case quite competently.
>
> But if you are looking for the very best, a lawyer with the credentials listed below might qualify. Your biggest challenge would most likely be affording her fees.
> * Personal recommendation by at least one unaffiliated lawyer
> * Martindale Hubbell AV rating
> * Contributor to recognized family law publications and lecturer to legal groups
> * AAML Membership
> * Where available, certification as family law specialist

Choosing a Traditional "Court-Based" Lawyer

A court-based lawyer's negotiating and courtroom skills can be game-changers. However, less readily apparent skills such as the ability to listen to clients and to understand their needs are also important. Those skills will affect clients not only emotionally but financially as well, because good attorney/client relations save legal fees. Likewise, a lawyer's organizational skills and use of support staff can speed up (or slow down) the progress of your case, and thus reduce (or increase) its cost.

Skills and Attributes to Consider in Choosing a Divorce Lawyer

Below is a list of qualities to consider when choosing a lawyer.
* Experience and knowledge of family law
* The power of persuasion
* Family law credentials and reputation
* Law firm affiliation: solo practitioners vs. firm members
* Compatibility, communication skills, and empathy
* Toughness vs. practicality
* Professionalism regarding opposing counsel, clients, and clients' children
* Reasonable fees
* The "X Factor": WISDOM

This list merits further discussion, so here it is:

Knowledge and Experience Regarding Family Law

Keep the following in mind regarding a court-based lawyer's experience.

- You want a lawyer whose practice has been dedicated at least 75% to family law for the last 5 years or more in your jurisdiction.
- The lawyer must have substantial experience with cross-examination and evidentiary rules acquired while handling contested matters.
- Age doesn't necessarily mean family law experience, because
  - Some young attorneys in law firm matrimonial departments may have more trial experience than general practitioners who have practiced longer, and
  - Some older attorneys may not have the experience they appear to because for some of them, law is a second career

You can find out how long a lawyer has practiced, at http://www.avvo.com.

The Power of Persuasion

A lawyer's "job #1" is to persuade opposing counsel in settlement negotiations, or a judge in court that her position is a sound one. To help you assess a lawyer's persuasive powers, ask yourself the following during an initial consultation:

- Does the lawyer appear confident?
- Does the lawyer command respect?
- Is the lawyer knowledgeable about family law?
- Is the lawyer easy to understand?
- Does the lawyer respond fully to questions?
- Does anything about the lawyer's manner suggest a lack of sincerity or sense of perspective?

Family Law Credentials and Reputation

A diploma from a top law school does not guarantee competence. Nor does any single credential. Recommendations from a local lawyer or other professional whom you trust are more useful. One measure of a lawyer's standing in the profession is her "peer review rating" at www.martindale .com. Look for lawyers with "AV" or "BV" ratings who list divorce or family law as a specialty.

The two best credentials for divorce lawyers are
- American Academy of Matrimonial Lawyers (AAML) membership
- Certification as a specialist in family/matrimonial law or family trial advocacy in the states that offer it, namely:[1]
  - California
  - Ohio
  - Florida
  - Indiana
  - Louisiana
  - New Jersey
  - New Mexico
  - North Carolina
  - Texas

Law Firm Affiliation: Solo Practitioners vs. Firm Members

The advantage of hiring a "solo" practitioner is "what you see is what you get." You won't be surprised, for example, by some kid you've never met showing up in court to "pinch-hit" for your lawyer at an important hearing.[2]

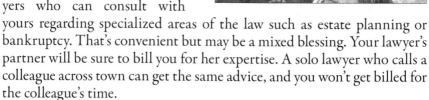

On the other hand, you save money when a law firm associate handles a routine court status conference at a lower hourly rate than your lawyer.

Law firms also may have lawyers who can consult with yours regarding specialized areas of the law such as estate planning or bankruptcy. That's convenient but may be a mixed blessing. Your lawyer's partner will be sure to bill you for her expertise. A solo lawyer who calls a colleague across town can get the same advice, and you won't get billed for the colleague's time.

If you hire a member of a firm, request that no one else handle settlement negotiations or substantive hearings, and that your lawyer won't involve

---

1. A number of other states allow private organizations to certify attorneys.

2. However, if you are considering a solo practitioner, make sure there is experienced support staff to help you when the lawyer is unavailable.

her partners in your case—other than for an occasional consultation—unless you agree to it.[3]

Compatibility, Communication Skills, and Empathy

You know how sometimes someone just doesn't seem to be on your wavelength? You want to make sure your lawyer isn't one of those someones. If something seems a little "off" during your initial consultation with a lawyer, that should sound an alarm.

A productive attorney/client relationship requires clear communication. To help with that, be sure to ask your lawyer questions about anything you don't fully understand. Misunderstandings lead to hurt feelings, and smoldering resentments. If that's what you're after, why not just stay married?

Finally, don't use your lawyer as a therapist. Mental health professionals, including qualified divorce coaches, do it better and cheaper. On the other hand, it's only natural to want a lawyer who displays some empathy.

Measure your need for empathy with the three questions below. If you answer question #1 "yes" and questions #2 and 3 "no," you might need a lawyer who is not averse to a little handholding . . . and someone to provide counseling as needed.

The Divorce Need-o-Meter:
Measuring Your Empathy Needs

1. Am I likely to need periodic reassurances on matters such as the following?
   A. My children will be okay
   B. I will be able to deal with new financial realities
   C. Some normalcy will return to my life
2. Do I have a therapist or counselor, and/or trusted friends and family members who can help me stay in emotional balance during my divorce?
3. Do I have experience in dealing with lawyers, litigation, or divorce that will make me more comfortable with the process?

---

3. Solely for the sake of uniformity, I will refer to your lawyer in the feminine. References to opposing counsel and mediators will be in the masculine. Gender references to judges will be all over the lot . . . a little like some judges I know.

Toughness vs. Practicality

You want a lawyer who can be tough when necessary. Experienced matrimonial lawyers aren't pushovers, but lawyers known for toughness alone often don't serve their clients' needs. You want an assertive lawyer, not a needlessly aggressive one. A lawyer's adaptability and practicality come in handy when you get to the negotiation phase of your case.

The barracuda is not your best choice.

Be wary of the lawyer called "the barracuda" or the one known as the nastiest SOB who ever owned a briefcase. Lawyers with those reputations too often prolong the hostilities at their clients' financial and emotional expense. Moreover, tough guy/gal posturing angers judges who can do without Cruella de Vil blowing smoke out her "porte-cigarette."

The vast majority of divorce cases are settled. Settlement nearly always saves money and emotional wear and tear for parents and children. Don't hinder settlement by hiring an unreasonable lawyer. Seek one with empathy, perspective and other aspects of "emotional intelligence."[4]

Professionalism With Regard to Opposing Counsel, Clients, and Clients' Children

It's unprofessional for lawyers to let grudges cloud their judgment or conduct, but occasionally it happens. Courtroom battles and tough negotiations can create hard feelings between lawyers. That's their problem unless those hard feelings turn your case into a jousting match between Lord Paynenthass and Lady Stigget-Enyorear. Ask your lawyer if she has any problem with the lawyer on the other side. If so, find out the extent of it. Seek an assurance that the lawyers' problem won't become yours.

---

4. For more on emotional intelligence and divorce lawyers, see http://www.markbaeresq.com/Press.aspx.

Professionalism also requires your lawyer to treat you with respect. In addition, she should be protective of your children, making sure that her tactics don't unnecessarily expose your children to risk of emotional harm.[5]

"Reasonable legal fees" (is there such a thing?)

Divorces cost too much, especially court-based divorces. In Chapter 7, we'll discuss how to work with your lawyer in a way that will limit legal fees. Before you choose that lawyer, however, you'll need information about her regarding:

- Hourly rates: The great majority of divorce lawyers charge by the hour. How much a lawyer charges hourly depends on factors such as experience, reputation and your geographic location. Learn the range of divorce lawyers' hourly rates in your area by speaking with divorcing or recently divorced friends, and by contacting some local law firms.

- Billing Increments: Most lawyers do not charge for the actual number of minutes they devote to a task, but rather for the portion or "increment" of an hour they spend. Increments usually consist of either one-tenth (.1) or two-tenths (.2) of an hour. For tasks that take only a few minutes, incremental billing produces charges at rates that exceed a lawyer's stated hourly rate. The section immediately below on "effective hourly rates" explains why that happens, and what you can do to avoid at least some of those excess charges.

- Retainers: Make sure that your fee agreement provides that any unused portion of your retainer will be refunded to you.

- Hourly Rate Changes: Find out if the initial hourly rates for your lawyer, paralegals, etc. will remain in effect throughout the case. If not, consider requesting that the rates not be raised for a minimum amount of time such as 6 or 9 months.

- Location: Lawyers in affluent communities may charge more than comparable lawyers with offices in more modest areas. If you are choosing between two otherwise comparable lawyers, limit billings for travel time by selecting the one whose office is closer to the courthouse. There's no need to pay a premium for your lawyer's fancy digs or upscale locale.

---

5. If your spouse seems intent on battling over child-related issues, use the *Talk to Strangers* short film and parents' guide to help dissuade him/her. Visit www .childcustodyfilm.com.

Dealing With Minimum Charges:
The "Effective Hourly Rate"

Question: When does a 3-minute call from a divorce lawyer who charges $300 per hour cost MORE than the same call from a $400/hr. attorney?

Answer: When the $300/hr. lawyer charges in increments of 2/10 of an hour, and the $400/hr. lawyer charges in 1/10 increments.

Wait . . . WHAT? Based solely on their hourly rates, you would expect "Attorney 300" to charge you $15.00 for that 3-minute call, and "Attorney 400" to charge $20.00.

But they won't.

Why? Because like most lawyers, they charge in increments. "Attorney 400" charges in increments of 1/10 (.1) of an hour (6 minutes), and "Attorney 300" uses increments of 2/10 (.2) of an hour (12 minutes).

Did you ever notice how the interest rate the credit card company reeled you in with isn't what you actually pay? That's because banks base interest charges on something other than your overdue balance. Most lawyers' hourly rates aren't what you actually pay either. That's because lawyers base their charges on something else besides the actual time they spend. That something else is a chunk of time called an increment.

Incremental billing adds dollars to your bill. That's because when lawyers bill in 6 or 12-minute increments, those increments become minimum charges. A lawyer using .1 increments charges a minimum of 6 minutes for anything she does on your case—even if it only takes 2 or 3 minutes. And a lawyer using .2 increments, bills even more in extra fees—a minimum of 12 minutes!

Put another way, clients pay more than their lawyer's hourly rate every time a .1 increment lawyer spends less than 6 minutes on a task, or a .2 lawyer spends less than 12 minutes.

Incremental billing creates another problem as well. Because the 6 and 12-minute minimum charges alter lawyers' hourly rates, they make it difficult to compare what different lawyers will actually charge you. A more useful tool for comparison is what I call the lawyer's "effective hourly rate" (EHR). EHR takes into account both a lawyer's hourly rate and the increments in which she charges.

To illustrate how EHR works, let's use the 3-minute phone call mentioned above.

"Attorney 400," who charges in .1 increments, will charge $40.00 for that call: $400 x .1 = $40.00 ($13.33 per minute)

But "Attorney 300," who charges in .2 increments, will charge $60.00 for the same 3 minutes: $300 x .2 = $60.00 ($20.00/minute)

To compare the two lawyers' 3-minute EHRs, simply multiply their per-minute charges by the 60 minutes in an hour. That yields a 3-minute EHR (are you sitting down?) of $800/hr. for "Attorney 400" and $1,200/hr. for "Attorney 300."

While your heartbeat returns to normal, remember that EHR exceeds a lawyer's hourly rate only as to tasks that take less than 6 minutes for .1 increment billers, and less than 12 minutes for .2 increment billers. For example, EHR doesn't apply to a half-hour meeting because it exceeds both the 6 and 12-minute minimum charges. Thus regular hourly rates will accurately measure the cost of that meeting at $200.00 for "Attorney 400" and $150.00 for "Attorney 300."

Nevertheless, minimum charges do add up. While they won't make "Attorney 400" cheaper than "Attorney 300" over the course of a divorce, they will substantially narrow the difference in cost between "Attorney 300" and a lawyer who charges $350.00/hr. but uses .1 increments.

You can't entirely eliminate the extra fees generated by incremental billing. But you can reduce them by:
- Finding out what increments a lawyer uses before retaining him. As our example shows, 12-minute increment billers rack up substantially more in extra fees than 6-minute billers. And very few of those 12-minute billers hit enough home runs to be entitled to that big a bonus. If you're considering a 12-minute minimum lawyer, make sure the extra charges will be offset by a lower hourly rate, special expertise, or some other benefit.
- Avoid generating minimum charges. For example, wait to call your lawyer until you have several things to discuss, rather than just one. And don't call your lawyer at all to check whether a hearing has been scheduled; contact a staffer instead.

We'll discuss lots of other ways to save on legal fees in Chapter 7.

The "X Factor": Wisdom

There's one more attribute to look for in a lawyer. And it's as significant as experience, legal
knowledge and credentials.   That attribute
is wisdom.

A smart, experienced lawyer, for example,
knows a host of courtroom and negotiating tactics. But a wise lawyer knows when to use them,
and just as importantly, when not to use them.
A lawyer's hard-nosed cross-examination in

Carefully assess a lawyer's
listening skills at the IC.

a temporary visitation hearing might temporarily benefit his client. But
what if that benefit comes at the expense of damaging the co-parenting
relationship? Is it worth it?

Similarly, a lawyer might "stonewall" during settlement negotiations in
order to pressure the other side into a minor concession. But a wise lawyer
might save time and money by focusing instead upon a path to an overall
settlement of the case.

Gray Divorce

In recent years, the number of over-50 divorces has increased dramat-
ically. Research shows that between 1990 and 2010 the over-50 divorce
rate doubled.[6] Folks in that demographic should make sure that they hire
attorneys who are familiar with, and will help them handle gray divorce
issues. Those issues include:

- Plans to retire . . . and retirement plans: As with couples of any age,
  carving two households out of one increases a couple's total living
  expense. That's of particular concern if you are close to retirement
  and life on a fixed income. Discuss with your lawyer (and financial
  advisor) whether plans to retire, which will substantially reduce
  income and may trigger pension elections, should be reevaluated
  in light of the divorce. Also, familiarize yourself with the following basic rules regarding retirement account withdrawals or
  "distributions."
  - With limited exceptions, retirement account distributions at any
    age are taxed as income.

6. Susan L. Brown & I-Fen Lin, *The Gray Divorce Revolution: Rising Divorce among
Middle-Aged and Older Adults,* 1990-2010 (2013).

- Retirement account distributions prior to age 59 ½ trigger a 10% early withdrawal penalty. Note that the penalty does not apply to distributions that are transfers from one spouse's retirement account directly to a retirement account owned by the other spouse as part of a divorce settlement.
- Beginning at age 59 ½ you may begin withdrawing funds from retirement accounts without the penalty assessed on withdrawals prior to that.
- Beginning at age 70 ½, you must begin taking "required minimum distributions" (RMDs) from your retirement savings.[7] RMDs are calculated by dividing the prior December 31 balance of each retirement account by a life expectancy factor determined by your selection of beneficiaries. While the first RMD is required by April 15th of the year after you turn 70 ½, all subsequent RMDs are required by December 31st. Thus if you delay the first withdrawal, you might have to take 2 withdrawals in a single calendar year, which could significantly increase that year's tax bill.

⚠ NOTE: RMDs (and other permissible distributions) to "qualified" charities are not subject to income tax. Thus, you get a tax break on otherwise non-deductible donations by not having to pay taxes on the distribution.

- Social Security benefit elections: The election to receive Social Security benefits can be a critical part of your financial planning. If at all possible, make those elections in cooperation with your spouse in order to maximize benefits for both of you, including your option to receive 50% of your spouse's benefit (without decreasing your spouse's benefit) if that amount is greater than the benefit you would have received based on your own earnings.
- Your estate plan: Find out whether any parts of your estate plan should—and can be—changed. Items to consider include:
  - Amendment of revocable trusts
  - Designation of insurance policy beneficiaries
  - Designations of other beneficiaries and elections regarding, e.g., survivor benefits in retirement accounts
- Assisted living and long-term care: Get help understanding existing or new assisted living or long-term care insurance policies and

---

7. RMDs are not required from Roth IRAs during your lifetime.

plans. Evaluate, for example, whether your divorce settlement might disqualify you from needs-based assistance in the future.
- Health considerations: Health, which is universally included among the factors to be considered in support and property division awards, can be particularly important for older spouses. If you reasonably anticipate infirmities, impairments or illness, make sure that the relevant facts are part of your settlement discussions. Keep in mind that such conditions may be intensified or accelerated by divorce-related stress.

Sizing Up a Lawyer: The Initial Consultation

Once you've assembled your short-list of lawyers, you're ready to interview some. When you call up for an initial consultation (IC), ask how you'll be charged for it. Since an IC is partly a "meet and greet," some lawyers charge a reduced rate. Others charge a reduced rate when asked if they do.

Be cautious with lawyers offering free consultations, as many lawyers consider that a bad practice that leads to advice based on incomplete information.

What to Look For at the IC

Besides providing an opportunity for advice regarding your case, the IC is your chance to learn these important things about a lawyer:
- Knowledge and experience regarding your circumstances: The IC gives you the chance to learn specifics about a lawyer's expertise and experience. For example, is the lawyer familiar with matters such as military benefits, royalties, or your spouse's construction business?
- Communication skills: Communication problems that appear in the relaxed atmosphere of an initial consultation will only worsen as your case progresses. Pay attention to whether your questions are answered clearly and thoroughly.
- Listening skills: Poor listening is one of the biggest sources of disconnect in any relationship. (Can you think of a failed relationship where listening skills were an issue?) Many lawyers are lousy listeners, so pay attention to how the lawyer . . . pays attention to what you have to say.
- Compatibility: You're not looking for a new BFF at your IC. But you must be able to connect with the lawyer well enough to ensure a

productive working relationship based on clear communication and mutual respect.

Preparing For an Initial Consultation

Obviously, the IC is a critical event in your divorce. Prepare for it as follows:

- Fill out a Statutory Criteria Summary (see Appendix 1): You can download it from www.divorcesimplystated.com. "Updates and Materials" to provide the lawyer a timesaving summary of your case.
- Select questions from the Initial Consultation Checklist: Following the Statutory Criteria Summary is this exhaustive checklist of questions that can be asked at an IC. Choose a handful to ask that are of particular importance to you.
- Bring key documents with you: Bring along 2 or 3 years of tax returns and a net worth statement (a list of assets and liabilities with estimated dollar values). If you use Quicken or other budgeting software, bring 2 or 3 years' worth of year-end spending summaries.
- Educate yourself with the right resources: As discussed in Chapter 1, nearly every state court system website provides information about how family matters proceed there. That's the best place to go for basic information about "divorce procedure" in your state.

Rating How Your Friends Rate Their Lawyers

Test the reliability of your friends' opinions of their lawyers with the following questions:

- Did the lawyer understand your goals and remember them as your case progressed?
- Were immediate concerns such as temporary support or visitation addressed quickly
- How quickly did the lawyer respond to your emails and phone calls?
- Did you feel your questions were answered frankly and in a way you could understand?
- Were you sufficiently prepared for meetings and court proceedings?
- Did you feel that you were kept informed of the progress of your case?
- Did the lawyer seem confident and persuasive in depositions, hearings, and settlement conferences?
- Did you feel that the lawyer's staff and associate attorneys were knowledgeable?
- Did you feel that the lawyer made a meaningful effort to settle your case?
- Did you feel that your lawyer tried to move the case along?
- Did you feel that the billing practices were fair?
- What did you like most/least about your lawyer?

Where to Find Attorney Right

Now that you have a better idea of what you want in a court-based lawyer, here's where to look for Attorney Right.[8]

Personal Recommendations

Once you've decided upon the type of lawyer and divorce that you want (ADR vs. traditional), begin assembling your lawyer shortlist with recommendations from attorneys you know personally. If you don't know any lawyers (or don't want to admit to knowing them), ask other professionals you trust such as mental health professionals who deal with local divorce lawyers.

It's also important to ask clients about their divorce lawyers to learn how the client was treated. However, be aware that clients can form unsound opinions of their lawyers for many reasons, including:
- Some clients blame lawyers for not reaching (sometimes unrealistic) goals.
- Narcissistic clients may blame others (especially their lawyers) for their woes; or conversely, tout their lawyers' brilliance to demonstrate their own brilliance in choosing them.
- Emotionally needy clients may exaggerate the job their attorneys did, perceiving them as faultless knights in shining armor.

Institutional Referrals

If you don't know a lawyer or anyone else who can recommend a divorce lawyer, you may wish to try a lawyer referral service. These services are maintained or authorized by state, county, and city bar associations in each state and U.S. territory. To find the closest one to you, visit the American Bar Association website, abanet.org. Select "Public Resource," then "Lawyer Referral Services," followed by the name of your state.

One note of caution: Many lawyers put their names on referral lists to build their practices. So be sure the lawyer has the experience and skills required for your case.

---

8. Before beginning your search, make sure that you are not forgetting free or discounted legal services that may be available to you through an employment- or union-provided legal services plan.

Bar Association Participation

Most lawyers who are active in family law committees or "sections" of state or county bar associations tend to stay current on developments in the law. However, mere membership in a family law section doesn't tell you much, other than it shows interest in family law. Most officers of the state bar association's family law section (past and present) are likely to be above-average family lawyers.

As mentioned in Chapter 3, family law sections usually contain a little-known "Fount of Family Law Knowledge." To tap into it, obtain contact information on Section officers from your state bar association's website. Call one of the officers and ask which Section members make presentations to the Section regarding family law recent developments. Those are likely to be energetic lawyers who know your state's family law as well as anyone. And the younger ones who don't yet charge top rates for their superior knowledge may be a great bargain.

Lawyer Rating Services, Professional Memberships, and Directories

The following resources provide useful information to evaluate lawyers' qualifications.

- Martindale Hubbell (www.martindale.com) with its 1.0-5.0 peer rating system is the most reliable lawyer directory/rating service. Its printed version, available in many libraries and law offices, contains (for those law firms that pay extra for it) information regarding each lawyer's professional achievements and practice areas.
- The American Academy of Matrimonial Lawyers at www.aaml.org offers a searchable database of AAML membership, which, as noted above, may be the single best credential for top divorce lawyers.
- State judiciary websites list lawyers certified in matrimonial law. In the states listed above that offer certification, this is another excellent indicator of family law expertise.
- National Board of Trial Advocacy is a non-profit body accredited by the ABA to certify lawyers in family law trial advocacy. Where court proceedings are expected, this is a significant credential. Some states have used it to qualify state-certified family lawyers.
- "Super Lawyers" at www.superlawyers.com and "Best Lawyers" at www.bestlawyers.com/Search. Inclusion on these lists is a relatively

reliable indicator of high competence. The lists are far from infallible, however. For example, "Super Lawyer" partners often promote their associates as promising younger lawyers known as "Rising Stars." That means that some of the "Rising Stars" (who later graduate to "Super Lawyer" status) are designated as such more because of where they practice family law than how well they do it.

- Avvo.com. Avvo and similar online sites rely principally upon information supplied by lawyers about themselves. Although Avvo may be the best of the lot, these sites are not nearly as reliable as Martindale.

By the way, if you're thinking about finding a lawyer in the yellow pages, don't. Use the phone book to find a lawyer's phone number, not to find a lawyer.

Revisiting the 'Quality Lawyer Bargain Table'

The very first "pearl of wisdom" discussed in Chapter 3 is called "Find the Quality Lawyer Bargain Table." You might want to go back there and review what makes a lawyer a (relative) bargain. Then try the following 3-step method to find a table full of them:

1. Visit www.aaml.org/find-a-lawyer.
2. Select your state to obtain contact information for members of the local chapter of the American Academy of Matrimonial Lawyers (AAML). That will give you access to quality matrimonial lawyers in your area. (If there are no AAML lawyers near you, call the closest one and ask for a referral to top matrimonial attorneys in your area who are members of law firms.)
3. Visit the law firm websites of the lawyers you find pursuant to step #2. Make sure that matrimonial law is the firm's specialty—or at least one of them. Then, locate the site's lawyer bio section. Skip past the pricey partners to younger, associate lawyers who practice matrimonial law.

If you discover an associate who fits the profile discussed in Chapter 3, congratulations! You've found yourself a high quality lawyer at a discount!

Unbundled Representation:
Saving Fees With Lawyers *a la Carte!*

In Chapter 5, we'll discuss cost savings associated with alternative dispute resolution. For example, mediations conducted without lawyers present can save money with a streamlined process that assigns the bulk of the legal work to one professional—the mediator.

Another valuable fee-saving technique is available in court-based cases. It's called "unbundled representation."[9] Also known as "discrete task" or "limited scope" representation, unbundled representation:
- Allows clients to control legal fees by retaining a lawyer to provide specified services, rather than handle all aspects of their case
- Allows lawyers to focus their participation on the areas where it will do the most good

Unbundled Representation Tasks

Certain services in divorce cases are relatively easy to separate from the others, and thus lend themselves readily to unbundling. Those services include:
- Conducting court proceedings such as temporary custody/support hearings, or trial
- Drafting court filings ("ghost-writing")[10]
- Drafting a settlement agreement
- Providing legal advice and opinions upon request
- Legal research
- Reviewing documents and agreements

A Recipe For Successful Unbundling

Successful unbundled representation arrangements require:
- A client who's able to manage certain tasks traditionally handled by lawyers

---

9. Unbundled representation should not be confused with the more traditional limited or "special appearance." The special appearance allows a party to contest the single issue of the court's jurisdiction over him/her without submitting to that jurisdiction. Several states have expanded their limited appearance rules to accommodate the trend toward unbundled legal services.

10. Note that even in states that allow some form of unbundled representation, "ghost writing" may not be permitted.

- A written agreement clearly stating the responsibilities of attorney and client
- A client fully educated as to how unbundled representation works, its benefits, and its limitations
- Adherence to state law and bar ethical rules

Cautions Regarding Unbundled Representation

Unbundled representation is not for everyone. Before going into an unbundled arrangement, make sure that all the specifics are reduced to writing and that both you and your lawyer are perfectly clear as to its scope. Be sure in particular to discuss with your lawyer potential downsides of such arrangements:

- An unbundled representation lawyer handling limited tasks may not be in a position to negotiate an overall settlement of your case
- Clients do not always know when to consult with a lawyer whose role is limited to providing advice, and thus may miss out on important guidance
- Clients who feel they can handle a particular task such as a "routine" court proceeding may find out otherwise when they hit the courtroom
- The line between the respective responsibilities of lawyer and client can become blurred

To find out if your state allows unbundled representation, visit the American Bar Association's website at http://americanbar.org/ and search the phrase "unbundling resources by state."

If You Feel You Cannot Afford a Lawyer . . .

As austerity budgets shrink legal assistance resources, it's more important than ever to know how to find free or subsidized legal services. Here's what to look for in your area:

- Publicly funded legal assistance programs:
    - The Legal Services Corporation is the largest funding source of legal assistance programs. You can find the LSC office closest to you at http://www.lsc.gov/.
    - The non-profit organization, Lawhelp provides a list of legal assistance resources in each state at www.lawhelp.org.

- ° Legal aid resources are also available on the American Bar Association website. Go to the "legal help" web page, http://www.abanet.org/legalservices/findlegalhelp/, select your state on the map, and then select "Free Legal help."
- Law school legal clinics: In these "legal aid clinics," law students supervised by professors provide free legal advice and assistance. You can find a list of your state's law schools at http://lawstudents.findlaw.com/. Then check the schools' websites to find out if they operate legal clinics that handle family cases.
- State bar association resources: Many state bar organizations fund or administer groups providing pro bono (free) legal services. In some states, residents can access such services online. Many state bar associations also maintain the lawyer referral directories mentioned above. Some of the listed lawyers are newer members of the bar, building their practices by charging "below-market" rates.
- Courthouse mediation: Limited court-sponsored mediation of child-related issues is free in some states. Other states such as Vermont, offer sliding scale fees to qualifying spouses. [1] In still others, a "court-annexed" ADR program refers cases to private mediators who charge below market rates. To find ADR resources in your state, go to the "family" page on your state's court system website. Search "ADR" or "mediation." And while you're there, look around. Many court system sites offer valuable information about court procedures and links to other useful resources.

---

1. Visit https://www.vermontjudiciary.org/GTC/Family/Mediation.aspx for more information.

Yes, there IS a quiz! Test what you have (or haven't) learned.

1. Which of the following distinguishes lawyer shopping from food shopping?
   A. Lawyers can be returned even if they're sour, bloated, or past their expiration date
   B. You're usually not allowed to squeeze lawyers before choosing them
   C. Both of the above

2. The best referral source for local divorce lawyers is:
   A. Your divorced Uncle Billy's website, StrangleShyster.com
   B. Your divorced Aunt Gladys's website, StrangleBilly.com
   C. A Yellow Pages display ad with a headshot large enough to tell if the lawyer really will "fight for your rights"
   D. A local attorney who can tell you which lawyers command the respect of the judges and other lawyers

3. Pro Bono is:
   A. Cher's PGA golfer daughter
   B. Cher's PGA golfer son
   C. Both A and B
   D. A U-2 tribute band
   E. A Latin term used to denote the providing of free legal services

4. Martindale Hubbell is:
   A. A male strip club in Hubbell, Michigan
   B. Robert Redford's character in "The Way We Were"
   C. A space telescope manufactured by Martindale, Inc.
   D. The leading directory of lawyers containing peer ratings, educational background and length of practice, plus additional details about lawyers and firms who pay to publish it

CHAPTER 5

Alternative Dispute Resolution: Saving Time, Money, and Your Sanity

"People with clenched fists cannot shake hands."

— Indira Gandhi

ADR can avoid many of the delays that plague court-based divorces.

ADR in Divorce

The term "alternative dispute resolution" (ADR) refers to several methods of settling legal disagreements outside the traditional "court-based" system. If you and your spouse wish to have more control of your divorce, and to settle it fairly and cooperatively, you should definitely consider ADR.

In ADR, lawyers usually play a smaller role than in court-based divorce.[2] Some folks feel that's reason enough to try it! But there's more: ADR is usually quicker, cheaper, and less adversarial than court-based divorce, which is why it's usually better for the participants—and their children.

Besides that, the court-based process relies on the "adversary system." That system dates back to Merry Olde England where the two not-so-merry methods of dispute resolution were "trial by battle" and "trial by ordeal." So today, hundreds of years later, court-based divorces retain some of each.

ADR Methods Used in Divorce Cases

The following ADR methods are used in divorce cases:
- Mediation
- Collaborative Divorce
- Cooperative Divorce

---

2. That's *not* true of arbitration, which while a form of ADR, is not *consensual* dispute resolution.

- Arbitration
- Court-Ordered Parenting Coordination

Mediation

Mediation is the most common form of divorce ADR. The two most popular types of divorce mediation[3] are:

- Facilitative mediation in which the mediator guides the participants to identify, analyze, and cooperatively resolve all issues.
- Evaluative mediation in which the mediator assesses the likelihood that the participants would achieve their respective goals if they went to court, and offers settlement recommendations based largely upon the likely outcome if they did. Evaluative mediation is very similar to the "pre-trial" process used in court-based divorce. At pre-trials, judges or experienced matrimonial lawyers, sometimes called "special masters," meet with self-represented parties and counsel (and sometimes represented parties as well) and recommend how the case should be settled, based again on likely outcomes at trial.

Neither facilitative nor evaluative mediators can dictate a particular result. If the participants are unable to reach agreement, they are free to proceed in court.

> ### From the Bizzaro-World Law Dictionary:
> Adversarial system—(1) The Anglo-American model of jurisprudence based on the clash of opponents. (2) The Anglo-American model of marriage based on the clash of opponents.

What Is a "Review Counsel" and Why Would I Need One?

Review counsel (sometimes called "consulting counsel") provide services to clients who are mediating their divorces. Usually, review counsel do not attend the mediation sessions. Instead, they have two principal roles:

1. To provide advice upon the client's request during the mediation process

---

3. A third, rarely used method is "transformative mediation," a process in which the participants control the course of the mediation and strive for "recognition" of the other party's needs, interests, and points of view.

2. To review (and sometimes prepare) the settlement agreement upon conclusion of the mediation

More specifically, if you mediate your divorce, your review counsel's job will be to:

- Support the mediation process and respect your desire for a fair result.
- Explain your rights and obligations in a way that mediators, who must remain neutral, cannot.
- Request that the mediator obtain any additional information or documents that counsel considers necessary.
- Help you choose reasonable goals. For example, if your review counsel advises that the facts and state law do not justify a claim against your spouse's inheritance, you can select a more realistic goal. Review counsel should not encourage clients to go for a "home run" result.
- Help you advocate effectively for yourself in the mediation.
- Propose settlement agreement language changes or new provisions to protect you.[4] For example, counsel might suggest an "indemnification" clause to protect you against your Ex's failure to pay a joint debt. Counsel should not try to alter basic terms that are reasonable.

If you are unable to afford review counsel, consider hiring a divorce financial planner or analyst (see Chapter 6) to help you define and achieve your financial goals in your mediation.

> Chapter 14 contains step-by-step instructions on how to negotiate your divorce settlement in both ADR and traditional divorces, whether or not you have a lawyer.

How I Mediate: Facilitative Mediation FAQs

Facilitative mediation is the more common of the two forms of private mediation, and is mainly what this chapter covers. Below are excerpts from a FAQ sheet I give clients for mediations that I conduct without lawyers

---

4. Note that in many states, mediators prepare a memorandum of understanding rather than the separation agreement itself. One of the review counsel then prepares an agreement based on the memorandum. The more efficient practice—provided that it is permitted in the jurisdiction—is for the mediator to prepare the agreement. This assumes that the mediator is a matrimonial attorney.

present. Note that each mediator has his own style, and that mediators' and review counsels' roles vary in different locales.

Q. How often will we meet, how long are the mediation sessions, and how many sessions will there be?

A. Sessions are typically 10 to 14 days apart and last about 2 hours. A mediator can't predict the number of sessions needed before knowing the facts of your case and how close you are to agreeing on key issues.

Q. Won't mediation be more, rather than less expensive if 3 lawyers (the mediator and 2 review counsel) are involved?

A. A successfully mediated divorce should be less expensive because one lawyer (the mediator) does the great majority of the work. Mediation also saves fees through quicker gathering of information and issue resolution.

Q. I have been primarily responsible for raising our children while my spouse has pursued a career in finance. How can I compensate for my lack of financial expertise?

A. Part of the mediator's role is to "level the playing field" by explaining legal and financial concepts. Good mediators don't accept cases if they believe a spouse is:
   • Severely "overmatched"
   • Incapable of understanding the issues
   • Unable to meaningfully participate in resolving the issues

If you are concerned that you might not be able to hold your own with your STBX, advise the mediator of that at the outset. Even if you don't have such concerns, make sure to ask questions throughout the process about anything you don't fully understand. If you continue to struggle with a concept, ask the mediator to explain it further after the session.

Q. How do I know that all the necessary information about my spouse's finances will be disclosed in the mediation?

A. Early in the process, mediators require information and documents from the participants. Additional information and documents are typically requested as the mediation progresses. The mediator may also recommend experts such as appraisers, accountants, and actuaries to provide additional information and analysis if necessary. Your review counsel can monitor compliance with, and propose additions to the mediator's requests.

Q. What happens if my spouse and I reach an impasse?

A. Mediators use a variety of techniques to deal with particularly difficult issues. For example, the mediator may suggest
- That participants reframe an issue or position in a less confrontational manner.
- Meeting with each participant separately, in a process called "caucusing." In caucus, the mediator can explore a participant's goals, concerns, and "bottom line" positions, and candidly help him/her re-think unrealistic positions and goals.

Advantages of Mediation

Mediation offers the following advantages:
- Limits the hostility fostered by the court-based adversary system
- Allows clients to maintain much more control than in court-based divorces
- Usually saves money by:
  - Beginning the settlement process immediately
  - Expediting the discovery process

Mediation cools the hostility that the adversary system encourages.

  - Dealing quickly and efficiently with disputes that arise along the way
  - Usually takes less time than court-based divorce
  - Empowers participants to fashion their own creative solutions in which they are more invested and thus more likely to honor
  - Attends to details that are often overlooked in court-based cases
  - Allows participants to handle their divorce in a private and confidential manner

When Mediation Doesn't Work

Despite its benefits, mediation will not work when:
- Participants are not emotionally prepared to resolve issues cooperatively in face-to-face meetings
- There is too large a disparity in the participants' financial sophistication

- One participant tries to use mediation to work around the legal system and impose his/her will on the other
- A participant insists upon unrealistic goals
- A participant won't agree to anything without first checking with review counsel

General Skills and Attributes Your Mediator Should Have

Mediators should have at least the half-dozen credentials and attributes listed below that were mentioned in Chapter 2 with regard to court-based lawyers. Note that the last 3 items on the list may be even more important for mediators than lawyers:

- Professionalism
- Family law experience and credentials
- Compatibility with clients
- Communication (including listening) skills
- Empathy
- Mediation-Specific Skills and Attributes

In addition to the above, the following are important attributes for a divorce mediator:

- Experience and training in mediating family matters
- Neutrality
- The ability to "reframe" issues in non-contentious ways
- The ability to guide participants to a fair and reasonable agreement
- The ability to get participants to focus on "interests" rather than "positions" that may or may not serve their interests
- Efficiency and practicality
- Familiarity with the range of likely outcomes had the parties chosen a court-based divorce
- Doesn't charge an arm and a leg (or any other body parts)
- Is a matrimonial attorney, though mediations of child-related issues only can be handled either by mental health professionals or lawyers familiar with the basics of child development)

Finding a Mediator

Use the following resources to find a mediator:

- Referrals from lawyers or mental health professionals who treat families in divorce. As is the case with lawyers, these professionals are the most reliable referral sources.

- Roster of "Advanced Practitioners" of The Association for Conflict Resolution (ACR), available at http://www.acrfamily.org/advanced-practitioners
- Local mediation societies. Contact ACR for information about mediation groups in your state.
- Referrals from former mediation clients.
- Where available, rosters of certified family mediators. No jurisdiction requires certification of private practice mediators. However, the following states require that mediators who receive court referrals meet certain training, experience, and educational requirements:[5]
  - Arkansas
  - California
  - New Hampshire

In addition, the following states offer voluntary certification for mediators:
- Florida
- New Hampshire
- South Carolina
- North Carolina
- Virginia
- Washington

If you live in one of the states immediately above, search your state court system websites for a roster of certified mediators.

What You Need to Know About Your Mediation

Before your mediation begins, you should know the following:
- Will the mediator provide educational material on mediation, including its voluntary nature, the mediator's impartiality, and confidentiality issues?
- Will the mediator provide forms or checklists to help you organize your financial information?
- In what circumstances will the mediator recommend review counsel?
- Is the mediator familiar with local judges and court customs?
- Who decides the order in which issues will be discussed?

---

5. In other states, such as Massachusetts, confidentiality laws apply only to mediations conducted by mediators who meet training and experience requirements.

- In situations where one spouse is less knowledgeable about financial matters, how will the mediator "level the playing field?"

What Your Mediator Owes You

As a participant in facilitative mediation, you can reasonably expect the following from your mediator:

- Availability to complete the mediation within a reasonable amount of time
- A written agreement specifying the obligations of participants and mediator, including the fee arrangement
- An unbiased approach to issue resolution
- Clear explanations of relevant legal and financial concepts and their applicability to your circumstances … and the patience to repeat those explanations if necessary
- Recommended rules of conduct such as
    ○ How and to what extent issues can be discussed outside mediation sessions, including each participant's right to end the discussion at any time
    ○ Prohibition of ex parte (unilateral) discussions between a participant and the mediator
    ○ Prohibition of threats of court action or other intimidating conduct
- Attention to marital relationship dynamics that affect the mediation
- Facilitation of a reasonable agreement that will pass muster with local judges
- Assistance with promoting your children's best interests, including (where applicable) counseling and other resource recommendations
- Supervision of disclosure of relevant information and documents
- Skillful use of mediation techniques such as caucusing
- If necessary, recommendations of accountants, appraisers, actuaries, or mental health professionals
- Preparation of
    ○ Settlement agreement, in states where permitted, which accurately memorializes the resolution of issues and contains reasonable protections for the participants
    ○ Memorandum of settlement in states where mediators do not draft agreements

What You Owe Your Mediator (and Your Spouse)

Your mediator and your spouse can reasonably expect the following from you:

- That you enter the mediation with a good faith intention to resolve all issues fairly and efficiently
- That you be willing to compromise when necessary
- That you not try to use the mediation process to obtain unfair advantage over your spouse
- That you not knowingly act against your children's best interests
- That you preserve and fully disclose
  - Relevant information relating to your finances
  - Other pertinent facts relating to your children and other non-financial issues
- That you comply with interim agreements reached during the process
- That you and your spouse agree in good faith upon how and what you will communicate to your children about your mediation and divorce
- That you choose review counsel who support the mediation process
- That you comply with all court orders in your divorce including "automatic orders" that prohibit property transfers, non-routine expenditures, insurance cancellation and removing children from the jurisdiction.
- That you communicate to your spouse and mediator any substantial changes in your financial or other circumstances

Determine Your Goals and Negotiation Strategy, and Avoid Being the Path of Least Resistance

Mediators facing an impasse may look for concessions from participants to help them reach agreement on a particular issue. Consciously or not, mediators sometimes take the "path of least resistance" by seeking more, or larger, concessions from the participant who appears to be more reasonable and flexible.

In mediation, you should be reasonable and flexible. However, you don't want to be perceived as weak when difficult issues arise. To avoid that, do the following before the mediation process begins:

- Decide on your goals (see the material on goals in Chapters 1 and 14) and how best to achieve them by:

  ° Identifying your essential needs regarding at least the "Big
    Three" divorce issues (and related issues listed in Chapter 1) that
    apply to you:
    (1) Amount of child support and/or amount and duration of
        spousal support
    (2) Division of property and debts including mediation and
        legal fees
    (3) (if applicable) Allocation of time and decision-making
        regarding the kids in a manner consistent with their
        best interests
  ° Deciding on your initial positions regarding the issues above that
    exceed, or are at the high range of what is acceptable to you. This
    will create "wiggle room" for concessions you can make without
    sacrificing your must-haves. In Chapter 14, we will discuss in
    detail how to create a complete negotiation strategy.
- Consult a divorce lawyer (even if you can't afford to hire review
  counsel) or a certified divorce financial analyst before you begin the
  mediation. Discuss whether and how you should adjust your goals
  and negotiation approach given your state's law, your circumstances,
  and how local judges would likely rule on your case if it went to
  trial. (See Chapter 14.)

If You Feel Pressured ...
Occasionally, overzealous mediators pressure participants into
poor decisions. If you feel that is happening to you and are having
difficulty sticking to your game plan, calmly but firmly express that
concern. If the pressure continues, state that you'd like to suspend
the session in order to consult with your lawyer or financial advisor.

Collaborative Divorce

Over the last 20 years, a second form of ADR known as "collaborative
divorce" has become increasingly popular. Collaborative divorce addresses
the items in the "When Mediation Won't Work" list above. Other than in
states that have adopted The Uniform Collaborative Law Act (see below),
most collaborative divorces are conducted privately. Private collaborative
divorces proceed generally as follows:

- Spouses negotiate settlements directly as in mediation, but in a
  series of "4-way" negotiation sessions with their lawyers present and
  participating.

- There is no mediator or other neutral third party to guide the process.
- Participants and their lawyers sign an agreement making settlement their primary goal and further providing that
  - Participants and lawyers will work cooperatively to resolve all issues
  - The parties will provide full disclosure of all relevant financial and other information
  - Aggressive techniques such as threatening litigation are forbidden
  - If the parties fail to reach agreement, the lawyers must terminate representation of their clients, thus providing both participants and lawyers an additional incentive to settle
- A "team approach" is used in which
  - Divorce coaches and child development experts are made available as necessary to help parents understand and deal with children's issues and concerns
  - If necessary, the parties agree upon additional facilitators such as appraisers, certified divorce planners and accountants

The Uniform Collaborative Law Act (UCLA)

State laws differ greatly in their use of collaborative dispute resolution. In 2009, The Uniform Law Commission sought to address this problem with The Uniform Collaborative Law Act (UCLA), which has since been enacted in:

- Alabama
- The District of Columbia
- Hawaii
- Nevada
- Ohio
- Texas
- Utah
- Washington

The Act's provisions (as amended in 2010) include:

- Voluntary referral procedures by state courts, including extended "stays" (delays) of pending cases while the collaborative process is ongoing
- Confidentiality of all communications (and thus prohibition of their use in court proceedings) if the collaborative process fails

• Minimum standards for collaborative agreements

Cautions Regarding Collaborative Divorce

Collaborative divorce offers an efficient way for divorcing parties to control their path to settlement. Nevertheless, the process has several potential downsides:
• Like mediation, it won't work if the parties are not emotionally prepared for face-to-face negotiation
• It won't work if the lawyers behave too much like . . . lawyers
• Parties who don't reach agreement must start over with new counsel

The last item, sometimes called the "disqualification requirement," distinguishes collaborative divorce from its sister ADR process, "cooperative divorce." The two processes are essentially the same except that if the cooperative divorce process fails, the parties' lawyers may continue to represent their clients in a traditional divorce. That distinction renders cooperative divorce acceptable to some lawyers who believe that mandatory disqualification punishes clients for failing to resolve all issues, and emphasizes reaching any agreement over reaching a reasonable one. For whatever reason, however, cooperative divorce has never really caught on.

Court-Ordered Parenting Coordination

Another type of ADR available in some states is court-ordered parenting coordination ("PC"). Unlike other forms of ADR, PC is not always voluntary. PC is:
• Used to resolve ongoing parental disputes, to formulate parenting plans, and to try to build durable co-parenting relationships
• Particularly useful where parents have failed to co-parent, comply with court orders, or protect children from parental conflict
• Often ordered by judges to monitor particularly difficult cases, in which case it is
    ◦ Not confidential
    ◦ Involuntary
• Administered by parenting coordinators who typically have
    ◦ Graduate degrees in law, psychology, counseling, or related disciplines
    ◦ Training in conflict resolution, child development, and similar areas
    ◦ Knowledge of state divorce law and procedure

       º Licenses (in states where available)
- A process that focuses on children's rather than parents' needs in resolving child-related issues

States Using Court-Ordered Parenting Coordination

As of this writing, the following states have PC. However, its use is expanding, so check with a local matrimonial lawyer to see if it has recently become available in your locale.

- Arizona
- Colorado
- Delaware (pilot program)
- Florida
- Idaho
- Kentucky (in certain counties)
- Louisiana
- Maryland (in certain counties)
- Massachusetts
- Michigan (some judges order PC despite the lack of an authorizing statute or court rules)
- Minnesota (has "parenting time expeditor" statute similar to PC)
- New Hampshire
- North Carolina
- Ohio (in certain counties)
- Oklahoma
- Oregon
- Texas

Arbitration Pros and Cons

In arbitration, a neutral lawyer chosen by the parties is paid to decide a case. The arbitrator receives testimony and other evidence in a hearing much like a court trial. Arbitration is the one form of ADR in which a resolution can be imposed on the participants.

Experienced arbitrators can be found on The American Arbitration Association website: https://www.adr.org/.

As with all divorce dispute resolution methods, arbitration has its pros and cons:
- Pro: Participants can choose the arbitrator.

- Pro: Participants have more control over scheduling.
- Pro: Arbitration hearings are typically scheduled more quickly than court trials.
- Pro: The pre-trial discovery process is expedited, avoiding the delays in exchanging information and documents that slow court-based cases.
- Con: Arbitration carries an additional expense—the arbitrator's fee.
- Con: Arbitration retains the conflict of adversarial proceedings.
- Con: Most states don't allow arbitration of "ultimate" child-related issues such as custody. In some jurisdictions, arbitration is limited to "post-judgment" issues (disputes that arise after the parties are divorced).[6]
- Con: Arbitration will not prevent the parties from ignoring the arbitration result and seeking a court trial if
  - State law does not allow "binding arbitration" of family cases in which arbitrators' decisions become a judgment of the court (the same as a judge's decision)
  - State law does allow binding arbitration but the parties will not agree that their arbitration will be binding

---

6. In recent years, some states have expanded the scope of divorce-related arbitration to include children's issues. A few such as New Jersey even authorize child custody to be arbitrated. Although more states are likely to expand the role of arbitration in family cases, jurisdictions permitting custody arbitration are likely to remain in the minority. As always, check with a local family law practitioner for the latest on your state's law.

Yes, there IS a quiz! Test what you have (or haven't) learned.

1. Modern courthouses have the following in common with the castles in Merry Olde England where our judicial system originated:
    A. Not so merry black-robed figures who decide people's fates from on high
    B. Even less merry guards at the entrance
    C. "Trials by ordeal"
    D. All of the above

2. ADR won't work if:
    A. You show up for your mediation session at a meditation center
    B. The lawyers in a collaborative divorce are not emotionally prepared to sit down together and simulate the behavior of human beings
    C. Mediation or collaborative divorce participants are not willing to work in good faith toward a fair result
    D. You live in the Middle Ages
    E. All of the above
    F. None of the above
    G. Some of the above but you're not telling which
    H. You expire before getting to the end of this question

CHAPTER 6

Using Financial Planners, Coaches, and Other Non-Lawyer Professionals

> *"Wise men don't need advice.*
> *Fools won't take it."*
>
> — Benjamin Franklin

Who Needs a Lawyer?

You do. If you can possibly afford to, meet with a divorce lawyer even if it's only for an initial evaluation of your case. When you make the appointment, ask what paperwork the lawyer needs to be able to give you a range of likely outcomes.

In any event, fill out and bring with you the Initial Consultation Checklist (See Appendix 2) that you can download from www.divorcesimplystated .com/updates-materials/. See material in Chapter 4 regarding "initial consultations."

If you can afford a bit more in legal fees, you have options to use a lawyer "part-time" rather than one who will handle your entire case:

- If your case is mediated, a "review counsel" can advise you as needed during the process, and prepare or review your settlement agreement upon its conclusion. (See Chapter 5.)
- In court-based cases, a majority of states now permit "unbundled" or "discrete task" representation where lawyers perform only specified tasks. These tasks can include contested court proceedings, legal research and settlement

Avoid getting crushed by legal fees. Use other professionals as well!

negotiation. (See Chapter 4 to learn how unbundled representation works.)

These options give you the opportunity to obtain an experienced divorce lawyer's assistance on a limited, "targeted" basis even if you can't afford to retain one. And that assistance will vastly improve your chances of achieving a positive divorce outcome.

A lawyer's help is particularly important to:
- Evaluate your case and advise you about a negotiation strategy, including likely outcomes
- Explain how to use the strengths of your case to your advantage, and minimize the impact of any weaknesses
- Explain how applicable law and courthouse customs will affect your case
- Represent you in contested court proceedings and depositions if they become necessary
- Make sure a spouse's business is correctly valued and its earnings accurately portrayed
- Prepare enforceable interim agreements
- Negotiate settlement
- Advise you regarding issues about which you may be unaware, such as
    - Tax ramifications of various settlement alternatives
    - Valuation and division of retirement plans
    - Life insurance to insure spousal and child support
    - Protection if your STBX files for bankruptcy
    - Enforcement of your settlement agreement
    - Protection of your rights as a military spouse
- Prepare a final settlement agreement (see Appendix 5) with clear, enforceable language that meets legal requirements in areas such as
    - Spousal support that qualifies for tax treatment as alimony, if applicable
    - Impact of cohabitation on spousal support
    - Property valuation
    - Retirement plans

Limiting Lawyer Time

In Chapter 7 you'll learn a host of ways to limit legal fees by
- Choosing the right lawyer for you and your case
- Using your lawyer's time wisely
- Maintaining a functional relationship with your lawyer

Chapter 7 also covers the use of "traditional" professionals such as accountants and paralegals to perform non-legal or "quasi-legal" work for less than lawyers charge, or even for free. This chapter covers some less traditional types of professionals who will save you money and help you maximize your results.

Divorce Coaches

Divorce coaches do not provide legal advice, and are not substitutes for lawyers. Coaches offer services that most divorce lawyers don't.[7] Meeting with a divorce coach (and one of the divorce financial professionals discussed below) before you hire an attorney will allow you to
- Gain a general understanding of how divorce works
- Begin divorce preparation so that your initial dealings with your lawyer are more efficient and productive
- Provide emotional support and if necessary, refer you to counseling

If you do go on to retain a lawyer, your coach can remain involved. In fact, coaches can be highly effective when working with cooperating lawyers.[8]

In addition to the above, divorce coaches can assist you by:
- Helping you make choices, including:
  - Whether you should be considering alternatives to divorce, and
  - Whether you are emotionally prepared to make life decisions, and if not, how you can become so

Divorce coaches can help you organize those mountains of paperwork.

---

7. Note, however, that your communications with coaches and financial planners/analysts are *not* privileged and thus can be "discovered" by opposing counsel.

8. This occurs, for example, in the collaborative divorce "team approach" discussed in Chapter 5.

- Facilitating your recovery from the end of your marriage
- Familiarizing you generally with the divorce process including the types of professional assistance you may need
- Helping you organize financial and other documents and information
- Helping you optimize your attorney/client relationship
- Helping you support your children and serve their interests
- Helping you forge a new co-parenting relationship
- Providing you with techniques to manage emotions and resolve conflict
- Helping you make sound, intentional life choices
- Empowering you to transition to a happy and productive post-divorce life

Finding a Divorce Coach

Many divorce coaches come from backgrounds in mental health, mediation and even law. Others are drawn to coaching as a result of their own divorce experiences. As with divorce planners/analysts and private practice mediators, there is no mandatory certification of divorce coaches. Thus, personal recommendations from other divorce professionals and former clients are particularly important in selecting a divorce coach.

Your divorce coach should have substantial experience in the field and have been trained and certified by a private organization such as The CDC College for Divorce Coaching.[9]

Certified Divorce Financial Analysts (CDFAs) and Certified Financial Divorce Practitioners (CFDPs)

Certified Divorce Financial Analysts (CDFAs) and Certified Financial Divorce Practitioners (CFDPs) provide financial advice and assistance during divorce less expensively than attorneys. The main difference between CDFAs and CFDPs is that CDFAs are certified by The Institute for Divorce Financial Analysts while CFDPs are certified by The Academy of Financial

Don't be a sad sack! You can limit legal fees by getting help from non-lawyers.

9. Help locating local divorce coaches is available at the CDC website: http://certifieddivorcecoach.com/

Divorce Practitioners. For ease of reference, I'll refer to both collectively as "CDFAs."

An experienced CDFA can help you by
- Organizing your financial documents
- Evaluating your current financial circumstances
- Helping you prepare your financial disclosure statement
- Explaining retirement plans including
  ○ Plan elections that determine the type of benefit you want such as whether it includes survivors' benefits
  ○ What will occur upon the death of the employee spouse
  ○ How to divide retirement plans using qualified domestic relations orders ("QDROs")
- Explaining tax aspects of divorce such as
  ○ How pre-2019 alimony can help both spouses save money
  ○ The value of tax exemptions (pre-2018) and tax credits relating to your kids
  ○ How to identify future costs "hidden" in securities, such as
    - Unrealized capital gains
    - Stock and bond fund "back-end" fees, commissions and penalties
- Analyzing current and long-term spending at various income levels
- Projecting the long term effect of various settlement scenarios, adjusted for inflation and other factors

In mediation and collaborative law cases, savvy spouses agree upon a single CDFA to provide the above-listed services to both of them. Sharing the expertise of a single expert is one of the ways ADR can save you money.

CDFAs should not be confused with experts known as "forensic accountants" who are hired to value business interests or determine the earnings of a small business. Traditionally, forensic accountants have been used most often in court-based cases to
- Help formulate a settlement negotiation strategy
- Provide expert testimony
- Evaluate the other spouse's expert testimony and provide litigation support if negotiations break down

Again, however, in circumstances such as where a closely held business must be valued, try to avoid costly "battles of the experts" by agreeing on a single expert.

Other Divorce Consultants

There are other experts with whom you can consult in either an ADR or a court-based case to help you better understand settlement alternatives and likely outcomes. Unlike the use of divorce coaches and CDFAs, using the following experts will generally not reduce your legal fees. However, their expertise can help you achieve your divorce goals and save or generate money for you in your settlement.

Forensic and Other Psychologists

Lawyers have long used forensic psychologists as expert witnesses in contested custody cases. But mental health professionals can also be used as consultants to
  * Assess parenting issues
  * Help improve parenting skills
  * Perform psychological testing
  * Interpret existing psychological test results
  * Recommend options such as
    ◦ Individual counseling
    ◦ Parenting and family counseling
    ◦ Parenting coordination (see page 82)
  * Evaluate sexual abuse and other domestic violence

Vocational Experts

Vocational experts perform "employability assessments" to determine a spouse's
  * Employability
  * Income potential
  * Highest level of occupational functioning
  * Need for training and education

A vocational expert's services are most often used where a spouse appears to be earning below his/her "earning capacity" (i.e., "dogging it") or otherwise earning less than he/she could be expected to. Vocational experts base their conclusions on factors such as
  * A spouse's history of higher income
  * A spouse's earnings that fall below industry norms
  * Potentially income-producing skills that a spouse chooses not to use

> ## Court Rules Regarding Expert Witnesses
> ⚠ Court rules require that expert witnesses be identified and the substance of their testimony disclosed. Failure to meet disclosure deadlines can result in exclusion of your expert's testimony if your case goes to trial.

Appraisers

Listed below are the types of appraisers most commonly used in divorce cases. (See Chapter 13 for material on business valuation, and Chapter 18 for help with finding an appraiser.)

- Real estate appraisers
- Appraisers of antiques, collectibles and artwork
- Appraisers of business interests

Other valuations are available if you can't afford an appraiser. But values from non-appraisers may be less reliable and are generally inadmissible in court except by agreement.

For example, realtors will provide "opinions of value" of a family home and other real estate. However, values from realtors eager for your signature on a listing agreement typically come in a bit higher than those of appraisers.

Sites like eBay can also shed light on values of antiques and collectibles for use in settlement discussions. However, prices from eBay-type sites or any source other than a testifying qualified expert, are inadmissible in court. If you do try eBay, use actual sales results (not asking prices) of items substantially the same as yours in nature and condition.

More reliable sources of information regarding value include:
- Antique and collectible dealers—you can find local antique dealers at: http://www.local.com/results.aspx?keyword=collectibles+shop&cid
- Price guides and valuation services including, for example,
  - Kovels price guides for antiques and collectibles at http://www.kovels.com/
  - Beckett Grading Services at http://www.beckett.com/grading/ or Professional Sports Authenticators at www.psacard.com
- Vendors at antique and collectible shows

- Auction houses offering free appraisals, hoping for a commission if you use them to sell the item

> ### Online Updates
> The law is evolving regarding the use of forensic computer experts to search electronic devices during the discovery phase of divorces. For free updates on this and other issues, visit http://DivorceSimplyStated.com.

Forensic Computer Experts

Computer forensic experts are occasionally used in divorce cases to examine computer hard drives in order to

- Locate documents, photos, and videos including emails and other electronic correspondence (including items "deleted" from the device)
- Determine information regarding the origination of computer contents such as
  - ° The identity of the preparer or originator of the item
  - ° The date of preparation or origination
  - ° Whether, when and by whom an item has been modified

As with all divorce professionals, hire only a computer expert with training, expertise and experience that relate to the issues in your case. The following computer experts should have the necessary training to perform divorce-related tasks.

- Certified Computer Examiners (CCE), certified by The International Society of Forensic Computer Examiners (ISFCE)
- Certified Forensic Computer Examiners (CFCE), certified by The International Association of Computer Investigative Specialists (IACIS), which specializes in law enforcement
- Professional Certified Investigators (PCI), certified by ASIS International

Yes, there IS a quiz! Test what you have (or haven't) learned.

1. This chapter is mainly about:

A. Finding more divorce professionals to pay

B. Facebook-friending that nerdy kid Sheldon who you gave wedgies in high school, when you find out he's a CDFA

C. Deleting from your draft box those poison pen emails to your spouse that you wrote to feel better but had the good sense not to send

D. Saving on legal fees by using non-lawyer professionals for certain tasks; and deciding what other professionals you may need

2. Pronounce out loud at your child's school Open House Night, and then unscramble the following key phrases from this chapter!

A. tacoviloan sexterp

B. revcodi shecoca

C. reinscof slopyhogstics

CHAPTER 7

Embracing the Tiger: How to Work With and Spend Less on Lawyers

"We are all born ignorant, but one must work hard to remain stupid."

— Benjamin Franklin

Five of the Best Ways to Cut Down on Legal Fees

There are a number of things you can do to save money on divorce lawyers. Here are 5 of the best of them:

1. Use ADR methods such as mediation or collaborative divorce to quickly begin work on settling your case.
2. If yours is a court-based divorce, choose an experienced litigator of family cases, but one who believes that most family cases should be settled.
3. In any type of divorce, avoid overpaying by researching family law-yers' hourly rates and "incremental billing" practices in your area.
4. Avoid legal fees by using non-lawyers for tasks that are primarily financial or child-related rather than legal in nature.
5. Control legal fees with an efficient attorney/client relationship.

We've already touched on #1—4, though we will revisit #3 here. Most of this chapter will focus on item #5; how to work efficiently with your lawyer to achieve a quicker, cheaper and better outcome in your case.

Financial Considerations in Choosing a Lawyer, Revisited

Chapter 4 included a list of tips on evaluating the cost of a lawyer. In case you spilled your energy drink on it, here it is again:

- Find out from divorced friends and local law firms what local divorce lawyers charge.

- Make sure that any unused portion of your retainer is refundable.
  - Lawyers in affluent communities may charge more than comparable lawyers with offices in more modest areas. Don't pay more for a lawyer's elegant digs.
  - All other things being equal, save fees on travel time by choosing a lawyer who is located closer to the courthouse.

  - ⚠ Billing Increments: Find out in what increments a lawyer charges to learn the lawyer's real or "effective hourly rate." Increments are what causes a 3-minute phone call with a lawyer who charges at $450/hr. and bills in 1/10 hour increments to cost less than the same call to a $350/hr. lawyer who bills in increments of 2/10 of an hour. (See material on minimum charges in Chapter 4.)

Keeping the Long Arm of the Law Out of Your Pocket: Saving Legal Fees by Understanding Your Fee Agreement

A lawyer's fee or "retainer" agreement should tell you most of what you need to know about how you'll be charged. Most states have ethical rules requiring lawyers to provide written agreements to family law clients. Even if your state doesn't require it, ask for a clearly written description of how you the billing works. Clarity benefits both attorney and client.

When reading your agreement, pay particular attention to the following:
- Hourly rates: Most divorce lawyers charge by the hour. The lawyer's rate as well as that of associate attorneys and paralegals must be clearly stated. If the agreement permits increases in the rates, ask the lawyer to keep the stated amount in effect throughout your case, or for at least 6 or 9 months. Finally, look for the billing increment language discussed above—the hidden fee inflator that catches many clients off guard.
- Flat fees: Some lawyers charge a flat fee for "simple" divorces. But many of those lawyers handle a high volume of cases, spending little time on any of them. Also, many flat fee agreements allow for additional fees if the case becomes more complicated than expected—something that may occur more often than not. In that event, make sure you understand
  - What constitutes an unexpected complication
  - How any increase is to be calculated

- Non-refundable retainers: If only some of a retainer (either the initial or any subsequent retainer payment) is used, will the unused portion be refunded? Unless the lawyer is the only competent/sober one in the county, don't agree to a non-refundable retainer. Find an attorney who charges you only for services actually provided.
  - Expenses: Be sure that your prior approval is required for major expenditures such as hiring an expert.
  - Travel time: Charges for trips to and from court are appropriate but paying your lawyer to drive home from court . . . not so much.
  - Premium billing: Beware of premium billing language that permits an additional charge if the lawyer achieves a "superior result." Lawyers don't hit enough home runs to earn bonuses.
  - "Communication fees": A very few law firms still charge a flat "communications fee" for phone calls, etc. in addition to the charge for time spent. These fees were originally intended to limit client phone calls. But lawyers' hourly rates these days compensate them quite sufficiently without the need for extras.

> ### From the Bizarro-World Law Dictionary
> **Retainer** (1) Something your orthodontist puts in your mouth that makes you gag. (2) Something your lawyer puts in his/her wallet that makes you gag.

Holding Down Legal Fees With a Productive Attorney/Client Relationship

Once you've hired a lawyer, you can save money with a productive attorney/client relationship. The relationship tends to work pretty well for lawyers—they get paid to play. It's your job to make it work for you.

Avoiding Familiar Relationship Mistakes

There are a number of ways to optimize your relationship with your lawyer. Start by avoiding mistakes from your last partnership—the one that sent you to a divorce lawyer in the first place. For example, DON'T:
- Harbor unrealistic expectations

- Be overly compliant or inattentive—a healthy relationship requires both partners to be engaged and mindful
- Be overly skeptical or contentious—make sure to participate in the relationship in a productive way
- Refuse to admit that you don't understand something
- Listen without truly hearing
- Blame your lawyer for delays and other things that aren't her fault
- Transfer feelings of victimization, betrayal, emotional need, etc. from your marriage to the relationship with your divorce lawyer

---

 A Lawyer's Top Ten List of Least Favorite Questions from New Clients

- If you're such a hotshot, why isn't your picture in the phone book?
- Do you mind if my parents, their attorney, and my "god-father" sit in on our meetings?
- Are we on the clock yet?
- Do I get a refund if you like ... screw up my case?
- Which one are you, Jacoby or Meyers?
- I thought you'd be ... bigger!
- When I put down my income on my financial disclosure statement, should I put what's on my tax returns or the real amount?
- You won't wear that outfit to court, right?
- Do any of the judges maybe owe you a favor?
- My brother-in-law's plumber knows a guy whose girl-friend's cousin only charges $500 for a divorce, soup to nuts. Can you beat his price?

Great Expectations . . . and Reasonable Ones

The first "relationship mistake" on the list above has to do with unrealistic expectations. Understanding the following will help you avoid them:

- Your lawyer can't change the facts of your case. She cannot, for example, magically increase your net worth, or transform your spouse into parent-of-the-year.
- Your lawyer is restricted by procedural and ethical rules that she must follow whether or not you think they make any sense.
- Your lawyer is neither interested in nor qualified to act as your therapist.

- Nearly everything in your case will take longer than you would like
  due to scheduling conflicts, court system inefficiencies, and life
  in general.

Mutual Obligations of Clients and Lawyers

Getting the most out of the attorney/client relationship requires that each
of you fulfill certain basic obligations to the other.

Your obligations to your lawyer are to:
- Fully disclose all relevant facts
- Notify your lawyer of any substantial change in your circumstances
- Communicate clearly and concisely
- Ask questions to make sure you understand what's going on
- Ask more questions to make doubly sure you understand
  what's going on
- Tell your lawyer about any misgivings you have concerning her
  advice or tactics
- Consult with your lawyer before any direct negotiations with
  your spouse
- Pay your lawyer's bills promptly, or make alternative arrangements
- Treat your lawyer with civility and respect

Your lawyer's obligations to you are to:
- Listen to and understand your goals, advise you as to their feasibil-
  ity and where appropriate, suggest alternatives
- Devise a plan to achieve your reasonable goals
- Keep you informed of all developments in your case
- Respond to your calls and emails within a reasonable period of time
- Use her experience and expertise to resolve your case as favorably
  as possible
- Consult with you before incurring any substantial expenses
- Use her time as efficiently as possible
- Make sure her bills are consistent with her fee agreement
- Keep your communications confidential
- Pay attention to your concerns and address them
- Treat you with civility and respect

Embracing the Tiger:
Keys to a Functional Attorney/Client Relationship
Both you and your lawyer must:
- Agree upon and follow a plan for your case while remaining flexible enough to make adjustments when necessary
- Ask questions to avoid misunderstandings
- Take notes at meetings
- Be respectful
- Be reasonably available to each other
- Keep each other informed

What Lawyers and Clients Should Not Expect from Each Other

It is not reasonable for you to expect your lawyer to:
- Misuse court procedures to harass your spouse
- Do whatever you ask, whether reasonable or not
- Allow you to act disrespectfully to the lawyer or her staff
- Act as your therapist
- Wait indefinitely to be paid

Likewise, your lawyer cannot expect that you will:
- Accept all of her advice without question
- Tolerate inattention or rudeness
- Allow her to ignore your reasonable goals

Ten Ways to Optimize the Attorney-Client Relationship

Below are specific steps you and your lawyer can take to get the most out of your relationship:
- Put in writing the agreed-upon goals in your case, and any revisions
- Establish ground rules such as an agreement to respond to each other's phone calls and emails within 24 hours.
- Agree that you will receive copies of all substantive correspondence and be kept informed of all developments.
- Limit communications with your lawyer to matters she can actually help you with. To avoid being charged 1/10 or 2/10 of an hour for a 3-minute phone call, don't call your lawyer in non-emergency circumstances until you have more than one topic to discuss.
- Be efficient at meetings with your lawyer by

- ° Having an informal agenda of topics to be discussed
- ° Making sure that you each have copies of your current financial disclosure statement
- ° Listening carefully to your lawyer's questions and answering them concisely
- Don't fret and fume—if one of you does something the other doesn't like, talk about it.
- Don't drown your lawyer in paperwork. Provide accurate information concisely.
- Ask your lawyer to explain legal concepts and terms she uses. Take notes, but if you've forgotten the explanation, ask again.
- With respect to court proceedings, make sure that you understand
  - ° The reason for the proceeding
  - ° The potential risks and rewards
  - ° Whether you might need to testify and if so, the details of the testimony including expected cross-examination (See Chapter 15.)
- Keep in a binder for quick access copies of key financial documents you've given to your lawyer. (This can also be helpful to your lawyer in court or at a deposition if she can't locate her own copies.)

Optimizing the Attorney/Client Relationship Item #11: Skip the Lawyer Basketball Games

There's one more way to optimize the attorney/client relationship. Ask your lawyer to consult you before getting other lawyers in the firm involved in your case. Otherwise, you may find yourself watching "Lawyer Basketball," played by 2 or more lawyers bouncing your case back and forth, and slam-dunking you with their bill.

How to Talk to a Lawyer

If your lawyer seems impatient when you speak with her, she may be behaving poorly. Or, you may be communicating poorly.

If it's the latter, try the following to communicate more clearly and concisely:

- If you are recounting a series of events, present them chronologically. The less your lawyer hears, "Wait—I forgot to tell you!" the better.

- If you are expressing a concern, state the concern first and then provide the details.
- Listen carefully to what your lawyer tells you.
- At the end of the conversation, state your understanding of any decisions that have been made.
- As always, ask questions!

Incurring Additional Legal Expenses

The cost of divorce can strain even the best attorney/client relationship. Those costs sometimes involve more than attorneys' fees. Among the most expensive add-ons are depositions[1] and expert witnesses. Before incurring such expenses, you must compare the likely costs with the anticipated benefits.

Deciding Whether a Deposition Is Necessary

Consider the following in deciding whether to take the deposition of your spouse or a third party:
- Can the same information be obtained using less expensive discovery methods such as interrogatories, document requests, or requests for admissions?
- To what extent does your lawyer need to ask follow-up questions that are not available with other discovery methods?
- What does your lawyer estimate the cost of a deposition will be in legal fees (including preparation time) and transcript expense?
- Can you agree with your lawyer on a time limit for the deposition?[2]
- Will taking your spouse's deposition cause the other side to take your deposition too, adding yet more expense?

Deciding Whether an Expert Is Necessary

Before retaining an appraiser, accountant, actuary, or other financial expert, find out the following:
- The expert's fee or hourly rate for
   o Research
   o Preparation of a report

---

1. For information regarding depositions, see "Divorce Procedure: The Steps to Your Divorce" on page 23.

2. Court reporters get paid by the transcript page. If you've ever seen a transcript, you know why. The pages have more white than Mount Everest in the snow season.

- ○ Testimony (both in court and at depositions . . . the rates may be different)
- How much of an impact will the expert's opinion likely have on the outcome of your case?
- What are the chances that the expert's opinion could harm your case?
- Should you hire your own expert (typical in court-based cases) or hire an expert jointly with your spouse (typical in ADR cases)?

Use Providers Other Than Your Lawyer or Paralegal

Another way to save on legal fees is to have someone other than your lawyer or paralegal perform non-legal or semi-legal services. With that in mind, consider the following:

- Communicate with office staff rather than your lawyer on scheduling and "housekeeping" matters such as
  - ○ Checking whether your accountant sent your tax returns to your lawyer
  - ○ Whether a motion has been filed or scheduled for hearing
  - ○ Whether opposing counsel has agreed to, or the court has granted a request for a continuance or extension of time
- Use a certified divorce planner, divorce financial analyst[3] or accountant to
  - ○ Help you prepare your financial disclosure statement
  - ○ Analyze tax and other financial implications of settlement options or proposals
  - ○ Advise you as to pension elections regarding survivors' benefits, etc.
- Use a therapist, or divorce coach to assist in resolving child-related issues, while the lawyers focus on financial issues.
- Use an actuary to value pensions.
- Use a mediator to resolve disputes regarding division of personal property.
- Use a discovery referee (where available) to resolve discovery issues such as disputes over what information and documents you and your STBX must exchange.

---

3. Find a CFDA in your area at: www.institutedfa.com

⚠ Be Your Own Paralegal

While paralegals' rates are much lower than those of attorneys, avoid fees altogether by having someone else perform paralegal tasks. Who? You!

Discuss with your lawyer performing tasks yourself such as gathering, copying, scanning and organizing documents. The documents typically gathered in divorce cases are listed halfway through Chapter 1 under the heading "Locating Key Documents."

If you don't have access to a scanner, see if you can arrange to use your lawyer's. Otherwise, consider buying one yourself to organize key documents electronically. You can recoup the cost plus more with what you save on paralegal charges.

Don't be a pawn in your divorce. Be your own paralegal!

With some direction by your lawyer or her paralegal, you can also summarize and analyze documents such as bank and credit card statements and even tax returns.

Using Legal Resources Wisely

Talk to staff about:
- Scheduling
- File organization
- Document production logistics
- Billing questions and payment arrangements
- Routine questions regarding your financial disclosure statement such as whether to include your STBX's solely owned property on your statement

Talk to your lawyer about:
- The law and how it applies to your case
- The progress of your case
- Your responses to discovery
- Regarding your STBX's responses to discovery
  - Information obtained that you feel is particularly important
  - Missing information
  - Advice or divorce 'war stories" you've heard that worry you
- Substantive questions regarding your financial disclosure statement such as
  - Whether and how to include discretionary bonuses in the income section
  - Whether to deduct selling expenses from the value of your home

Where to Find Financial Documents and Information

Look for financial documents in your home where they are normally kept. Then look in as many other places as you can ... as soon as you can. While this may not be pleasant to do, it can save time and money down the road having your lawyer track the documents down.

Make copies of as many documents as you can. If you suspect that your spouse might conceal information, decisive action may be necessary. Consider consulting with a forensic computer expert about seeking a court order to inspect your spouse's computer.

For documents you cannot locate, there are a number of resources available:
- Documents recorded on Land Records such as deeds, mortgages, liens, etc. are located in your Town, City, or County Seat Clerk's Office and should also be accessible online. There are also several electronic document retrieval services such as www.fastdeed.com and http://datastore.netronline.com/ that access public records for a fee.
- Information regarding military pay and allowances such as Basic Allowance for Subsistence ("BAS") and Basic Allowance for Housing ("BAH") is available at http://www.military.com/benefits /military-pay/allowances/
- Estimates of your Social Security retirement, disability, and survivors' benefits are available from the Social Security Administration at http://www.ssa.gov/myaccount/
- Your filed federal income tax returns must be retained by the preparer for at least three years. You can also call IRS at 1-800-908-9146 or order them online at https:// www.irs.gov/taxtopics/tc156.html
- Probate Court documents (wills, trusts, accountings, inventories, etc.) relating to pending or closed estates are available in the Probate or Surrogate's Court[4] located in the municipality or county where the decedent resided at death. Note that "ancillary estates" may also have been opened in other states where the decedent owned property.
- Your bank and credit card records can often be obtained online through your bank or credit card company for at least the last 12 months. You may also be able to get copies (and sidestep the

---

4. A list of U. S. probate courts appears at http://estate.findlaw.com/probate/state -probate-courts.html

bank's fee schedule) by asking nicely at your local branch where, BTW, you've stood in line for years without once complaining. Alternatively, share access to online accounts with your spouse using temporary passwords. However, make sure to consult your lawyer first about what limitations and safeguards will be necessary.

- Local real estate prices and other property information regarding sale prices of homes similar to yours ("comparables" or "comps") are available from local realtors. You might also be able to access recent home sale prices online, though be sure that those prices relate to comps. Be wary of online services that supply information regarding sales (though not necessarily "comparable" ones) and those that supply "fair market value" estimates.

- ⚠ Loan applications may be found in the files of the attorney who handled the transaction. If you have refinanced your home in the last few years or your STBX has borrowed for a business, these applications containing statements under oath as to income and asset values can be a treasure trove of information.

- Retirement plan information and plain language information regarding your account should be available from the plan administrator. Information regarding the largest plans, which are guaranteed by The Pension Benefit Guarantee Corporation (PBGC), can be accessed at http://www.pbgc.gov/wr/trusteed/plans.html.

- Life, homeowners, valuable items, and umbrella insurance policies can be obtained from your insurance agent or insurance company.

Begin Organizing For Success With a Goals Statement

One of Chapter 2's basic truths is that while organization doesn't guarantee you'll have a functional divorce, disorganization usually guarantees that you won't. The first thing you need to organize is . . . you. Start with a list of your divorce goals. The Sample Goals Statement provided in Chapter 1 should help you write your own.[5] So here it is again:

---

5. Note: The items in this Goals Statement are examples only, and are NOT intended to be used as goals in your case.

Sample Goals Statement

- Shield the children from the divorce conflict as much as possible
- Divide time with the children as practically as possible
- Determine if the children need counseling
- Provide for sufficient spousal and child support to stay in the house until a specified event such as children leaving for college
- Allocate responsibility for the children's extracurricular activities, camp, tutoring, religious training, etc.
- Require each of us to contribute to college education according to our respective abilities
- Divide our assets 50/50, except that I keep my investment account that includes money I inherited
- Allocate the debts fairly between us
- Establish methods to resolve any disputes regarding the sale of our home after the divorce
- Look for off-the-books cash receipts in STBX's business, possibly using a forensic expert
- If there's an audit of our joint tax returns, protect me from paying deficiencies resulting from STBX's business
- Protection for me if STBX files for bankruptcy
- Prevent additional home equity line borrowing except by agreement
- Require life insurance coverage to ensure support
- Provide for children's health insurance and non-covered expenses

As you can see, a Goals Statement need not specify how your goals are to be achieved. That will be for you and your lawyer to decide, weighing the potential benefits of a course of action against its costs. See Chapter 14 regarding negotiation strategies.

⚠️ Needs vs. Positions

You're more likely to achieve your goals if you can express them in terms of needs rather than positions. For example, let's say you want to maximize your time with your kids who live primarily with your STBX. This might lead you to demand "joint physical custody."

"Joint physical custody" is a position. Your desire is to spend as much time with your children as you can. Focusing on that will help avoid rigid positions (and hot-button legalisms) that can obstruct settlement.

How to Prioritize Your Goals

Very few people achieve all of their divorce goals, so it's important to prioritize them. Weigh the importance of each of your goals by asking yourself the following questions:

- Is my goal (e.g., spousal support of a specific amount or percentage) realistic given the circumstances?
- Is my goal important enough to me that I would be willing to give up something important to achieve it?
- Might pursuing my goal (for example, getting an item of personal property that has emotional significance to my STBX) harm prospects for overall settlement?
- Is there another way to state my goal that will be less threatening to my STBX?
- Is my goal something that the divorce process is intended or able to achieve?
- Is my goal motivated by what's in my or my children's interests as opposed to malice toward my STBX?
- Might achieving my goal sacrifice long-term interests to a less important "win" in the present? For example, would limiting my STBX's time with the children come at the expense of the children's interest in maintaining strong ties to both parents?

You may need a lawyer's advice to answer these questions. Prioritizing goals is an important task. Don't hesitate to seek help with it.

Questions For Your Lawyer

Writing out a Goals Statement will also alert you to matters you need to know more about. Make a list of those issues for discussion with your lawyer. It might include, for example:

- To what extent should spousal support payments be modifiable as to amount or duration?
- What happens if our financial circumstances change substantially?
- How does cohabitation affect spousal support?
- What happens if one of us wants to move out of the area?
- Can my settlement agreement include a method for resolving post-divorce disputes without going to court?
- Can penalties for non-compliance with our agreement be established now?
- Can my agreement include provisions for pet care and custody?
- Can I get a contribution from my STBX to my attorney fees?

Organize With a Divorce Binder

Divorces involve a pile of documents. You can make sure you're able to access the important ones quickly with a divorce binder. Even in our electronic 21st Century, binders provide an easy way to organize and share documents with your lawyer, mediator, or collaborative attorney.

Start with a single 1½-inch binder. Pick up numbered binder dividers—a 12-set if your case is court-based; a 10-set if you are in ADR. Then set up your Table of Contents as follows:

Divorce Binder Sections

Court-based Cases

1. Financial Disclosure Statements
2. Atty./Client Correspondence/Memos
3. Court filings
4. Discovery Requests and Responses
5. Parenting Issues
6. Support Calculations
7. Assets and Liabilities
8. Financial Exhibits
9. Non-Financial Exhibits
10. Agreements and Orders
11. Tax Return Excerpts
12. Research and Notes

ADR Cases

1. Financial Disclosure Statements
2. Atty./Client Correspondence/Memos
3. Court Filings
4. Parenting Issues
5. Support Calculations
6. Assets and Liabilities
7. Agreements and Orders
8. Tax Return Excerpts
9. Education
10. Research and Session Notes

Writing Your Marital History

Your lawyer may ask you for a "marital history" or chronology. If she doesn't have her own form, prepare one in outline form like the one below. You get no points for style, so the fewer words, the better.

1. Personal background

- Date of marriage, separation(s)
- Prior marriages and ages of children from prior relationships
- Events contributing to the breakdown of the marriage[6]
- Approximate dates of any marriage counseling
- Significant professional achievements such as promotions, awards, and industry recognition
- Health including significant illnesses or disabilities
- Substance abuse or mental health issues

2. Financial history and highlights

- Values of assets owned and debts owed at the time of the marriage
- Employment histories with positions held, dates, and incomes
- Significant financial events such as inheritances,[7] acquisition of property, and squandering or waste of assets
- Bankruptcy
- Educational background

3. Children's issues

- *Pendente lite* parenting plan
- Areas of co-parenting agreements and disagreements
- Children's talents and achievements
- Children's special needs and related matters such as individualized education plans (IEPs), physical therapy, or counseling
- Children's expressed desires regarding sharing time with parents
- Anticipated significant child-related expenses such as orthodontia, car purchase, tutoring, Bar/Bat Mitzvah, travel for athletics or other events or competitions

---

6. Before doing this, see the material below regarding whether a chronicle of spousal misconduct is worth your time and money.

7. In a majority of states, inheritances are not considered "marital property" that a court can distribute. Connecticut and Massachusetts are exceptions to the rule.

Mess Makes Stress: More Organizing Tips For Your Divorce and Divorce After-Life

- Check out personal finance software such as MoneyLine or Quicken. Besides helping you organize, PF software can save you lots of that fun time you spend paying bills.
- Consider using your financial disclosure statement to help take control of your finances. Though totaling up your expenses can be disheartening, use what you learn to stay within a budget in the future.
- Manage your time efficiently with electronic or paper To Be Done lists.
- Handle paperwork (once) with 1-touch paper management techniques.
- Organize your correspondence, bills, and account statements in color-coded folders.
- Keep your Divorce Binder handy . . . to you, not your kids!

Staying Relaxed and Healthy

Obviously, good health and stress reduction involve more than organization. The steps listed below are not only good for you; they will foster a more productive, efficient, and thus less expensive attorney/client relationship.

- Learn relaxation techniques such as yoga and meditation. If you haven't tried meditation, there are, of course, apps and sites to show you how, such as Headspace ("the world's first gym membership for the mind") at https://www.headspace.com or "Headspace-on-the-go" (IOS and Android) at https://www.headspace.com/headspace-meditation-app.
- Maintain an exercise schedule. If you're not the gym type, there are plenty of apps for cardio, core exercises, etc.

- Eat well. You don't have to shop at high-end organic grocery stores to
    - Eat a balanced diet with plenty of fresh fruits and vegetables
    - Lay off soda and other sugar-laden products
    - Drink lots of water

- Seek counseling. If you don't need therapy during a divorce, you probably never will. Check with a qualified therapist to see if you might.
- Have some fun once in a while!
- Avoid isolation. Nothing good comes out of brooding at home. And your networking opportunities there are pretty much limited to mail carriers, repairmen and the kid from down the street selling magazines.

- Sleep like Chuck. My dog Chuck is a very accomplished sleeper. He's much better at it than I am, and he doesn't worry half as much as I do. So connect the dots. Try the following to help you sleep like Chuck:

Chuck, an accomplished sleeper, avoids ill health associated with the lack of it.

  - Establish a pre-sleep routine built around relaxation, such as a hot bath, meditation, or light reading. Avoid bright lights, including TV. And turn off all electronics.
  - Don't drink alcohol, smoke cigarettes or drink caffeinated beverages within 4 to 6 hours of bedtime. Try not to take in liquids for a few hours, so you don't wake up in the middle of the night to get them back out.
  - Experiment with the thermostat to find your best sleep temperature—a degree or two can make a big difference.
  - Don't nap within 8 hours of your bedtime. However, if you've had a bad sleep night, a 20 or 30-minute nap sometime the next day can be surprisingly rejuvenating.
  - If possible, catch up on lost week-night sleep with extra sleep on the weekends.

○ If nothing else gets you to sleep, try reading Chapter 9 on taxes. That should do it.

Keeping an Eye on Yourself

Wouldn't it be cool if there were apps to monitor your sleep and other lifestyle habits? Well, there are, of course. Check out a fitness-tracking app such as Jawbone UP, Fit-bit, or Pillow-Neybox to chart your physical activity, as well as sleep and eating habits.

Avoid Unnecessary Confrontations That Damage the Attorney/Client Relationship

No matter if your arrangement with your lawyer is traditional, ADR-based or unbundled, problems can arise. Some of your lawyer's conduct may seem insensitive, lazy or inattentive to you.

And some of it may be. But her conduct may not be as inappropriate as you think. Below is a list of things lawyers do that might irritate you, accompanied by reasonable explanations for them. If you encounter such conduct, discuss it with your lawyer. It may turn out to be justified or at least explainable.

- At the beginning of your case, your lawyer may be busy with other matters. If there are no urgent issues early in your case, it makes sense for your lawyer to be giving priority to court hearings, settlement negotiations, or trial preparation in cases that are further along.
- Your lawyer may appear insensitive to you. Veteran divorce lawyers often become desensitized to the emotional aspects of divorce. However, this may be a blessing in disguise if it sends you to a mental health professional who does emotional support better and cheaper.
- Your lawyer will not always agree with you as to which details of your case are important. She may be right to focus on the "big picture" that is likely to decide your case.
- Even if you have emphasized that you wish to settle, your lawyer may continue to reference what a judge might do in your case. This is simply a "yardstick" that lawyers use during settlement negotiations.

- You might feel that your lawyer is either too friendly or too antagonistic to opposing counsel. However, your lawyer may simply be using the tactics she feels will be most effective.

Deciding Whether to Fire Your Lawyer

Despite your best efforts, your relationship with your lawyer may continue to be unsatisfactory. Changing lawyers isn't the end of the world; if there's one thing the world has no shortage of, it's divorce lawyers. However, changing lawyers invariably causes duplication of effort and thus additional expense. So how do you know if it's time for a barrister trade-in? Read on!

Confronting Attorney/Client Relationship Problems

Make a list of the things that bother or worry you about your lawyer. They might include, for example, hefty bills that have brought little result, or your lawyer failing to:
- Return phone calls or reply to emails quickly enough
- Fully explain legalities
- Fully explain her strategy
- Update you on developments
- Attend to pressing needs such as temporary support

Before throwing back your lawyer and reeling in another . . .
- Candidly discuss your concerns in an attempt to remedy the problems, including finding out how your own conduct may be contributing to the dysfunction
- Weigh the cost of paying another lawyer to get "up to speed" on your case
- Try to reduce your lawyer's role by suggesting to your spouse that you resolve some of your issues by ADR

- ⚠️ Get a 2nd opinion from another lawyer regarding whether
  - Your current lawyer is pursuing necessary discovery
  - Your current lawyer's settlement "game plan" is valid
  - Your case is proceeding at a reasonable pace
  - Your case has become unnecessarily contentious
  - Your lawyer has been responsive to your reasonable needs and goals

○ Your lawyer has kept you informed and prepared for what
   may come next
○ Your lawyer's assessment of likely outcomes in your case
   is accurate
○ Reasonable *pendente lite* orders and agreements have
   been obtained
○ The lawyer would be willing to take your case, or can recommend competent counsel who will

---

A Half-Dozen Ways You May be Pissing Off Your Lawyer

You may not be the only one suffering in your attorney/client relationship, especially if you're doing this stuff:

- Acting on advice from others that conflicts with your lawyer's advice
- "Goin' Rogue:" negotiating directly with your spouse without first consulting your lawyer
- Failing to disclose important information to your lawyer
- Drowning your lawyer in unnecessary paperwork
- Calling your lawyer at home after hours
- Calling your lawyer certain other things at any hour

As mentioned, there could be reasons for conduct by your lawyer that you find objectionable. Explanations might include a temporarily heavy case-load, health issues or some of the reasons mentioned above. If you can't find a reasonable explanation for the conduct—or a work-around—you will have to at least consider making a change. As Chuck would say, there are plenty of tennis balls in the sea.

Yes, there IS a quiz! Test what you have (or haven't) learned.

1. This chapter could have been called:
   A. "Mission Impossible: Getting Along with a Lawyer"
   B. "Death by Divorce: How to Avoid Choking on Retainers, Drowning in Paperwork and Mauling by Tigers"
   C. "How to Sleep Like a Dog"
   D. "Will This Book Ever End?"

2. Activity: To make absolutely sure your children won't decide to leaf through your divorce binder, slip a sheet of paper between the front cover and the plastic overlay, bearing any one of the following titles:
   A. "Sweat Equity: Jobs Kids Can Do Around the House."
   B. "Why Algebra Matters"
   C. "SQOOMBA! 25 Zoomba Square Dance Routines for Cardio, Core, and Cornpone"

CHAPTER 8

Preparing and Analyzing Financial Disclosure Statements

"Seldom, very seldom, does complete truth belong to any human disclosure."

— Jane Austen

Introduction to the Financial Disclosure Statement

The financial disclosure statement, or "financial affidavit," is the most important document in your divorce. It is heavily relied upon by divorce lawyers negotiating settlement, and by family court judges deciding cases.

Disclosure forms provide a summary of each spouse's financial circumstances. The forms typically require detailed information regarding income, expenses, assets, and liabilities.

The following states provide a short form disclosure statement for "lower income" spouses:
- Florida for individuals whose gross annual income is less than $50,000
- Connecticut for individuals with both gross annual income and net assets of less than $75,000.00
- Massachusetts for individuals whose gross annual income is less than $75,000

Proper preparation of a disclosure statement takes time. You can save attorney and paralegal fees by preparing a solid first draft yourself (with help from a divorce financial analyst if possible) early in your case, or even before it begins. In this chapter, you'll learn how to:
- Prepare your disclosure statement accurately
- Show your finances in the most advantageous way
- Analyze your spouse's disclosure to make sure it shows

     ᵒ All income, including "perks" and "add-backs"
     ᵒ The full value of all assets

Finding Your Financial Disclosure Statement Form

You can access disclosure statement forms on your court system's website.[1]
Your search of the site should go something like this:
- Locate the "Forms" page.
- Select "Family" or "Domestic Relations" forms.
- Find "Financial disclosure statement," "Financial affidavit," "Net worth statement," or something similar.
- If necessary, choose the "short" or "long" form that applies to you.

> **⚠ Saving Lots of Time on Your Disclosure Statement**
>
> Some state financial disclosure forms automatically add numbers in each section and post them to the form's subtotal summary. Test your state's form to see if it contains these functions. If so, you're in luck! You just saved yourself a bundle of time having to re-calculate subtotals each time you change a number.
>
> TIP: Print and save your work frequently using the "Save As" feature to make sure your work is preserved.

Before beginning work on the form:
- Gather the information and documents discussed below
- Review the financial disclosure form in its entirety to avoid inserting numbers in one section that you find out later belong in another
- Ask your lawyer, financial planner or divorce analyst questions such as
     ᵒ How do I deal with self-employment income?
     ᵒ Can I reduce my income with expenses like child-care?
     ᵒ For expenses like food, clothing, etc., should I separate what is for the kids and what is for me?

---

1. Many states permit use of disclosure statements that are not on the court form as long as they substantially conform to the court form. If you have retained a lawyer, check to make sure your lawyer uses the court form before beginning to fill it out.

- ○ Can I include as expenses items that I have been putting off because I can't afford them, like home repairs and auto repair?
- ○ Should I include my house on my statement even though it's in my STBX's name?
- ○ Can I show 50% of the value of jointly owned property?
- ○ Should I include
  - Jointly owned property?
  - My spouse's retirement plan?
  - Trusts or inherited property?
- ○ How do I handle the discretionary bonus that I might or might not get this year?
- ○ I haven't earned much yet this year from my seasonal business. Should I put what I've earned so far, or base my income on last year's totals?
- ○ Should I include, as a liability, money my parents gave me during the divorce that they told me to pay back when I can?

Documents Needed for Disclosure Statement Preparation

The following documents will contain much of the information you will need to prepare your disclosure statement:

- 24 to 36 months of
  - ○ Checkbook registers
  - ○ Bank and stock, etc. account statements
  - ○ Credit card statements
- Your most recent retirement account statements (including IRAs)
- Summaries from Amazon.com, PayPal, and other online stores and payment resources

*Save yourself grief on your disclosure statement: Ask your lawyer, financial planner, or divorce analyst any questions you have **before** you begin!*

- Statements for bills being paid in installments—include the payments in the expense section of the disclosure statement and the current balance in the liabilities section
- Income and business tax returns (2 to 5 years' worth)
- Most recent mortgage interest and property tax payment records

- Appraisals or other estimates of value for real estate, collectibles, artwork, etc
- Homeowners' insurance valuable item schedules

Filling Out Your Disclosure Statement

Disclosure statements typically include the following 4 areas, each of which will be discussed below:

1. Income
2. Expenses
3. Assets
4. Liabilities

Income

Because support is "income-driven," income is easily the most important number on your disclosure statement relating to support. Thus, it's crucial to show it accurately and in a way that's fair to you, as discussed below.

Pay Stub Pitfalls

Divorce clients and lawyers alike often use an income figure based on the client's most recent paystub. That can be a serious mistake. If you are a wage earner, discuss with your lawyer how to:

- Avoid understating the taxes you will pay for the year based on a (pre-2018) paystub that claims too many exemptions.
- In a manner that's fair to you, present income that varies due to commissions, discretionary bonuses, overtime, seasonal work, etc.
- "Back out" deductions on your paystub that are impermissible for support calculations, such as voluntary pension contributions.
- Include the FICA deduction that is omitted from a late year paystub if you have reached the maximum annual income amount subject to FICA ($127,200 in 2017). In such situations, show your annual net income more accurately by dividing the total FICA paid (based on "year-to-date" figures on the paystub) by the total number of pay periods in the year.
- In determining your weekly or monthly income (some states require weekly numbers, some monthly), use the proper number of pay periods; e.g. does the paystub of a wage earner who is paid "twice a month" represent 1 of 24 or 1 of 26 pay periods per year?

If you are self-employed with irregular income, your year-to-date numbers at any point in the year may not accurately forecast your annual income. If so, discuss with your lawyer, accountant or a certified divorce planner how to show your income in a way that is fair to you. Your options include basing your income calculation on:

- Your previous year's income, especially early in the year
- Year-to-date income and expense numbers
- Where permitted, a projection of the current year's numbers

---

 What Does "Net Income" Mean?

"Net income" can be a misleading term for the self-employed because it can be used to mean either:

- Gross revenues less business-related expenses, OR
- Gross revenues less
  - Business-related expenses AND
  - Personal income taxes

If you are self-employed, make sure that you have deducted all business-related expenses from the income number shown on your disclosure statement. Then, in states where support is based upon "net income," ask your lawyer or tax preparer to calculate the amount of income taxes to be deducted from THAT.

Expenses

Calculating your expenses will likely be the most time-consuming part of preparing your disclosure statement. Use your check register, credit card statements, Amazon.com account, online payment services such as PayPal, etc. to identify your expenses. Find out if local custom allows you to include expenses that you usually have but have been unable to afford recently. If not, note those expenses in footnotes or an attachment.

You're likely to have expenses that don't fit the headings on the disclosure form. If so, add a supplemental page to list such expenses and then "bring forward" the total of the expenses on that page to a line on the form for "other expenses."

Children's Expenses

If you are seeking child support:
- Identify and separate your children's expenses from your own
- Jog your memory regarding child-related expenses with a foray into your children's rooms. Don't worry. It's not snooping. It's *research.*
- Visit http://www.cnpp.usda.gov/tools/CRC_Calculator/default.aspx to get USDA child-raising cost estimates based upon factors such as number of children, locale and income.

Use the following list of children's expenses to make sure you don't leave anything out of your expense section:
- Child care
  - Day care and pre-school facility fees and activity expenses
  - Babysitters
- Medical/Health
  - Unreimbursed expenses (not covered or subject to insurance deductibles)
  - Unreimbursed costs of medications, vitamins, inhalers, etc.
  - Unreimbursed therapy, dental, and orthodontia (including appliances)
- Clothing
- Education
  - Private school tuition
  - Boarding school room and board
  - Books, supplies, and activity fees
  - Religious school
  - Tutors
  - Field trips and special functions (school dances, proms, performances)
  - Lunches
- Extracurricular activities
  - Athletics (lessons, fees, uniforms, equipment)
  - Arts (lessons, instruments, supplies, clothing)
  - Group activities (clubs, Scouts, orchestras, etc.)
  - Hobbies (lessons, equipment, materials, etc.)
- Summer and vacation camp activities and programs
  - Room, board, and fees
  - Transportation
- Entertainment
  - Movies

- ° Special events (theatre, athletic events, etc.)
- ° Toys, books, magazines, CD and DVDs, electronic games, downloads, etc.
- ° Trips (skiing, etc.)
- Special celebrations (graduations, religious functions, etc.)
  - ° Gifts, outfits, supplies, and accessories
  - ° Birthday and holiday expenses
  - ° Gifts for other children's birthdays and special celebrations
- Automobile expense
  - ° Insurance
  - ° Registration
  - ° Gas, maintenance, and repair
- Travel
- Miscellaneous
  - ° Electronic/wireless device expense and fees (smart-phones, computers, iPads, chargers, flash drives, internet fees)
  - ° Grooming, haircuts, toiletries/cosmetics
  - ° Gym fees

Don't Lose the Forest For the Trees

Take a step back from your disclosure statement and consider whether the income and expense totals make sense. For example, if your expenses are substantially more than your income, see if the difference can be explained by

- Unpaid credit card balances and other unpaid bills
- Other money you've borrowed
- Inclusion of expenses that you normally have but have not been incurring lately because the divorce has caused a cash shortage
- Inclusion of expenses paid by your STBX, parents or others. (Ask your lawyer about providing an explanation in such circumstances with a footnote or attachment.)

If you cannot account for the disparity between income and expenses, consider revising your figures.

Liabilities

Making a list of your debts or "liabilities" seems easy enough to do. Painful perhaps, but easy. However, things can get complicated if you fail to:

- Understand the difference between expenses and liabilities. Expenses are costs that you will continue to incur regularly. Liabilities are debts you already owe, such as medical bills or credit card prior balances.[2]
- Avoid "double-dips." These often appear on disclosure statements inadvertently, for example where
  - An auto loan balance listed in the liability section has already been deducted from the car's value in the asset section
  - A mortgage balance listed as a liability has already been deducted from the fair market value of the family home

Showing such loans again as liabilities in the liability section has the effect of reducing your net worth twice for the same loans.

Assets

In the majority of states, your disclosure statement should only include assets in which you have an ownership interest.[3] Thus, your spouse's retirement plans, leased cars and the like probably don't belong on your disclosure statement.

The value of most assets is straight-forward. But some can be shown in a way that is more favorable to your position. Here are the most noteworthy examples:

- Real estate: If your marital home or other real estate is being sold and you will get the proceeds or the majority of them in the settlement, you may be able to reduce the value of what you will receive by the amount of
  - Certain fix-up expenses incurred
  - Realtor's commissions
  - Projected capital gains taxes
- Retirement accounts: Retirement funds are generally subject to income taxes when withdrawn.[4] (And if you make a withdrawal

---

2. Note that while a credit card prior balance is a liability, accruing interest and fees can be included in your expense section.

3. As with all aspects of your disclosure statement, confirm that your state law is consistent with the general rules mentioned here.

4. The Roth IRA is an exception. See Internal Revenue Service Publication 590.

from a retirement account prior to age 59½ that is not related to your divorce, the IRS has another surprise for you: a 10% penalty!) It is generally permissible to reduce retirement account values on your disclosure statement by estimated future income taxes so long as you note the amount of the reduction on the statement. As always, however, check with your lawyer to determine the practice in your state or locale.

- Partnerships: If you are a member of a partnership, ask your lawyer whether your ownership interest must be valued. In this connection, try to find out whether a recent appraisal is available. Keep in mind that valuations of "pass-through" businesses[5] based on income prior to the 2017 Tax Cut and Jobs Act are most likely no longer useful.

  Bear in mind that if you own a "minority interest" in a partnership, the value of your interest can be reduced or "discounted" because you can't control partnership business decisions such as whether to sell the company or property that it owns. That makes your interest less valuable and your disclosure statement should reflect that lower value.

- Assets with nominal or undetermined values: Assets that have little or no value may still need to appear on your disclosure statement. To avoid claims that you failed to fully disclose all assets, err on the side of caution regarding property such as collectibles that you think have little or no value. Depending upon local custom, state that the value of such assets is "undetermined" and/or "believed to be nominal."[6]

Reviewing and Revising Disclosure Statements

Once you have completed your draft disclosure statement, review it carefully. Step back from the details to see if it jives with your overall financial circumstances. Check in particular for the common mistakes and issues listed below. (Apply the same analysis when you get your spouse's statement.)

---

5. See Chapter 12.

6. Note that term life insurance policies generally believed to have no cash or "surrender" value, may have "return of premium" features allowing refund of a portion of premiums upon expiration.

Mistakes to Avoid and Issues to Consider Regarding Your Disclosure Statement

- If spending exceeds available cash (take-home pay, credit card charges, loans, gifts, bank withdrawals, etc.), where's the money coming from?
- Why is there no mention of a retirement plan in the asset section even though the income section shows a retirement deduction?
- Have you double-dipped mortgage or car-loan balances?
- Do you show earnings for assets you list such as stock accounts?
- Is the amount of taxes deducted on your disclosure statement substantially different from what your tax return reflects because, for example, your spouse's income substantially altered your effective tax rate?
- Did you use a monthly figure for a weekly expense or vice versa?
- Did you treat a semi-monthly paycheck (24 pay periods per year) as if it were bi-weekly (26 pay periods per year)?
- Did you neglect property such as savings bond wedding gifts in your safe deposit box?

Most of these mistakes and inconsistencies are typically caused by sloppiness rather than dishonesty. But it may not appear that way if you are cross-examined at a deposition or court hearing. So be sure to:

- Review your draft disclosure statement carefully before turning it over to your lawyer
- Update your disclosure statement to reflect any substantial changes while your case is pending

Analyzing Your Spouse's Disclosure Statement

Determining Income of a Self-Employed Spouse

Determining the "real income" of self-employed spouses (salary or "draw" plus perks personal expenses run through the company, dividends, etc.) can be a formidable task. But your knowledge of your spouse's business can help a great deal with it.

Take your time and prepare your disclosure statement carefully to avoid mistakes.

Income and expenses are found in company financial statements ("financials") and tax returns. But they:
- Include "paper deductions" such as depreciation
- Exclude cash receipts
- Make company-paid personal expenses look like business expenses; which, left undiscovered, reduces both the business-owner spouse's earnings and the business's value

I've had clients with information about cash receipts and company-paid expenses add substantially to the amount of income a spouse claimed he/she earned from a business. Make sure to share what you know with your lawyer or financial advisor!

Tax Reporting by Various Types of Businesses

The manner in which income is taxed and reported to IRS depends on the type of business:
- Unincorporated businesses such as sole proprietorships and limited liability companies ("LLCs"): Income and expenses are shown on "Schedule C" of the individual's Form 1040 income tax return; no other federal income tax returns are required.
- C Corporations: Form 1120: The corporation files a tax return and is subject to tax. C corporations can create "double taxation": a tax on the corporation's earnings and a second tax on dividends received by the shareholders. However, shareholders of a C corporation who receive a share of the company's profits as dividends rather than compensation, typically pay taxes on those dividends at a lower rate than they would have paid on salary or other compensation.
- Subchapter S Corporations: The corporation files a Form 1120S. However, the corporation is not taxed. Instead, the income is "passed through" to the shareholders and taxed at ordinary income tax rates, much like unincorporated sole proprietorships, partnerships, and LLCs. If your spouse operates a "Sub-S," LLC, sole proprietorship or partnership, get help from a tax professional.
- Partnerships: Partnerships file Form 1065 "informational" tax returns but it is the partners, not the partnership, who are taxed. Note that a partner is taxed on his "distributive share" of income whether or not he receives it. This can create "phantom income" that is shown on tax returns and taxed as income even though the partner doesn't receive it. In that situation, tax returns actually overstate income.

Income Add-Backs: Increasing Your Spouse's Income With "Disallowed Expenses"

Business owners are permitted to reduce the business' income by deducting expenses that are "ordinary and necessary" to production of business income. IRS disallows deductions for expenses that are only partly business-related or not related to the business at all. However, expenses such as the following may be "disallowed" and added back to

Stay awake! We're nearly done with disclosure statements!

taxable compensation for purposes of calculating both taxes and support (see discussion below):

- Home and family members' cell phone bills
- Vehicle expense such as
  - ° Gas, repair and maintenance for non-business vehicles
  - ° Gas, repair and maintenance for business owned vehicles not being used for business purposes
  - ° Depreciation and insurance on non-business vehicles
- Commuting expense
- Primarily personal travel and lodging expense[1]
- Personal expenses incurred on combination business and pleasure trips[2]
- Expenses of family members or other companions during business trips
- Personal meals and entertainment
- Dues to clubs and fraternal or veterans' organizations
- Expenditures not "ordinary and necessary" to the business
- "Consultant" and other fees paid to family members who perform no services for the business
- Inflated home office expense
- Travel expense purchased with frequent flyer miles
- Hobby losses (losses generated by a "business" that has operated at a loss for 3 of 5 years)
- Personal legal expenses

---

1. Note that IRS has different rules for travel within, and outside the U.S.

2. IRS Publication 463 contains specific rules for allocating time between business and personal days on combined business and pleasure trips.

- Political contributions
- Fines and penalties such as automobile moving violations and parking tickets

⚠ Business Expense Deductions That Family Judges May "Add Back"

Judges determining child or spousal support are not required to accept all business deductions, even some that are allowed by IRS to reduce taxable income. Deductions that are permissible for income tax purposes but which a judge may nonetheless "add back" to income for purposes of calculating support can include the following:

- Accelerated depreciation: Some courts will disallow certain "paper deductions" such as accelerated depreciation that don't involve an outlay of cash in the current year[3]
- Entertainment and travel allowances deducted from business income to the extent that such allowances reduce the taxpayer's usual expenses
- Voluntary contributions to retirement plans
- Home office deduction
- Excessive auto expenses[4]
- Some amount of travel and entertainment
- Any other expenses that appear excessive or inappropriate to the business

Scrutinizing Wage and Salary Earners' Incomes

It's not only self-employment income that should be analyzed in connection with support calculations. In the circumstances listed below, it is also important to scrutinize a wage earner's income.

---

3. This applies particularly to "accelerated depreciation" as opposed to "straight-line depreciation." Don't panic over the terminology—ask your tax preparer for further explanation.

4. Note that if a taxpayer attempts to deduct both actual auto expense and the IRS business mileage rate ($.54/mile in 2016), IRS will disallow one of them.

Factors in Determining a Wage Earner's Income For Support Calculations

Judges typically consider the following issues and items of additional compensation to adjust the earnings shown on a wage earner's W-2:

- Whether and how to factor in overtime
- Whether discretionary bonuses and other incentives should be included
- Identifying tax costs of assets to be transferred in the property settlement
- The impact of work hours that vary from one pay period to another
- The impact of seasonal work
- Non-cash perks such as use of company car
- Expense accounts
- Commissions and tips
- Whether payroll deductions such as mandatory retirement account contributions (generally a permitted deduction for support purposes) vs. elective contributions (generally not permissible) can be used to reduce income available for child or spousal support

Analyzing Your Spouse's Assets

In addition to income, some numbers in the asset section of your spouse's disclosure statement may require a closer look. They include:

- Whether the asset values are consistent with information you have (or will obtain through the discovery process) including information appearing on
  - ○ Loan applications
  - ○ Homeowners' or renters' insurance personal property schedules
  - ○ Safe deposit box inventories
  - ○ Tax returns
  - ○ Statements from financial institutions
  - ○ Receipts and bills of sale
- Whether the asset values have been reduced by projected taxes, selling expense, etc. and, if so, whether such reductions conform to state law and customs of your local courthouse
- Whether any mortgage or other loan that has been deducted from the asset value has been double-dipped as a liability
- Whether any assets are missing
- Whether the values add up—check the arithmetic!

Reporting Inaccuracies on Your Spouse's Disclosure Statement

Once you've completed your review of your spouse's disclosure statement:
- Prepare a list of comments and questions for your lawyer (arranged in the order in which the items appear on the disclosure statement) or (legibly) annotate a copy of the disclosure statement itself.
- Make your comments concise and your annotations legible.

If you find discrepancies between your spouse's statement and the real world, consider meeting with your lawyer to underscore their importance.

 Yes, there IS a quiz! Test what you have (or haven't) learned.

1. This chapter is mainly about:
   A. Snooping around my kids' rooms to find out what they manage to spend their allowance on within hours of getting it
   B. How to stay awake reading unbelievably boring and complicated stuff about disclosure statements—what's next, a chapter on taxes?
   C. How to prepare my financial disclosure statement properly and consistent with my goals, and to test my spouse's statement for omissions and inaccuracies

2. Pronounce out loud while riding on public transportation and then unscramble the following key phrases from this chapter:
   A. Thros morf lessudirco meettants
   B. Snesubis Snepexes
   C. Emicon dad-kacbs

CHAPTER 9

Taking Advantage of Divorce Tax Rules

"Anyone who lives within their means suffers from a lack of imagination."

— Oscar Wilde

Thumb Tax: A Thumbnail Sketch of Divorce Tax Savings

You can save tax dollars and make the tax code work for you during your divorce in a variety of ways, including:
- Inserting tax-friendly language in your settlement agreement
- Considering the "hidden cost" of capital gains taxes in your property settlement
- Properly using tax rules

All of the above will be covered in this chapter. But some of it's pretty complicated. (Gee, what a surprise!) Like other dense material in this book, it's here partly to alert you to things you should discuss with your lawyer or a tax professional. They will help you do what's necessary to make these tax-saving techniques work for you.

The 2017 Tax Cuts and Jobs Act (TCJA)

A discussion of taxes in divorce must include the 2017 Tax Cuts and Jobs Act (TCJA). The changes in that law radically altered the role of taxes in divorce.

What Hasn't Changed:

The TCJA doesn't change everything. A number of important aspects of divorce taxation remain intact. As discussed in more detail in Chapter 13, the most important of those are:

- Asset transfers: Transfers of property as a result of your divorce ("transfers incident to a divorce") continue with minor exceptions not to be taxable as "taxable events." For example, a spouse signing over stock to her spouse as part of a divorce settlement is not taxed on any "capital gain."[5]
- The family residence: Sizable chunks of "capital gain" (essentially profit adjusted for prior home sales) continue to be exempt from tax on the future sale of your family home.
- Retirement plans: Transfers of interests in retirement plans such as 401(k) plans and pensions that are otherwise insulated from claims of creditors and other "third parties," continue to be permitted in divorce. Accounts must be transferred by way of qualified domestic relations orders or "QDROs". For more on division of retirement plans and other property, see Chapter 13.

What Has Changed: The Alimony Deduction

For many years, child support has been treated differently under the Internal Revenue Code (IRC) than alimony. Because support of children is considered a parent's obligation, no tax benefit has been considered necessary to encourage parents to pay it. Spousal support, on the other hand, has been encouraged by giving a tax deduction to payers ("obligors") who follow certain rules that "qualify" the support as alimony.

The elimination of the alimony tax deduction as to obligations in agreements signed, and court orders entered after 2018 is by far the most important of the TCJA's divorce-related changes. (That's right, the alimony change was written to take effect on January 1 2019—a year later than most of TCJA's provisions.)

---

5. However, unlike in other situations, the "cost basis" that's used to calculate taxable capital gain (profit) when the recipient sells the property remains the same rather than increasing. That means that the "unrealized gain" will eventually be taxed when the recipient spouse sells the property. Finding out the original cost basis will alert you to this hidden tax cost.

For those who have signed separation agreements by December 31 2018, or have been divorced by that date, the old alimony rules remain in effect. See material on the old rules—as well as more on the new ones— in Chapter 12.

Before the TCJA, matrimonial lawyers used alimony (known in some states as "spousal support" or "maintenance") to increase support dollars for recipients while reducing the cost to obligors. That's possible because alimony has been deductible by the obligor and included in the recipient's taxable income. There's an overall tax savings—and thus more money for the spouses—because more often than not, obligors deduct alimony in a higher tax bracket than the bracket in which the recipient pays taxes on it.

The alimony deduction has helped lawyers settle divorce cases by taking some of the sting out of paying alimony. Support-paying spouses became willing to pay more once they realized how much in taxes the alimony deduction would save them. For the same reason, having less money for spousal support after 2018 will make some obligors less willing to pay as much support and thus their cases more difficult to settle.

Which brings new relevance to the question attributed to cowboy/philosopher Will Rogers:
"If 'pro' is the opposite of 'con,' what's the opposite of progress?"

From the IRS Dumb Tax Deductions Dept.
(Don't Try This at Home, or You May Not Be Home for Long!)

Reason for audit: Taxpayer deducted $424 for purchase of a "La-Z-Boy" reclining chair as a "retirement plan contribution."

Taxpayer's explanation: "When I retire next year, I intend to sit in my La-Z-Boy all the live-long day. So I should get to deduct it because that Bad Boy is my whole retirement plan."

Other TCJA Divorce Changes

But wait—the new law did more than just trash the alimony deduction!

Another IRC provision that helped settle pre-TCJA divorces allowed divorcing spouses to allocate between them their children's dependent exemptions. This provision has served the same purpose as the alimony deduction, though on a much smaller scale. Assigning exemptions to the parent who benefits most from them can increase the amount of income available to both parents. The new law's repeal of these exemptions (worth $4,150 per child in 2017) eliminated another divorce money-saving tool.

One other deduction that eased the financial pain of divorce has also bitten the dust. Under pre-TCJA law, taxpayers could deduct certain legal fees incurred for:
- Tax planning advice
- Creating taxable income such as alimony
- Obtaining an interest in a spouse's retirement plan
- Obtaining other taxable income such as royalties and residuals
- Identifying and collecting tax refunds

Sorry, that train too has left the station, carrying the legal fee deduction with it.

Other Tax Rules That Can Impact Your Divorce

You should be aware of several other IRC provisions that might affect your divorce:
- The Child Tax Credit: This is a tax credit available to parents and others with dependent children. The TCJA increased the credit from $1,000 to $2,000 per dependent child, until 2026, when it "sunsets" (expires). The credit begins to phase out for married taxpayers filing jointly who have adjusted gross income (AGI) exceeding $400,000, and $200,000 for all other taxpayers. To claim the credit for a calendar year, you must meet the following requirements.
  - Have a child under 17 as of December 31 of that year
  - Claim the child as a dependent on your income tax returns
  - The child must be your child, stepchild, foster child, adopted child, brother, sister, stepbrother, stepsister, or a descendant of one of these individuals (e.g., grandchild, niece or nephew)
  - The child must not have provided more than half of his/her own support during the year
  - The child must be a U.S. citizen, U.S. national, or U.S. resident alien
  - The child must not file a joint income tax return for the year except to claim a refund.
- Head of Household income tax filing status: Divorced parents with custody of a child are entitled to Head of Household ("HOH")

filing status that results in lower taxes than filing as "Single" after the divorce or "Married Filing Separately" during the marriage. Except in "split custody" situations (see Chapter 10) where each parent may claim HOH status based on having custody of one or more children, only one parent is entitled to HOH status.[1]

Note that to qualify for Head of Household status, you must
- Have a child living in your home for more than half the calendar year
- Provide more than half the cost of maintaining the household
- Be unmarried as of December 31 or have lived separately from your spouse for more than 6 months
- Have been a U.S. citizen or resident alien for the entire tax year

- Child and Dependent Care Credit: This credit for custodial parents is worth up to 35% of child care expenses with a maximum of $3,000 for one child and $6,000 per year in all, if
  - The child is under age 13 or disabled
  - The child lived for more than half the year with the parent claiming the credit
  - The claiming parent incurred child care expenses that enabled the parent to earn
  - Child care payments are not made to the parent, spouse, the child's parent or a child under age 19[2]

Your Tax Deduction Coupon Book

Think of the Internal Revenue Code as a coupon book—but with discounts on taxes instead of pizza. And you won't need the cardiologist all those free pizza promotions might require! But, you *will* need a tax professional to make sure you qualify for the savings.

Buy 10 Pizzas Get One **FREE**

Al's Grease Pit & Fructose Emporium

- Lifetime Learning Credit (LLC): Subject to income limits, you can claim this credit up to $2,000 per tax return for qualified education expenses paid for each dependent eligible student. The

---

1. See IRS Publication 504, *Divorced or Separated Individuals.*
2. See IRS Publication 503 for numerous additional restrictions on using this credit.

LLC is phased out as income increases. The LLC is available for an unlimited number of years, subject to a cumulative total of $10,000, provided that you do not elect the American Opportunity Credit (see below) in the same year for the same student.

- American Opportunity Credit (formerly The Hope Credit): Subject to income limits, you can claim a credit of up to $2,500 per eligible dependent student (including yourself). Like the LLC, the AOC phases out as income increases. The AOC differs from the LLC as follows:
  - The AOC is computed on a per student basis while the LLC is computed per family
  - The AOC is available for only 4 years per student while the LLC has no year limit
  - Unlike the LLC, 40% of the AOC may be refundable (in the event that your AOC exceeds what you owe in taxes for a particular year)

> ## What's the Difference Between a Tax Credit and a Tax Deduction?
> A tax deduction reduces the amount of your income that will be taxed. Tax credits are worth more because the amount of the credit is subtracted directly from the taxes you owe.

Tax Savings Tips

Careful drafting of your settlement agreement, proper preparation of your tax returns and even the timing of your divorce can help you save on taxes. Specifically, be sure that your settlement agreement conforms to the following:

- Allocation: Divide up the following between you and your spouse:
  - Mortgage interest deductions on jointly owned homes[3]
  - Property tax deductions[4]
  - Entitlement to income tax refunds

---

3. TCJA reduces from $1,000,000 to $750,000 the amount of a mortgage loan for which interest is deductible.

4. TCJA caps the allowable annual deduction for property taxes plus income taxes at $10,000.

- ○ Responsibility for deficiencies on past joint tax returns, making sure that you are "indemnified and held harmless" as to any taxes for which your soon-to-be-Ex is responsible
- Consistency: To avoid a tax audit, your tax return must be consistent with your former spouse's return as to the items above as well as how much alimony ordered before the TCJA was paid and received.
- Timing: If your final hearing date is late in the year and filing a joint tax return would save taxes, consider
  - ○ Postponing a late-year final hearing until the following January
  - ○ Proceeding with a late-year final hearing but asking the judge to delay the effective date of the judgment until January

---

 More from the IRS Dumb Tax Deductions Dept.
(Don't Try This at Home, or You May Not Be Home for Long!)

Reason for audit: Taxpayer deducted $329 in airfare as "tax advice"

Taxpayer's Explanation: *"I flew to Albuquerque for Thanksgiving with my Cousin Sheldon the accountant. During halftime of the Dallas-Seattle game I said, 'Tell you what, Shelly—taxes is a bitch.' And Sheldon tax-advised me: 'No sh*t'!"*

Protecting Yourself from Your STBX's IRS BS

You may be concerned that your soon-to-be-Ex has exposed you to IRS problems on your joint tax returns by under-reporting income, overstating deductions or other tax misbehavior in connection with his/her business. You may be particularly worried if you are a company officer or director of that business.

If you have such concerns, take the following steps to protect yourself:
- Be held "harmless": Provide in your settlement agreement that your spouse "indemnify and hold you harmless" against any tax deficiencies (and related accountants' and attorneys' fees) relating to your spouse's income or deductions.
- Consider filing separately: If you are still married at the end of a calendar year during your divorce, consider filing a separate tax return to avoid being on the hook for any of your spouse's tax shenanigans. Get advice beforehand however, because "married filing separate" status

- ° Increases the tax you will owe
- ° Can disqualify you for certain tax benefits
- Quit! Resign (by email or a written, notarized letter to your spouse) as an officer or director of companies controlled by your spouse to avoid personal liability that corporate officers and directors may have in the following situations.
  - ° Failure to pay wages within the time periods required by state law, which under some states expose corporate officers and directors to liability for as much as three times the wages owed ("treble damages") plus attorneys' fees
  - ° Failure to properly withhold income and FICA taxes
  - ° Failure to pay minimum wages or overtime, which can also result in treble damages and attorneys' fees
  - ° Failure to maintain Workers' Compensation insurance
  - ° Liability for corporate debts incurred after the corporation's privileges have been forfeited for failure to pay taxes or file reports.
- Joint ownership: Talk to a tax professional about keeping the former marital residence in joint names after your divorce. That will qualify you for the same $500,000 exclusion of capital gain when the home is sold that's available to married couples. However, continuing joint ownership can create headaches, so only use it if
  - ° There is likely, upon sale of the home, to be substantially more than $250,000 in capital gain (essentially sale price less your cost adjusted for sales of earlier homes, selling expenses, etc.)
  - ° You have clearly divided up responsibility for taxes, mortgage, utilities, maintenance, repair, capital improvements and all other expenses relating to the home
  - ° You fully understand how your state's law will change the nature of your joint ownership, which might permit, for example, someone named in your spouse's Will to become your new joint owner should your spouse die before the house is sold
  - ° You are, and are likely after the divorce to remain on, reasonably good terms with your spouse

---

Home for ... a Tax Holiday

With proper planning, you can get the full $500,000 capital gain exclusion on the sale of your *jointly owned* home, even after your divorce. (see Chapter 13.) As with all tax saving techniques, have a tax advisor show you how.

Common Tax Mistakes During Divorce

In addition to protecting yourself against problems arising from your spouse's reporting of income and deductions, be aware of the following tax traps for the unwary:

- Securities: Dividing securities (stock, bonds, etc.) in a way that results in you paying a disproportionate amount of capital gain taxes upon sale
- Tax-free assets and retirement accounts: Getting the short end of the stick in your settlement negotiations by trading tax-free assets such as money market accounts, for retirement funds that are potentially less valuable because they are
  - Taxable upon withdrawal
  - Subject to penalty if money is withdrawn before age 59 ½.
- Alimony issues: In pre-2019 divorces, you can run into difficulties by:
  - Failing to provide that alimony terminates upon the death of the recipient (unless state law requires termination automatically upon death)
  - Failing to consider the recipient's hefty tax bill created by an "alimony payoff" by which the obligor pre-pays months of alimony in return for termination of the alimony obligation (see Chapter 12)
- Squandering exemptions: Wasting pre-2018 dependency exemptions (and related child tax credits) by transferring them from a spouse who can use them to a spouse who can't
- Bad timing: Creating a "taxable event" with a settlement agreement that provides for a property transfer to occur more than 6 years after the divorce
- Inaccurate pay-stubs: Relying upon pay stubs to prepare your financial disclosure statements (or evaluate your spouse's) that inaccurately portray income due to, for example, mortgage interest and property tax deductions not figured in on the pay stubs
- Unallocated support: Risking disallowance of the alimony deduction by ignoring (in a pre-2019 divorce) complex IRS regulations regarding "unallocated alimony and child support" that substitutes a single deductible payment for separate payments of alimony and child support

---

 Yes, there IS a quiz! Test what you have (or haven't) learned.

1.This chapter is mainly about:
   A. Why we have to watch the Dallas Cowboys every Thanksgiving
   B. Qualifying for the Butterball Deduction by inviting an accountant to Thanksgiving
   C. How to take advantage of divorce tax-saving opportunities

2. The reason that alimony, but not child support, used to be taxable to the recipient and deductible by the obligor, is:
   A. Because some Congressman who was getting divorced, wanted a tax break
   B. Because some divorcing oil company executive reminded Congress that the Constitution guarantees oil company executives tax breaks for everything
   C. Because child support, unlike alimony, was considered an absolute obligation and thus not appropriate for tax incentives

3. Pronounce out loud while stopped for a driving infraction, and unscramble the following key phrases from this chapter!
   yanimol ciddonute
   drow beljums

CHAPTER 10

Providing for the Custody, Care and Comfort of Your Children

*"Would you tell me, please, which way
I ought to go from here?'
'That depends a good deal on where you
want to get to,' said the Cat."*

— Lewis Carroll, *Alice in Wonderland*

Caring For Your Children During Divorce

One of the most difficult aspects of divorce is that your children need extra attention just when you may be least able to provide it. Your challenge as a divorcing parent is to attend to your children's fears and anxieties despite feeling preoccupied—if not overwhelmed—by your own problems.

Telltale Signs of Distress in Children

Be on the lookout for the following behavioral changes that may indicate anxiety, stress, insecurity, or depression in children:
- Altered sleep patterns or eating habits
- Declining performance in academics, athletics, or other activities
- Frequent and/or broad mood changes
- Acting out through anger, aggression, defiance or other misbehavior with peers, teachers or family members
- Withdrawal from family and friends
- Lethargy or disinterest
- Regressive behavior
- Becoming accident prone
- Excessive catering to parents, which may signal self-blame for the divorce

Dos and Don'ts of Breaking the News to Your Children

How, what, and when you first tell your children about the divorce will affect the way they see and understand everything that comes afterward. So, to use legal terminology . . . try not to screw it up.

Here are the Dos and Don'ts of your first discussions about the divorce:
- Don't talk to the children about the divorce until you are emotionally prepared to discuss it in a calm, reassuring manner.
- Agree with your STBX about when and what the children will be told—initially, at least, by the two of you together.
- Try to anticipate questions the children might ask and agree upon the answers.
- See a therapist or divorce coach if you can't agree with your spouse on how, when, or what to tell the children.
- Consider telling teenage children about the divorce before the younger ones because children in different stages of development require different approaches; for example
  - Older children should be told before they hear it elsewhere or figure it out themselves.
  - Younger children often don't need to know until separation or some other event that requires explanation.
- Gather materials for your children and yourself about assisting children through divorce, such as
  - The American Bar Association's (ABA) handbooks: "My Parents Are Getting Divorced" and "What Your Children Need Now!"[5]
  - The American Academy of Matrimonial Lawyers' "Children's Bill of Rights" (See Appendix 3.)
  - For a story-book approach for younger children, see also http://www.childcentereddivorce.com/kids/
- Together with your spouse, be positive and reassure the children that:

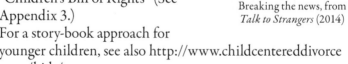

Breaking the news, from
Talk to Strangers (2014)

---

5. Available at http://shop.americanbar.org/ebus/

- ○ Both of you will continue to be involved in their lives
- ○ You can work cooperatively as their parents
- ○ The divorce is not their fault and has nothing to do with anything they have done (a message that bears repeating during the divorce)
- Be honest but DON'T discuss things that are unnecessary or that are likely to upset or worry them, such as
  - ○ An extramarital affair or other fault for the divorce
  - ○ Money problems
- Tell your children about arrangements you've made for both parents to spend time with them. (Avoid Lawglish terms like "custody," "visitation," or "primary residence.")
- Assure them that you will try your best to answer any questions they have.

The "right" answers depend upon your children's ages, maturity and temperament. Mental health professionals and divorce coaches can help you formulate those answers. If at all possible, do this with your co-parent for the sake of consistency and to demonstrate to your children that you will continue to be their parents after the divorce.

Questions Your Children May Ask About Your Divorce

One thing you can expect is that your kids will ask you about your divorce when you least expect it. So be prepared ahead of time for questions like:

- "What does divorce mean?"
- "Why do you have to get a divorce?"
- "Is the divorce my fault?"
- "Will you and Mommy [Daddy] get back together again?"
- "Why can't you make up?"
- "Will we have to move?"
- "Can we all still live here together in the house?"
- "Will I have to change schools?"
- "Is Mom/Dad going to move away?"
- "Will we still go to Grandma's for Thanksgiving?"
- "Who will be home when I get home from school?"

Divorce Parenting No-No's

Try to avoid making the following mistakes with your children during your divorce. But don't beat yourself up if you screw up in a bad moment. It's okay—everyone does it. Instead, use those incidents as learning experiences that strengthen your resolve not to let them happen again.

- Don't complain to your children about their other parent.
- Don't use the children to convey messages to their other parent.
- Don't ask the children (directly or indirectly) to choose with which parent they prefer to live or spend time.
- Don't try to "insulate" the children entirely from the divorce because
  ◦ It won't work
  ◦ Depriving children of basic information will only increase their anxiety
- Don't arbitrarily make rules that are inconsistent with their other parent's reasonable rules.
- Don't give the children false hope that you and your STBX might reconcile.
- Don't treat children as confidants or therapists. Children (and not only the younger ones) need to be reassured that normalcy will return to their lives and that they can feel safe and loved. Maintain the boundaries that will allow you to continue to fulfill those needs.

What is Child Custody?

The term "child custody" involves two concepts:

- Legal custody: Determines who makes decisions—and how—regarding the children
- Physical custody: Determines how much time the children spend with each parent and thus how much day-to-day child-care responsibility each parent has

Types of Legal Custody

The types of legal custody are:

- Joint legal custody: The parents share decision making regarding the health and welfare of the children, including schooling, extra-curricular activities, medical decisions, and the like. Joint legal custody also entitles each parent access to their children's educational, health, and other records.

- Sole legal custody: One parent has the right to make child-related decisions.
- Hybrid legal custody: Arrangements such as one of the following
  - One parent has the right to make child-related decisions except as to certain matters.
  - Parents share decision-making except as to specified matters.
  - Parents share decision-making, but one parent has the right to decide in the event of an impasse.

Legal Presumptions Regarding Custody

In the states listed below, it is presumed that in certain circumstances, joint legal custody is in a child's best interests. In states such as Connecticut, the presumption applies only if the parents agree to joint custody. In other states, the presumption means that parents arguing against joint custody have the burden of proving that it is more likely than not that joint custody is contrary to the children's best interests. Evidence that joint custody is not in a child's best interests would include, for example, a history of the parents being unable to parent cooperatively.[6]

States With Joint Custody Presumptions[7]

- Alabama
- Arizona
- California
- Connecticut
- District of Columbia
- Florida
- Idaho
- Kentucky
- Louisiana
- Minnesota
- Mississippi
- Nevada

---

6. Some judges feel that legal presumptions are unimportant in child-related matters where the ultimate issue is what's in a child's best interests. An experienced local attorney knows which judges those are and thus can help you weigh probable outcomes in your case.

7. In states such as Alabama, California, Connecticut and Mississippi, the court has no authority to award joint custody unless at least one parent requests it. In Oregon, joint custody can be awarded only if both parents request it.

- New Mexico
- Tennessee
- Texas
- Wisconsin

Types of Physical Custody

Just as there are several forms of legal custody, there are several forms of physical custody:

- Sole physical custody: One parent has the great majority of
  - Time with the children, and
  - Day-to-day child care responsibilities

  Note that in extreme situations when a parent poses a risk to a child, the other parent may have exclusive care of the children and the other parent's time with the children, if any, will be ordered to be supervised by a capable third party.

- Joint physical or "shared" custody: Each parent has specified rights to have the children with him/her. This can range from a "50/50" time split to the children having their "primary residence" with one parent, subject to a parenting plan schedule of time with the other parent. Note that an agreement or court order regarding physical custody can determine a child's school district.
- Primary physical custody or "primary residential parent": These terms usually refer to the fact that the children's "home" is with one parent.
- Alternating custody: A joint custody arrangement in which the parents take turns living with the children for extended periods of time, such as two weeks with one parent followed by two weeks with the other parent. Input from a mental health professional is especially helpful with alternating custody, as it is not appropriate for all children.
- Bird-nesting: A type of alternating custody in which the children remain in the home and the parents alternate residing there. This requires that each parent have an alternate residence.
- Split custody: An arrangement in which not all the children have their primary residence with the same parent, resulting in the children being "split up" from each other.

Orders and Disorders

Some psychological traits, whether or not they are considered mental disorders, make settlement negotiations difficult and perilous. But settlement is still worth a try, especially if children are involved. If you do manage to agree on some children's issues in such a case, make sure to do the following:

- Immediately put the agreement in writing.
- Avoid any vagueness or "wiggle room" in wording. Parents suffering from Narcissistic Personality Disorder, for example, will exploit to their advantage any lack of clarity, so be specific and precise regarding matters such as
  - Pick-up and drop-off times and places
  - Responsibility for transporting the children
  - Exactly what "day-to-day" decisions can and can't be made by the parent who has the children with him/her
  - Submit any agreements to the court with a motion for a court order so that the agreements can be quickly and effectively enforced with the court's contempt power.

If a court hearing becomes necessary because agreement can't be reached, ask your lawyer to prepare detailed "proposed orders" to submit to the court. This will:

- Underscore your concerns about your STBX's penchant for manipulation and/or avoidance of responsibility
- Provide the detail you need (if the court rules in your favor) that court orders often lack

The Shortest List of All:
How Judges Decide Child-Related Issues

In making decisions regarding children, the standard used by judges is:

- The best interests of the children ("BIC")

That's it, a one-item list. The devil, as they say, is in the details.

"BIC" Factors Judges Consider

Among the most significant "details" of the BIC standard are the factors judges may consider in applying it:

- The child's age and gender

- The parent's ability to provide the child with basic necessities such as food, shelter, clothing, and medical care
- The parent's ability to meet the child's physical, emotional, developmental, educational, and special needs
- The parent's mental and physical health
- The emotional ties between parent and child, including a parent's history as primary caregiver
- The parent's ability to provide a loving, stable, consistent and nurturing relationship
- The parent's lifestyle and ability to provide a stable environment
- A history of child abuse or neglect by a parent or household member
- The preference of a child of suitable age (often age 12 and up) and maturity
- The quality of the child's established home, school and community environments, and the importance of maintaining continuity
- The child's sibling relationships
- Whether a parent is likely to foster the child's relationship with the non-custodial parent
- Whether a parent has attempted to alienate a child from the other parent
- The availability of extended family
- Logistical considerations such as the ability of each parent to make appropriate child-care arrangements (or to provide child-care themselves), and the distance between the parents' residences
- The application of principles of developmental psychology
- Any other factors relevant to the child's best interests

Avoiding Battles Over Child-Related Issues

Despite their divorce, most parents must continue to co-parent. Except in situations in which cooperation is impossible such as when a parent poses a risk to a child, parents have the responsibility to cooperate in creating a parenting plan that is in the children's interests.[8]

---

8. If you feel that you and your co-parent may be unable to resolve child-related issues, see my short film *Talk to Strangers* (available at www.childcustodyfilm .com). Encourage your spouse to do the same. The film is accompanied by "The *Talk to Strangers* Pocket Guide for Parents" from which some of the material above is excerpted, and which contains additional strategies for sparing your children the trauma of court battles regarding them.

If you are unable to resolve children's issues with your co-parent, a judge will do it for you. Here are some reasons to avoid that if at all possible:

- The custody evaluation process can humiliate, frighten and compromise your children, and cause them enduring emotional harm.
- Custody cases are tremendously expensive. Parents must not only pay their own lawyers, but in some cases, they must also pay attorneys to represent the children and/or guardians *ad litem* (GALs). GALs can be appointed for children unable to act in their own interests due to age or other factors or who are otherwise in need of protection.
- Trial outcomes are difficult to predict.
- A judge's orders after trial rarely contain the crucial details and fine-tuning that parents who resolve the issues themselves include in their agreements.

Avoiding the Custody Evaluation Process

Talk to Strangers (2014) portrays how intrusive and humiliating the custody evaluation process can be for the children trapped in it.

```
          DR. HARDIN
  Your  mother  loves  you  very
much,  you  know.  She  always
will.

            EMILY
  Yeah, she always loved my Dad
too  . . . until she didn't anymore.

            DR. HARDIN
  I'm curious. Why do you feel it's your mother's fault that
your parents can't agree on custody? Did your father tell you
that?
```

Custody Battles: A Perfect Storm For Harm to Children

Children need very specific things from their divorcing parents. A "Kids' Top 4 List" of divorce needs would read something like this:

- An end to their parents' fighting
- An end to uncertainty about where and with whom they will be living
- A return to some degree of normalcy

- Security in knowing their parents will continue to love and
care for them

Custody battles put children at risk for emotional harm because they
delay or prevent children from getting the very things that they need most
during divorce. That's because custody battles:
- Increase the parents' conflict.
- Require children to suffer through evaluation procedures that
frighten, humiliate and compromise them.
- Add months to divorces, thus prolonging the children's anxiety and
delaying any return to normalcy.
- Leave parents hostile to each other for years, severely damaging
prospects for cooperative post-divorce co-parenting. Even children
who receive assurances of their parents' love may question why that
love isn't strong enough to create cooperative parenting in place of
hostility.

So perhaps the first question to ask yourself if you are considering a custody battle is this: Do you love your children enough not to fight over them?

Hopeful, Out-of-the-Box Solutions

Hope Fuller knows that her husband's proposal to
evenly divide time with the children would be a logistical nightmare. Her lawyer has told her not to negotiate because she will "win" at trial. But Hope knows
how custody battles damage children and that there
are no guarantees that she will get the result she
wants. So she asked her lawyer for some out-of-the-
box solutions. He suggested:
- "Flip schedules" that reverse the school year
plan for all or some of the summer, allowing for
more quality time for the "out parent" without
disturbing school week routines
- "Bird-nesting" arrangements in which children
remain in the family home and the parents
rotate in and out of it
- Trial parenting plans lasting for a month or two
while the divorce is pending that reveal quickly
what will and won't work

Ten Questions to Ask Before Fighting Over the Kids

For many years, I've required clients considering custody litigation to consider 10 questions. If it's your co-parent who seems intent on fighting over the kids, see if he or she has answers to the following:

1. Do you want your children to endure months of anxiety and uncertainty as to where they will be living and whether they will have the relationship they want with each of their parents and their siblings?

2. Do you want your children subjected to interviews by attorneys, mental health professionals and court personnel in which they will feel afraid, conflicted, and pressured to be loyal to both their parents?

3. Do you want your children subjected to the possibility of inquiry by these professionals about the most personal aspects of their lives, including their fears and frailties?

4. Clinical studies have shown that exposure to high conflict between parents places children at risk for serious psychological harm. Do you want to risk harming your children with a high-conflict custody battle?

5. Do you want your inability to resolve your differences to serve as a model of parenting for your children?

6. Do you want intimate details of your life to become a matter of public record?

7. Do you want a stranger deciding how much you will see your children and how you will make decisions concerning them?

8. Do you want a substantial portion of your assets used as fees for attorneys and expert witnesses with no guarantee that you will be happy with the result?

9. Do you want to give up attention to detail that a negotiated agreement will have but that a judge's decision will not?

10. Do you want to engage in costly, time-consuming and rancorous litigation that can make future cooperation between you and your co-parent extremely difficult at best and the resumption of amicable joint parenting nearly impossible?

Improving Communication With Your Co-Parent

In the early days of a divorce or separation, before lawyers are hired and positions harden, you and your co-parent can establish a spirit of cooperation with productive discussions of child-related issues. Consider the following ways to accomplish that:

- Keep your conversations under control by agreeing ahead of time what issues will be discussed.
- Focus on current issues without dredging up old problems, conflicts or vulnerabilities.
- Don't assume that your co-parent's motivations or intentions are hostile.
- Remain calm, and try to understand your co-parent's standpoint.
- Ask questions to better understand how your co-parent feels about an issue—and why.
- Don't interrupt. Make your co-parent feel that his/her concerns are being heard.
- If the conversation deteriorates to the point that further discussion will only make things worse, express that concern and politely end the conversation.

When Less (Communication) Is More

If communication between you and your spouse has become routinely contentious, it might benefit you (and your kids) to cut down on it, at least until things cool off. A number of apps and sites help with that by facilitating co-parenting during and after divorce. Some of these programs offer a free or low cost basic plan together with a premium plan that includes more options. At a minimum, any such program should serve as a buffer between you and your spouse, and allow you to:

- Create parenting time schedules
- Share child-related information such as schedule changes
- Schedule extracurricular activities, doctor's appointments, etc.
- Provide messaging that avoids in-person confrontations between antagonistic parents

Check out, for example, https://www.ourfamilywizard.com/, 2houses.com and custodyxchange.com. You might also want to find out if a particular program includes help keeping track of child support obligations and payments.

Parenting Goal Statements

If you are able to communicate productively about your kids, begin your new co-parenting relationship by agreeing upon some shared parenting goals and beliefs. Writing a "Parenting Goal Statement" redirects the focus from the parents' conflict to the children's needs. A Parenting Goal

Statement can also create momentum for the ultimate goal; a "Parenting Plan" that will become part of your settlement agreement.

Parenting Goal Statements should include most, if not all, of the following:
- We will shield our children from our conflict.
- We will not use our children as messengers.
- We will not use our children as confidants.
- We will not put our children in a position of "choosing sides."
- We will keep child-related issues completely separate from financial ones.
- We will not criticize each other to or in front of, our children. (Devaluing each other can cause children to wonder what is wrong with them for loving such unworthy parents.)
- We will each nurture our children's love for the other parent.
- We will agree beforehand what information we will share with the children regarding the divorce.
- We will encourage our children to express their feelings, but we will make the decisions.
- We will share information about our children's well-being, school-work, activities and schedules.
- We will make our best effort to have similar, consistent rules for the children.
- We will reassure our children that they will continue to have two parents who love them.
- We will reassure our children that the failure of our marriage is not their fault in any way. (This is especially important when child-related issues are in dispute and children may feel that if not for them, their parents wouldn't be fighting.)
- Because our children will suffer as long as issues remain unresolved regarding them, we will try to resolve those issues quickly and in a way that reflects the values stated above.

Parenting Plans: What Should Be in Them?

Parenting plans should address all non-financial matters regarding the children, including the following (see Appendix 5 for sample parenting plan provisions):
- Legal custody including responsibility for decision-making
- Physical custody, including

- ○ A parenting schedule allocating each parent's time with the children (see discussion below)
- ○ Where applicable, a designation of the children's "primary residence"
- Statement of shared parenting goals or beliefs regarding matters such as religion, health, and safety issues, etc.
- Obligations to parent cooperatively in the children's best interests, including
  - ○ Sharing school, extracurricular, medical and other information
  - ○ Being flexible in handling scheduling and other issues that arise unexpectedly
- Relocation: What happens if the primary custodial parent wishes to move from the area with the child?

Parenting Plan Schedules

Parenting plan schedules should cover:
- School year weekend and midweek time
- School year vacations
- Holidays and three-day weekends
- Summer vacation
- Special days: Mother's and Father's days, parents' birthdays; children's birthdays; traditional family gatherings
- Language regarding flexibility in handling changes in parents' or children's schedules
- If desired, a review of the schedule periodically or by a certain date

Virtual Visitation

More and more non-custodial parents are supplementing time with their children using Skype, FaceTime and other electronic means. Florida, Illinois, North Carolina, Texas, Utah and Wisconsin have virtual visitation laws and another 20 or so states are considering them. Even if your state doesn't have a statute, you can include virtual visitation in your settlement agreement or ask a judge to order it.

Additional Parenting Plan Provisions

Depending upon how much specificity you want or feel is necessary in your agreement, additional provisions can be included to preserve the children's well-being and to ensure the non-custodial parent's continued and meaningful involvement in their lives. Such provisions can cover:

- Bedtime and homework routines
- TV and online restrictions, etc.
- Responsibility for transporting children
- Phone and virtual parenting time via texting, message boards, Facetime, Skype, etc.
- Religious upbringing and training
- Counseling or therapy for children
- Access of grandparents and other relatives
- A parent's first option or "right of first refusal" to have the children if the other parent can't be with them as scheduled per the parenting plan
- Shared approach to discipline
- Transferring clothes, school material, special toys, etc.
- Matters of concern such as dangerous activities and travel limitations
- Restrictions regarding housemates and access of relatives or others who may put the children at risk
- Role of subsequent spouses and significant others in communications regarding the children
- Appointment of a child therapist or other third party to mediate or otherwise help solve problems that arise

See Appendix 5 for sample language.

Parenting agreements can include a wide range of topics beyond scheduling; from activity choices, to bedtimes, to transporting the kids.

When You May Need the Court to Be Involved

Parents should settle child-related differences as quickly as possible. Children's interests are served by speedy resolution of divorces and an end to, or at least a reduction of their parents' battling. However, the court's intervention may be necessary to protect children when there is:

- A history of or verifiable potential for domestic violence or neglect
- Untreated mental illness or continuing substance abuse
- The presence of third-parties in the household who put a child at risk
- Parents who are chronically unable to parent cooperatively
- Any other circumstances that pose a risk to a child's health or welfare

When Child-Related Issues Remain in Dispute

If, despite your best efforts, child-related issues cannot be resolved by agreement, you may have to testify at
- A deposition during which you will be questioned by opposing counsel
- A *pendente lite* child custody or access hearing

No one looks forward to being a witness. But if you are required to testify, think of it as an opportunity to show that you will be an effective witness if your case goes to trial. Strong testimony can also help persuade your spouse to settle. In Chapter 15, you will learn how to help your case with effective testimony.

The Inside Scoop: What You Might Be Asked at Trial About Child-Related Issues

In order to testify effectively, you must prepare for the types of questions you are likely to be asked. You can expect questions regarding custody and other child-related issues to include the following:
- Your and your spouse's strengths and weaknesses as parents
- Whether you consider your spouse to be a good parent and the reasons for your opinion
- Whether one parent has been the "primary" parent
- Which parent has been chiefly responsible for child rearing tasks such as
    - Meal preparation
    - Buying the children's clothing and necessities
    - Assistance with homework and school projects
    - Getting the children up and out in the morning

- ○ Nighttime routines including baths, bedtime stories, etc.
- ○ Transporting the children to activities
- ○ Participating in parent/child activities such as coaching, scouting, and field trips
- ○ Communicating with teachers, coaches, health care providers, instructors, tutors, etc.
- ○ Providing guidance and religious training
- ○ Selecting and scheduling extracurricular activities
- ○ Setting up play dates
- The children's preferences regarding spending time with their parents
- The children's current routines (including temporary parenting plan) and what changes might be beneficial
- The likely impact on a child of a change in the current living situation
- Whether you have the workplace proximity and work schedule flexibility to attend teachers' conferences, athletic, music, etc. events, and other children's activities
- Health issues, disabilities or habits of either parent that affect the ability to parent
- Whether either parent exhibits conduct or characteristics that may put the children at risk, (e.g., emotional disorders, anger issues, or substance abuse)
- Specific events (including altercations between you and your spouse) that demonstrate either fitness or unsuitability as a custodial parent
- What support systems (grandparents, child care providers, etc.) are available to each parent
- Details of your children's lives regarding schools and teachers, academic performance, children's hobbies and interests, identities of their close friends, etc.
- The nature of your and your spouse's relationships with the key adults in your children's lives such as teachers, physicians, therapists, tutors, music and arts teachers, and coaches
- Your children's special needs, if any
- Similarities and differences among your children
- Which parent is more likely to provide a stable environment and continuity in the children's education, home life and community involvement
- Sensitivity of both parents to the impact of the divorce on children and appropriateness of conduct during the divorce (e.g., not using

children as messengers, disparaging the other parent, arguing in front of the children, etc.)
- What more could be done to help the children handle the divorce, including how you feel about counseling for them
- Whether joint decision making is doable given your relationship with your spouse
- How you feel you and your spouse will co-parent after the divorce, including what each of you could do to improve the co-parenting relationship

The Child's Preference

In nearly every state, a child's preference is among a number of factors a court can consider when deciding custody cases. The importance of those preferences depends on the facts of the case. Those facts include the child's age and ability to intelligently form and express preferences and feelings.

State laws and customs vary widely as to how children's preferences are expressed, and under what circumstances. As a general matter, judges try to strike a delicate balance between:
- The child's interest in being shielded from the harsh realities of courtroom testimony; and
- The parents' interest in knowing the child's preference and to have that preference evaluated or "tested," as testimony of any other witness would be.

As with all child-related issues, judges base their decisions on the best interests of the child. Judges have a great deal of discretion in deciding how a child's preference will become known and the weight the court will afford it.

The Uniform Marriage and Divorce Act (UMDA) provides guidelines that have been adopted in whole or part by many state statutes, whether or not the states have formally adopted the UMDA. Those guidelines provide that:
- The judge may interview the child in chambers.
- The judge may, but is not required to have the lawyers present.
- The interview must be recorded by tape or a court reporter, and the lawyers can access transcripts.
- The judge can also interview experts such as mental health professionals, provided that the parents have
  ○ Access to the experts' opinions

    º The right to cross-examine the experts

If you are facing a custody hearing, familiarize yourself with your state's law regarding children's preferences. That includes the following:[9]

- Where is the child heard? In most states, judges can interview children regarding their preferences in the judge's chambers rather than a courtroom. Such "in camera" interviews are intended to lessen the child's distress and to protect her from having to openly choose sides. In states such as New Mexico and Ohio, if children are interviewed, it must be in chambers, not a courtroom. However, California, North Carolina and Utah allow children to testify in court.
- Who may or must be present when the child is interviewed? Colorado, Indiana, Kentucky, Louisiana, South Carolina, Texas and Wyoming permit the parents' counsel (and appointed child's counsel or guardian *ad litem*) to be present for chambers interviews. New Mexico and Oklahoma prohibit counsel from being present.
- May the child also be questioned by someone besides the judge? This is permitted in states such as Minnesota and Oregon. In Delaware, Minnesota, New Jersey, Oklahoma, Oregon and Pennsylvania, counsel can submit questions for the judge to ask the child.
- Must the interview be recorded and if so, who has access to transcripts? Once again, the answers to this question vary widely:
  - º Arizona, Georgia, Illinois, Maryland, Missouri, Montana, New Jersey, Oklahoma, Virginia and Washington require a record although in some of those states parties may agree not to have the interview recorded.
  - º Kansas permits, but does not require a record. New York requires transcripts to be made but does not allow parents to access them. New Jersey allows the parties access to transcripts but in Oklahoma the parties can have transcripts only if the judge's decision is appealed.
- Is there a specific age at which a child's preference becomes particularly important? Here's a sampling of rules applied in various states:

---

9. Information provided in this section is derived in part from "The Preferences and Voices of Children in Massachusetts and Beyond", Vol. 50, *Family Law Quarterly* (a publication of the Section of Family Law of the American Bar Association) No. 3, Fall 2016.

- ° Connecticut judges pay attention to children's preferences to the extent that the children are mature enough to form and articulate a preference. Age 12 is sometimes considered the threshold for meeting those requirements. Judges give considerable weight to a 14-year-old's preference.
- ° Georgia requires judges to consider the preferences of children between ages 11 and 14, and allows children over 14 to choose the custodial parent unless the court finds that parent unfit.
- ° In Oklahoma, there is a rebuttable presumption that 12-year-olds can form intelligent preferences regarding custody.
- ° Nebraska judges must consider a preference based on sound reasoning from a child regardless of age. Tennessee courts can consider the preference of children aged 12 and over.
- Is appointment of an attorney or guardian *ad litem* required for a child being interviewed? Vermont, for example, requires this.

A Testimony Pearl

Among the questions above that you might be asked in a custody or child access proceeding is one concerning your child's preferences regarding spending time with you and their other parent. If you do testify about the children's preferences, be prepared for the next area of inquiry regarding how you know what those preferences are, and whether you have influenced them.

On the other hand, such a question may "open the door" for you to repeat what others, such as teachers or neighbors have told you the children have told *them*; testimony that might otherwise be excluded as "hearsay." See Chapter 15 for a detailed discussion of testifying.

Modification of Child Custody

Either parent can ask a court to modify child custody, access and related orders, either prior to or after a divorce decree is issued. Generally, the requesting parent must establish that:

- There is a substantial or "material" change in circumstances
- As a result of the changed circumstances, a change in custody or access would be in the child's best interest

Substantial changes in circumstances can include the following:
- The non-custodial parent requests a change after the child has lived with the non-custodial parent for a substantial period of time by agreement
- The custodial parent has engaged in conduct detrimental to the child, such as criminal activity or substance abuse
- The custodial parent's judgment or ability to care for the child has substantially declined due to illness or some other reason
- The preference of a child of suitable age and maturity has changed
- The child's residence is not safe for the child physically, mentally, or emotionally, and it would be more harmful to leave the child where he/she is than to move him/her to the other parent's home
- One parent alienates a child from the other parent
- A parent habitually fails to abide by the parenting plan[10]
- The custodial parent has or wishes to relocate (see "Relocation" below)
- Any other change in circumstances that jeopardizes a child's health, safety or welfare

Limitations on Custody Modification

Some states limit how many times a parent can attempt to modify custody. For example, in Minnesota:
- Except in extraordinary circumstances, "or as agreed to in writing by the parties, no motion to modify a custody order or parenting plan may be made earlier than one year after the date of the entry of a decree of dissolution or legal separation containing a provision dealing with custody. . . ."[11]
- If a prior modification motion has been heard, "no subsequent motion may be filed within two years after disposition of the prior motion on its merits."[12]

Find out if your state has rules like Minnesota's, and what, if any, exceptions there are to those rules.

---

10. Note, however, that custody will not be changed simply to punish a parent.

11. Minnesota Statutes sec. 518.18(a). The exceptions to Minnesota's limitations on frequency of child custody modification proceedings are: "persistent and willful denial or interference with parenting time, or has reason to believe that the child's present environment may endanger the child's physical or emotional health or impair the child's emotional development. Minnesota Statutes sec. 518.18(c)

12. Minnesota Statutes §518.18(b)

Relocation

One of the most heart-wrenching controversies regarding children arises after a divorce when a custodial parent wishes to move a significant distance away from the other parent. These cases arise most often when:

- The custodial parent or his/her new spouse is transferred by an employer
- A custodial spouse who cannot find work locally is offered a job a substantial distance away
- A custodial spouse wishes to relocate to be closer to family or other support systems

Many states require that parents wishing to relocate with children file with the court a notice of intent to move. The other parent is then entitled to a hearing. All states use the BIC standard in determining whether to allow the relocation.

The Toughest Question

A parent wishing to move in a relocation case can be put in an impossible position when asked whether he/she will move regardless of whether the child is permitted to relocate. Answering either "yes" or "no" can both unfairly prejudice the parent. As a result, the American Academy of Matrimonial Lawyers has proposed that the question not be allowed in relocation cases and state legislatures have begun amending their statutes accordingly.

Key Relocation Case Facts

As noted above, judges' decisions generally come down to the BIC standard. State statutes (laws passed by state legislatures) as well as case law (law made by judges) enumerate factors such as the following for determining a child's best interests:

- Whether the relocation is proposed in good faith and is necessary
- The primary custodial parent's reasons for wishing to relocate and the other parent's reasons for opposing relocation
- Whether the child's health, educational and extracurricular activity opportunities would be comparable to her current situation if relocation occurs
- The preference of a child of suitable age and maturity

- The extent to which the child's relationship with the non-custodial parent might be damaged
- The distance of the proposed relocation
- Whether the child's special needs or talents will be sufficiently attended to if relocation occurs
- The hardship and expense the non-relocating parent would experience
- The extent to which the custodial parent is likely to foster the child's relationship with the noncustodial parent if relocation occurs
- Whether it is feasible for the non-custodial parent to relocate as well
- How relocation is likely to impact extended family relationships
- Any other factors relevant to the child's best interests

Illegal Relocation Provisions

The following provisions regarding relocation, even if agreed to in writing by both parents, are illegal and thus can't be enforced by a court:

- Provisions that automatically change custody if a custodial parent improperly relocates. Such provisions impinge upon the court's ultimate right to decide custody issues.
- While agreements may require that a parent wishing to relocate with a child obtain court approval, provisions flatly forbidding a custodial spouse from moving out of state after the divorce violate the parent's constitutional right to travel among the states. [Note that Wyoming is an apparent exception to this rule. See Watt v. Watt, 971 P.2d 608 (Wyo. 1999).

Key Relocation Case Legalities

Besides weighing the facts listed above, judges must be aware of two key legal principles:

- Definition of "relocation": State law definitions of relocation vary, with some focusing on how far the parent has or wishes to take a child, and some on how long:
  - Florida's definition: "relocation of a child to a principal residence more than 50 miles away from his or her principal place of residence . . ."[13]
  - Missouri: "a change in the principal residence of a child for a period of ninety days or more . . ."[14]
  - Michigan: ". . . a parent of a child . . . shall not change a legal residence of the child to a location that is more than 100 miles from the child's legal residence . . ."[15]
- Burden of proof: As discussed above in connection with joint custody, legal "presumptions" and "burdens of proof" put one of the parents at a disadvantage. Note that state relocation laws allocate burdens of proof in a variety of ways:
  - Missouri: "The party seeking to relocate shall have the burden of proving that the proposed relocation is made in good faith and is in the best interest of the child."[16]
  - Wisconsin: ". . . the burden of proof is on the parent objecting to the move or removal."[17]
  - Indiana: "The relocating individual has the burden of proof that the proposed relocation is made in good faith and for a legitimate reason.[18] If the relocating individual meets the burden of proof . . . the burden shifts to the non-relocating parent to show that the proposed relocation is not in the best interest of the child."[19]

Third-Party Visitation Claims

The U.S. Supreme Court's 2000 decision in *Troxel v. Granville* made it more difficult for grandparents and other "third parties" such as other relatives to gain visitation rights with children.[20] The Court emphasized that fit parents have the right to object to grandparent visitation and indicated

---

13. Fla. Stat. §61.13001(a)
14. Missouri Statutes §452.375
15. Mich. Comp. Laws §722
16. Missouri Statutes §452.375
17. Wisconsin Statutes §767.481(3)(a)(3)
18. Indiana Code §31-17-2.2-5(c)
19. Indiana Code §31-17-2.2-5(d)
20. 530 U.S. 57 (2000)

that "special factors" must be shown to justify visitation by grandparents over the parents' objections. After the *Troxel* case, about half of the states made it more difficult for grandparents to obtain visitation rights. Those states either:

- Established a presumption that the parents' denial of visitation was reasonable, or
- Increased the grandparents' burden of proof to show otherwise

"Standing" of Third Parties to Seek Visitation

In a number of states, courts will not entertain third-party visitation claims unless the claimants establish their right or "standing" to seek visitation by establishing one of the following facts:

- The parents are divorced, legally separated, or a divorce is pending
- A parent has been missing for a specified period of time
- A parent has abandoned the child
- The child was born out of wedlock
- A parent is deceased, incarcerated, incompetent or has had his/her parental rights terminated
- Neither parent is raising the child[21]

Once a third party makes it over the standing threshold, he/she bears the burden of establishing the right to visitation. Either by statutory or case law,[22] third parties are required to show both of the following:

- Visitation is in the child's best interests.
- Additional circumstances that rebut the presumption favoring parents.

---

21. By contrast, New York is particularly permissive regarding "standing," allowing a non-parent access to the courts where "equity would see fit to intervene." N.Y. Dom. Rel. Law § 72(1).

22. This is an area where you will need a lawyer to advise you regarding your state's law. Reading a statute can be misleading. For example, many state statutes require simply that visitation be in the child's best interests. However, case law interpreting those statutes has added additional requirements consistent with *Troxel*. Those states include: Alaska, Arizona, California, Colorado, Delaware, Idaho, Kentucky, Louisiana, Massachusetts, Michigan, Missouri, Montana, North Carolina, Ohio, Vermont, Virginia, and Wisconsin.

What Must a Third Party Claiming Visitation Prove?

The "additional circumstances" a third party seeking visitation may be required to prove since the *Troxel* decision include the following:

- That the parental determination is not in the child's best interest (Colorado)
- That grandparent visitation would not significantly interfere with any parent-child relationship (Maine, Minnesota, North Dakota, Pennsylvania, South Carolina, South Dakota, West Virginia, and Wyoming)
- That a substantial relationship has been established between the grandparents and the grandchild or, at the least, the grandparents have attempted to establish such a relationship (Alaska, Arkansas, California, Iowa, Kansas, Maine, Mississippi, and Oregon)
- That grandparent visitation has been unreasonably denied or restricted (Nevada, Alabama, Illinois, Mississippi, Missouri, and South Dakota)
- The parent objecting to grandparent visitation is unfit (Iowa, Montana, and Oklahoma)

Factors Considered in Third Party Visitation Claims

Judges consider some or all of the following in determining whether a grandparent or other third party is entitled to visitation:

- The nature and stability of the relationship between the child and the grandparent seeking visitation
- The amount of time grandparent and child have spent together
- The potential detriments and benefits to the child from granting visitation
- The effect granting visitation would have on the child's relationship with the parents
- The physical and emotional health of parents and grandparents
- The stability of the child's living and school arrangements
- The wishes and preferences of the child
- Parental unfitness
- Significant harm that would result to the child in the absence of a visitation order

Third-Party Custody Claims

Although state statutes and case law vary widely, some rules and principles regarding the rights of grandparents and others to seek custody (rather than simply visitation) have gained acceptance in a majority of states:

- Parents who are not unfit, and are able and willing to care for a child are usually presumed to be more appropriate custodians of their child than non-parents.[1]
- As a result of the presumption in favor of parents, grandparents usually have the burden of establishing some degree of unfitness on the part of a parent against whom they are claiming custody.[2]
- If the court makes a finding that a parent is unfit, the court will apply the best interests of the child standard.
- There is a built-in tension between the "parental preference rule" favoring parents' rights, and the best interests of the child rule that is the ultimate standard in child custody matters.
  - Some courts resolve this conflict by holding that the parents' rights must yield in situations where a non-parent can better serve the child's interest.
  - Many courts, however, will not consider a grandparent's claim until the presumption in favor of parental custody has been rebutted.
- Asserting a close and nurturing relationship with a child is generally not sufficient. However, grandparents with whom a child has been living for an extended period can make a persuasive case for custody. The grandparents' claim is further strengthened if the child was placed with the grandparents by agreement with the parents. In those circumstances, it is the parent who may bear the burden of proving both of the following in seeking a custody change.

---

1. An exception is Iowa's statute that grants grandparents with whom a grandchild resides in a stable relationship, the same standing as parents. In *Hernandez v. Hernandez*, 265 P.3d 495 (Idaho 2011), The Iowa Supreme Court upheld the statute's constitutionality.

2. States where parental unfitness need not always be proved include New York and California. In California, if granting custody to a parent would be "detrimental" to a child who has been living in a stable environment with a person "who has assumed on a day-to-day basis, the role of his or her parent, fulfilling both the child's physical needs and the child's psychological needs for care and affection, and who has assumed that role for a substantial period of time," the court may transfer custody away from parents without a finding that they are unfit. Cal. Fam. Code sec. 3041(a).

- A change in circumstances has occurred (see modification below).
  - The best interests of the child require a change in custody.
- A parent's lack of financial resources will not be considered unless it reflects a lack of fitness such as substance abuse or emotional problems.

Is It Easier For a Third Party to Get Custody Than Visitation?

Not really, but it might appear that way.

Some state third party visitation statutes contain requirements that seem more difficult than those in custody statutes. That's partly because visitation sought with children of parents who are not unfit is seen as an incursion on the parents' rights. Custody claims, on the other hand, arise most often where there is reason to believe that one or both parents are unfit and thus the children's interests are considered more important than the rights of such parents. And proving these more serious allegations of lack of fitness are more likely to result in a custody change.

"Standing" Rules Regarding Custody

A number of state statutes provide that third parties do not have standing to seek custody unless they can show at least one of the following:

- The third party has acted as a *"de facto* parent*"* or stands *"in loco parentis"* to the child. [3]
  - Arizona
  - Delaware
  - Kentucky
  - Minnesota
  - Montana
  - Oregon

---

3. The Latin terms *"de facto* parent*"* and *"in loco parentis"* are often used interchangeably. Technically, there is a difference. Grandparents who are *in loco parentis,* meaning that they are acting in the place of a parent, have taken control of a child's upbringing in the temporary absence of the parents, but with the parents' permission. A *de facto* parent is simply a third party acting as the child's parent.

  ° Pennsylvania
  ° South Carolina
- The child is living with the third-party claimant: California, Idaho
- Death of both parents: Texas
- The child is not in the custody of one of the natural parents: Illinois

Factors Favoring Third-Party Custody

Certain circumstances strengthen a grandparent's custody claim:
- Lack of fitness or persistent neglect by the objecting parent(s)
- Abandonment of the child by the objecting parent(s)
- The grandparents have raised the child for a significant period of time
- One of the parents consents to the grandparents' custody
- Other extraordinary or exceptional circumstances

Factors Considered in "Grandparent Custody" Cases

Once grandparents (the term "grandparents" is often used as shorthand to include all third parties claiming custody) have hurdled the *standing* obstacle, judges may consider the following factors in custody cases:
- The fitness of parents and grandparents
- The respective abilities of the parents and grandparents to attend to the child's safety, welfare, and physical and emotional health
- The history and nature of the relationship between the grandparent(s) and grandchild, including any periods when the child has resided with the grandparents
- The wishes of the child, if the child is of sufficient age and maturity to make decisions for himself or herself (often beginning around age 12)
- Evidence of abuse or neglect by the parent(s) or grandparent(s)
- Evidence of substance abuse by, or emotional disturbance or mental illness of, the parent(s) or grandparent(s)
- The child's present living situation, including potential threats to the child's well-being from members of the household, neighbors, etc.
- The child's adjustment to the home, school, or community, and importance of maintaining continuity
- The respective abilities of the parents and grandparents to foster the child's love and affection for, and contact with, the other

- The geographical distance between the child and the parent(s) or grandparent(s)
- Any other factors relevant to the child's best interests

Assisted Reproductive Technology

The increasing number of children born as a result of assisted reproductive technology (ART) has sent matrimonial lawyers scurrying for answers to new questions. Their task is complicated by the wide disparity in state laws, including states that provide little or no guidance in defining a "legal parent."

To be safe, parents should adopt children to whom they have no biological relationship. This is true whether the child is born through surrogacy, or procedures such as *in vitro* fertilization. In view of the developing state of applicable law, even parents named on a birth certificate would be wise to becomes.

See Chapter 16 for more on ART.

Federal Laws Regarding Custody, Safety, and Rights of Children and Spouses

State laws govern the majority of divorce-related issues. However, two other types of laws seek to bring uniformity to disputes where two or more states or countries are involved:
- Federal laws enacted by Congress: Where federal and state laws conflict, federal law prevails under the constitutional law doctrine of "preemption." Federal laws can be found in The United States Code, which contains all laws enacted by Congress.
- "Uniform laws": These are laws proposed for state adoption by The National Conference of Commissioners on Uniform State Laws (NCCUSL), also known as the "Uniform Law Commission." They contain the word "uniform," and strive for
  ○ Predictability
  ○ Avoidance of disputes over which jurisdiction's law applies
  ○ Equal treatment of litigants regardless of where they reside

Unlike federal law, "uniform acts" may be adopted by state legislatures in whole or in part. Since a uniform act is not a federal law, your state's version of any uniform act can be found among your state's "Statutes" or in its "Code," usually with the word "uniform" as part of the title.

Issues relating to well-being and safety of children and spouses, and to child custody are particularly likely to be the subject of uniform acts and federal law. Such issues are covered by the following:

- The Uniform Child Custody Jurisdiction and Enforcement Act (UCCJEA): Adopted by all states (and the District of Columbia) except Massachusetts, the UCCJEA complements and is often applied together with a federal statute, the Parental Kidnapping Prevention Act (PKPA).[4] Together, these laws seek to
  - Thwart interstate kidnapping of children by a parent
  - Establish rules to determine which state has jurisdiction and which state's law applies in custody disputes where the parents live in different states
  - Provide uniform procedures to register and enforce custody orders across state boundaries
  - Avoid conflicting custody decrees in different states
  - Avoid repetitive litigation of custody orders
- The National Child Search Assistance Act:[5] Eliminates waiting periods for missing child reports including family abduction cases.
- The Hague Convention on the Civil Aspects of International Child Abduction ("Hague Abduction Convention"): An international treaty enacted to speed the return of a child who has been abducted from the country of habitual residence to another country, and to ensure that each country respect the custody and visitation laws of the others. Signatories include the U.S., Australia, Canada, Israel, The Russian Federation, South Africa, Zimbabwe Mexico, and most other Western Hemisphere countries, and most European countries.
- The International Child Abduction Remedies Act (ICARA):[6] Implements The Hague Abduction Convention in the U.S.
- The Uniform Deployed Parents Custody and Visitation Act: Addresses issues regarding deployed members of the military by
  - Requiring a deployed custodial parent to notify the other parent within 7 days of notice of the deployment

---

4. 28 USC Sec. 1738A et seq.
5. 42 USC 5779 et seq.
6. 42 U.S.C. 11601

- ° Establishing expedited procedures to address child-related issues of deployed parents
- ° Allowing deployed parents to grant temporary custody rights to grandparents and other third parties
- The Uniform Parentage Act: Intended to facilitate the identification of fathers in order to obtain child support orders, including actions brought by non-parent "interested parties."
- The Uniform Interstate Enforcement of Domestic Violence Protection Orders Act: Intended to expedite the enforcement of out-of-state restraining orders against abusive spouses.
- The Uniform Status of Children of Assisted Conception Act: Intended to provide uniform rules for establishing parentage by defining the legal mother and father in cases of assisted conception.
- The Indian Child Welfare Act: Intended to limit the removal of children from custody of Native-American families.

 Yes, there IS a quiz! Test what you have (or haven't) learned.

1. This chapter is mainly about:
   A. International children's uniforms
   B. Whether grandparents should be left standing
   C. Whether visiting a third party in one weekend is too much partying
   D. Caring and making suitable arrangements for children of divorce
2. Pronounce out loud during your child's music recital, and unscramble the following key phrases from this chapter!
   A. drith taryp griths
   B. nijto stuydoc stipumperon
   C. tincoolear assec

CHAPTER 11

Understanding Child Support

"If you think you will, you might. If you think you won't, you're right."

— Unknown

Child Support Guidelines

Federal law requires each state to maintain Child Support Guidelines (referred to here as "Guidelines" or "CSG") that calculate the amount of child support to be ordered in a particular case. Those calculations are based primarily upon
- The parents' incomes
- The number of minor children

There's more to it than arithmetic, however, because a number of variables come into play:
- State laws vary as to how long child support is required.
- "Deviation criteria" in a particular case can render the Guidelines inapplicable.
- Since CSG support depends on income, calculation of a spouse's "real income" is critical and requires analysis of (for example)
    ○ An employee spouse's bonuses, commissions, overtime, use of a company car, and "perks" such as reimbursed expenses that include personal as well as business related items.
    ○ The total benefit that a self-employed spouse derives from a business that, for example:
        ▪ Pays personal bills
        ▪ Provides other perks such as leased vehicles
        ▪ Retains earnings rather than distributing earnings to the spouse
        ▪ Reduces its "bottom line" by "paper deductions" such as depreciation

Duration of Child Support

In many states, the child support obligation lasts until a non-emancipated child graduates high school or reaches age 18, whichever comes later. However, in New York and Indiana, child support can extend to age 21 whether or not a child has graduated from high school. In states such as Texas, parents remain responsible for child support so long as a child remains in high school, regardless of age.

More often, parents are not required to support indefinitely a child who remains in high school past his or her 18th birthday. Typical child support "end-dates" include:

- Arizona, California, Connecticut, Delaware, Florida, Illinois, Ohio, South Carolina: High school graduation or age 19
- Michigan: High school graduation or age 19 ½
- North Carolina, Georgia: High school graduation or age 20
- Missouri: High school graduation or higher education graduation

In other states, child support is not deemed to end at a single age:
- New Jersey: Unless an existing support order specifies a termination date, child support does not end until the court determines the extent to which child support should extend beyond age 18.
- Massachusetts: Child support will end at age 18 unless the child remains principally dependent on the custodial parent, is employed full time, or is in the military. Thereafter, it ends at age 21 or 23 for full-time students in college or a trade school. As in a number of states, child support can be required for longer for disabled children.

Child Support That Ends Prematurely or Extends Indefinitely

Emancipation terminates child support even prior to the state's termination age. A child's emancipation usually occurs as a result of one of the following:
- Marriage
- Military enlistment
- Financial independence
- Court order of emancipation

At the other end of the spectrum, many states provide for indefinite child support for physically or mentally disabled children.

Amount of Child Support Under Child Support Guidelines

As with duration, state law regarding amount of child support varies significantly. There are, however, a number of common features. Typically, state child support guidelines:

- Provide a formula for calculating child support based on the income of one or both parents and the number of children
- Include instructions as to how the child support amount is affected by factors such as health insurance and child care expense
- Require the judge to order the amount of child support determined by the CSG formula unless the judge finds that it would be inequitable or unjust due to "deviation criteria"
- Define deviation criteria (see below) and specify in what circumstances the Guidelines will not apply
- Define
  - Whether items such as future bonuses and other employment-related "perks" should be included in income for purposes of CSG calculations
  - What can be deducted from the parents' incomes (e.g., mandatory pension contributions, union dues, etc.) to determine the incomes to be used in CSG calculations
- Calculate payment of child support arrearages
- Require periodic revisions to insure that the Guidelines reflect changing economic realities in the state
- Require publication of a booklet (available on many state court websites) explaining the state's rules regarding the items above and including
  - A chart showing the support payable according to number of children and incomes
  - A support calculation worksheet
- Provide for a child support amount based on the state's census income data when there is no reliable information regarding the obligor's income

CSG Formulas

At this writing, 34 states use the "Income Shares" formula to calculate child support:

Alabama, Arizona, California, Colorado, Connecticut, Florida, Hawaii, Idaho, Indiana, Kansas, Kentucky, Louisiana, Maine, Maryland, Michigan, Missouri, Nebraska, New Jersey, New Mexico, New York, North Carolina, Ohio, Oklahoma, Oregon, Pennsylvania, Rhode Island, South Carolina, South Dakota, Utah, Vermont, Virginia, Washington, West Virginia, and Wyoming

The Income Shares formula:
- Determines a total child support obligation for both parents based on their incomes
- Calculates the obligation of the non-custodial parent ("the obligor") based on the percentage that his/her income bears to the total of both incomes

Delaware, Hawaii, and Montana use the "Melson Formula," which is a more complicated version of the "Income Shares" formula. The remaining states use the "Percentage of Income" formula that calculates child support solely upon the income of the non-custodial parent.

CSG Deviation Criteria

As mentioned above, certain factors called "deviation criteria" allow a judge to order more or less than the amount calculated under the CSG. Typical deviation criteria include the following:
- Extraordinary expenses for medical care and/or maintenance of the child
- Extraordinary parental expenses
- Extraordinary child care expenses for medical or other reasons
- Atypical amounts of time spent with the parents, such as 50/50 arrangements
- The paying (non-custodial) parent's income is so high that the formula amount would exceed the needs of the children
- Extraordinary disparity in parental income
- Extraordinary assets or debts
- Contributions or gifts of a spouse or domestic partner
- Needs of a parent's other dependents such as their own parents or children of a prior marriage or other union
- Child support paid for children of other relationships

- Shared physical custody that either substantially reduces the custodial parent's expenses for the child or substantially increases the noncustodial parent's expenses[7]
- Low-income obligor and custodial parent
- A child's special needs (e.g., a disabled child) or special expenses (anything from special medical needs to special activities that aid the child's development, such as art or music lessons, travel, and school extracurricular activities such as athletics, band and clubs)
- Income of other adults in the household, which some states such as Texas, require to be coupled with an additional deviation criterion)
- A child's extraordinary income (stranger things have happened!)
- Travel expenses for exercising parenting time

Defining Income For Support Calculations

Federal law requires that all of the child support obligor's income be included for purposes of calculating child support. State Guidelines and cases interpreting them have deemed that to include:

- Salary, wages, tips, overtime, commissions (including draws against commissions), profit sharing, deferred compensation
- Bonuses and severance pay
- Non-cash "perks" and reimbursements such as free housing, meals and vehicles that reduce personal living expenses
- Independent contractor income
- Retained earnings of Subchapter S corporations
- Interest, dividends, partnership distributions and recurring capital gains[8]
- Trust income
- Pensions and annuity income
- Armed Forces Reserve and National Guard pay
- Social Security, veterans', and G.I. benefits
- Workers' compensation, unemployment and disability insurance benefits
- Scholarships, fellowships, and living expense subsidies

---

7. An *equal* time-sharing is typically *not* required for a finding of shared physical custody.

8. A capital gain is essentially the profit made when property is sold, with some adjustments. "Recurring capital gain" is profits from, for example, investments, and is distinguished from one-time capital gain such as the profit realized upon sale of a principal residence, which should not be included in income when calculating support.

- Forgiveness of a debt or use of property at less than market or customary cost
- A new spouse's income to the extent that it directly reduces a parent's expenses
- Spousal support from a former spouse
- Money, goods, or services provided by friends or family
- Prizes and winnings from gambling and lotteries

Reducing an Obligor's Income When Calculating Support

Some state statutes provide for specific reductions of the amount of income used in support calculations. For example, New York's Child Support Standards Act allows income to be reduced by the following:
- Certain unreimbursed employee business expenses
- Spousal support or child support paid per an order or written agreement in another case
- Public assistance
- Supplemental security income

Determining Income of the Self-Employed

CSG calculations can be complicated for self-employed business owners whose "real income" is hard to determine. Income and expenses can be found in the business's financial statements ("financials") and on various tax returns, depending on the nature of the business entity.

In Chapter 8, we looked at how those entities report income. Chapter 8 also includes techniques for identifying the "real income" of self-employed individuals that is not readily apparent from financials or tax returns. Since determining "real income" is so crucial to calculating support correctly, you might want to revisit that material. In any event, it's critical that you get help from a divorce lawyer, CDFA and/or business appraiser to determine not only your spouse's actual income but also the value of his/her ownership interest in the business.

Child Support Helpers

You can get help online with monitoring child support obligations and payments. Sites like supportpay.com can be especially useful if your agreement provides for a base child support amount plus expense sharing for things like medical expenses, extracurricular activities, lessons, camp, etc.

Additional Child Support

Many spouses negotiate settlement agreements that provide for child support in addition to the CSG amount.[1] Such additional child support can include contributions to:

- Health insurance premiums and coverage of uninsured or partially insured expenses such as mental health therapy and counseling
- Private school and tutoring
- Extracurricular expenses such as athletics (including participation fees and equipment), art and music lessons (including instrument/material expense), related travel and other expenses
- Post-high school education, including contributions to tax sheltered college savings accounts such as "529 accounts"

Negotiation of such "extras" can also include allocation between the parents of valuable tax benefits, including:

Child Support Guidelines don't prevent parents from negotiating "extras" such as sports activity and equipment fees.

- In pre-2018 divorces, tax exemptions for children, subject to phase-outs at higher income "threshold levels" that vary according to the taxpayer's filing status
- Federal child tax credits (CTC) for low and middle income families of as much as $2,000 for a dependent child, available if
  - The child is under 17 as of December 31st
  - You claim the child as a dependent on your income tax returns[2]

---

1. Because child support extras are typically tied to the actual cost of, for example, extracurricular activities, not a flat amount, the amount of the co-parent's contribution increases as the cost of the activity increases. This operates as a built-in "cost-of living" increase that child support payments usually don't have.

2. The requirement that you claim the child as a dependent distinguishes the child tax credit from the Child and Dependent Tax Credit (DTC) for children who are under age 13 or disabled, or the Earned Income Tax Credit (EITC) designed for low-income individuals and families. Neither the DTC or the EITC can be transferred in a divorce settlement; only the custodial parent may claim them.

- The child is your child, stepchild, foster child, adopted child, brother, sister, stepbrother, stepsister, or a descendant of one of these individuals such as a grandchild, niece, or nephew
  - The child did not provide more than half of his/her own support during the year
  - The child is a U.S. citizen, U.S. national, or U.S. resident alien
  - The child does not file a joint income tax return for the year except to claim a refund
- State child tax credits in New York, Oklahoma, North Carolina and California
- Assignment by one parent to the other of Head of Household income tax filing status in shared custody cases

Modification of Child Support

Family courts can modify child support amounts that the parties have agreed upon or a judge has ordered when the following occur:
- There has been a substantial or "material" change in the parents' circumstances and abilities to support the child—typically a change in income.[3] In some states, a substantial change is defined as a change that would cause a deviation from the Child Support Guidelines of more than a certain percentage. For example
  - In Connecticut, a change in circumstances requiring the child support amount to be modified by more than 15% will trigger modification.
  - A Minnesota court has held that a 20% (and $75) variance from the Child Support Guidelines created a presumption of a change in circumstances requiring modification.
- There has been a substantial change in the needs of the child, including educational or health expenses.
- The child support being paid does not comply with the current Guidelines.
- There has been a change in custody or primary residence.

Many parents believe that child support obligations are automatically reduced when one of several children attains majority. However, "It ain't necessarily so." It depends upon the language used in your court order or separation agreement.

---

3. In states such as Oregon and Washington, the change must be "unforeseen" or "unanticipated."

For example, language stating that child support shall be "$250 per month for each of the parties' two children" assigns a specific amount of child support per child. Thus, when the older child attains majority, the obligor may reduce the payment from $500 to $250.

However, a provision that the obligor pay "$500 per month for the parties' two children cannot be automatically reduced when one child no longer qualifies for child support. It may very well be a basis for the obligor to seek a downward modification of the child support, but the obligor must continue to pay $500 per month unless and until a modifying court order is obtained.

NOTE: If you anticipate the need to reduce child support (or spousal support for that matter), make sure to file your modification motion as close as possible to the event that you feel entitles you to a reduction. Support orders are often not retroactive further back than the date of the filing of a motion to modify.

Finally, note that parents cannot limit the court's power to determine child support. Thus, settlement agreement provisions prohibiting child support modification are generally invalid.[4]

Enforcing Child Support Orders

A number of laws offer assistance in enforcing child support orders:

- The Uniform Interstate Family Support Act (UIFSA) makes it much easier for custodial parents to obtain initial child support orders and/or to modify or enforce them when the obligor parent lives out-of-state. UIFSA facilitates enforcement of out-of-state orders by establishing a "home state" with continuing exclusive jurisdiction over the case. Judges from two states often confer by phone to decide which of their states will be the home state. Note that UIFSA was amended in 2001 and 2008, so different states apply different versions of it.
- State "long-arm jurisdiction" statutes can be used by an "initiating state" to keep child support proceedings in the state where the child support recipient lives. This can occur even when the obligor lives elsewhere if the obligor had at some point established "sufficient contacts" with the initiating state. In deciding whether a state

---

4. Some state courts, in limited circumstances, will uphold such a provision if agreed to by a child's attorney or guardian *ad litem*.

may exert authority over a non-resident under UIFSA, a court can
consider whether [5]
   ○ The obligor has resided with the child in the state
   ○ The obligor has resided in the state and provided prenatal
     expenses or support for the child
   ○ The child resides in the state as a result of the obligor's actions
   ○ The obligor engaged in sexual intercourse in the state and the
     child may have been conceived as a result
   ○ The obligor asserted paternity in the putative father registry filed
     with the appropriate agency within the state
   ○ Any other legal basis exists for the state's exercise of personal
     jurisdiction over the obligor to obtain this result

> ### ⚠ A Child Support Enforcement Pearl
> Qualified Domestic Relations Orders (QDROs) are
> court orders that allow assignment to one divorcing
> spouse of some or all of the other spouse's retirement
> plans. What most people (including most lawyers) don't
> know is that under The Employee Retirement Income
> Security Act ("ERISA"), QDROs can also be used to en-
> force child support orders out of retirement plan assets.

State support enforcement agencies assist support recipients in both intra-
state and inter-state child support proceedings. These agencies have an
array of weapons to enforce support orders, including the ability to:
   • Summon the obligor to appear at court proceedings in which an
     agency representative represents the recipient at no or nominal cost
   • File property liens
   • Report child support debts to credit agencies
   • Suspend drivers' and other licenses
   • In UIFSA cases, ask the obligor's state to begin proceedings there

Some state agencies will also assist obligors to reduce support in appropriate circumstances.

---

5. Because state long-arm statutes differ, judges' application of the UIFSA factors
differ as well.

Protecting Rights of Child Support Recipients

If you will be receiving child support, protect your rights as follows:

- Wage Garnishment: Many states allow child support recipients to elect a "wage garnishment" or a "wage order" by which employers deduct child support directly from the obligor's pay and forward the support to the custodial parent. Especially where there is a history of failure to comply with temporary orders, ask for a wage order.

- Direct deposit: If you don't use wage garnishment, provide in your settlement agreement that child support be paid via direct deposit from your Ex's account into yours. This will increase dependability and eliminate lost or late checks issues.

- Life Insurance: Require in your agreement that your Ex maintain life insurance naming you trustee or guardian of the children until child support (including college education expense) terminates. Your attorney, accountant, or an actuary can calculate the "present value" of the stream of child support and thus the amount of insurance needed to insure it. Your agreement can provide for one or more reductions of that amount as the remaining child support obligation is reduced over the years.

- Security Orders: Where there is reason to believe that the obligor may not comply with a spousal support order, courts in some states can require the obligor to provide security for payments.

- Attorneys' Fees: Most state statutes provide that attorneys' fees may be awarded in contempt proceedings. But it generally remains up to the judge whether to award fees—and to decide the amount. If you are a support recipient, provide in your agreement that the obligor will pay your reasonable attorney's fees in any proceeding in which an arrearage is established.

- Interest and Penalties: Support recipients may seek language in their settlement agreements providing for interest and even an additional monetary penalty to be assessed for willful (and perhaps repeated) failure to honor the support obligation.

- Motions for Contempt: Support orders, whether resulting from a judge's decision or a settlement agreement incorporated into a divorce decree, are enforceable by the court's contempt power. Post-judgment motions for contempt give support recipients a streamlined remedy to collect arrearages. Penalties in contempt proceedings include imprisonment of chronic offenders.

- Maintaining Accurate Records: Both spousal support recipients and obligors should keep records of payments. They will be needed in proceedings to collect arrearages.

The Bankruptcy Bugaboo

If you are worried that your spouse might file for bankruptcy after your divorce to evade child or spousal support obligations . . . relax. Bankruptcy does not "discharge" (wipe out) family court orders for:
- Child support
- Spousal support
- Attorney's fees incurred to obtain child or spousal support

Note also that the discharge of debts in bankruptcy frees up additional funds for support and also eliminates excuses for chronic missing or late payments of existing orders. So your spouse's bankruptcy may contain a silver lining!

See Chapter 13 for more on the impact of bankruptcy on property settlement and other aspects of divorce.

Yes, there IS a quiz! Test what you have (or haven't) learned.

1. This chapter is mainly about:
   A. How to garnish the salad at your Divorce Celebration Party
   B. Making a last minute material change to your Divorce Celebration outfit
   C. The factors that affect the calculation of child support orders, and ways to protect your rights with respect to it

2. What phrase used in this chapter might have been most helpful in avoiding your failed marriage?
   A. Uniform acts
   B. Retained earnings
   C. Deviation criteria

3. Pronounce out loud to your book club and then unscramble the following key phrases from this chapter:
   A. votinaide iritacre
   B. dilch poputrs snideluige
   C. dilch poputrs ridutoan

CHAPTER 12

Understanding Spousal Support

*"There is not a woman
born who desires to eat
the bread of dependence."*

— Susan B. Anthony

Trending in Spousal Support: How Much and for How Long?

Spousal support, also known as "maintenance" or "alimony," is intended to assist the less financially secure spouse after a divorce—or prior to the divorce if the spouses have separated. In the latter case, the support is referred to as "temporary" or *"pendente lite"* support and lasts until final orders are entered in the divorce case.

In Indiana, Louisiana and Texas spousal support (when it is awarded at all) is awarded only to remedy severe financial hardship. In most other states, the amount of spousal support depends on the spouses' past financial and non-financial contributions to the marriage, current circumstances and future prospects, plus a list of other factors a judge may consider under state law (see below). Easily the most important of those factors are the spouses' incomes. In fact, as discussed below, some states use formulas by which support amounts are calculated solely as percentages of income.

The duration or "term" of spousal support has been hotly debated in recent years and a number of states have shortened duration. Other states have adopted formulas by which support duration is calculated strictly on the basis of the length of the marriage (see below).

Even in states that do not have guidelines or rely on formulas, length of marriage is generally the most important factor in determining duration of spousal support. This is also the case in Canada, where for marriages lasting less than twenty years, the suggested support term is 6 to 12 months per each year of marriage.

During the last ten or so years, a number of states have introduced "alimony reform" legislation. This legislation is designed in part to eliminate "lifetime," "indefinite" or "permanent" spousal support. Nevertheless, in a majority of states, long-term marriages still qualify for "permanent" or "unlimited" support.

Of course, definitions of "long-term marriage" vary among the states. For example, in Florida where there is a rebuttable presumption of permanent support in "long-term marriages," the term is defined as marriages exceeding 17 years. In California, indefinite spousal support is often awarded in marriages of more than 10 years. In most other states, indefinite support requires marriages of more than 20 or 25 years.

Types of Spousal Support

Many of the states that have changed their spousal support laws distinguish among several types of support:

- Permanent periodic or "lifetime" spousal support: Paid on a regular (usually monthly) basis until the death of either party or the recipient's remarriage. Reserved for long-term marriages, permanent spousal support is typically subject to modification upon retirement or other substantial changes in circumstances and is subject to state law regarding cohabitation discussed below. The term "permanent alimony" can also mean alimony awarded at the conclusion of a divorce as opposed to temporary or *pendente lite* alimony paid while the divorce is pending.
- Transitional support: Also referred to (regrettably) as "rehabilitative alimony," transitional support is paid for a limited period after divorce to enable job training, certifications, etc. leading to employment intended to render assistance unnecessary. It can also be awarded to parents working part-time while raising young children.
- Lump sum support: A fixed amount that is usually, although not always, paid at one time. Because the amount is fixed, it does not terminate upon remarriage. It remains in effect even if the "obligor" (paying spouse) dies, becoming a debt of the obligor's estate.
- Reimbursement support: Paid to compensate an ex-spouse who supported the obligor through school or job training.

- Unallocated alimony and support: A single tax deductible payment (in pre-2019 divorces) that includes both spousal and child support. To qualify for the deduction, unallocated alimony payments must adhere to a complex set of IRS requirements. Otherwise, they will be subject to "recapture" of the tax benefits (discussed below).

> ### What's the Difference Between "Spousal Support," "Maintenance," and "Alimony"?
>
> The term "spousal support" as used in this book includes payments to or on behalf of a spouse or ex-spouse by agreement or court order in a family case.
>
> "Spousal support," "spousal maintenance" and "alimony" all appear in state statutes, but their meaning varies. For example, in some states "spousal maintenance" refers to temporary support only. Be sure to familiarize yourself with your state's terminology.
>
> "Alimony" is also the term used in The Internal Revenue Code (IRC) for spousal support that qualifies in pre-2019 divorces for the tax treatment discussed later in this chapter. Thus payments can be both alimony under the IRC and "maintenance" or "support" under state law.

Spousal Support Formulas

In recent years, the idea of uniform spousal support guidelines has gained in popularity in some states. In addition, The American Academy of Matrimonial Lawyers (AAML) has proposed that judges and lawyers use the following formula to calculate the amount of spousal support:

> 30% of the obligor's gross income minus 20% of the recipient's gross income, provided that the recipient's total income including alimony does not exceed 40% of the parties' combined gross income.

As of this writing, only a handful of states (including those listed below) have adopted statutory formulas or rebuttable presumptions regarding spousal support amount and/or duration. In some other states, only courts in particular counties use spousal support formulas. While each state's approach to spousal support is different, the sampling below gives you an idea of the range of those approaches. As always, your best source of information regarding your state's law is an experienced matrimonial lawyer.

> See Chapter 14 for a detailed discussion of how to negotiate spousal support both in ADR and traditional divorces, whether or not you have a lawyer.

States that Use Spousal Support
Formulas, Guidelines, or Presumptions

Statutes in the following states include formulas, guidelines and presumptions that limit the amount and duration of spousal support, and the situations in which it can be awarded.

- California: California Family Code Section 4320(k) states that one of the goals of alimony is for the supported party to be self-supporting within a "reasonable period of time." While the reasonable period of time is defined as half the length of the marriage, the statute further states that its goal is not to limit the court's discretion to order support for a greater or lesser length of time. California Family Code Section 4336 requires the court to retain jurisdiction indefinitely for purposes of alimony in marriages of "long duration," which is presumed to mean marriages of at least 10 years. Read together, these sections create the possibility of lifetime alimony after a 10-year marriage, so long as the recipient is working toward "self-sufficiency."

- Colorado: Pursuant to Colorado's alimony guideline statute,[6] in a marriage of at least three years where the parties' combined gross income is less than the greater of $240,000 or the highest income contained in the Child Support Guidelines (currently $124,000), "spousal maintenance" is calculated at 40% of the higher income party's monthly adjusted gross income less 50% of the lower-income party's monthly adjusted gross income—provided that the amount paid does not exceed 40% of the parties' combined monthly adjusted gross income.

- Florida: There are rebuttable presumptions...
  - Against any spousal support in short-term marriages (less than 7 years)
  - For indefinite spousal support in long-term marriages (more than 17 years)

- Illinois: For couples with a combined gross annual income of less than $500,000, maintenance is 30% of the payor's gross annual income minus 20% of the payee's gross annual income, provided that the sum of that amount plus the recipient's gross income does not result in a payment exceeding 40% of the parties' combined gross income. Maintenance duration is calculated by multiplying

---

6. CRS Section 14-10-114, entitled, "Spousal Maintenance-guidelines," effective January 1, 2014.

a range of percentages times the number of years of marriage. The range begins at 20% of the number of marriage years for marriages of less than 5 years, to a possibly indefinite term for marriages of longer than 20 years.

- Maine: Maine has a rebuttable presumption that, absent unusual circumstances, no spousal support will be awarded in marriages of less than 10 years. General spousal support awarded in marriages exceeding 10 years is subject to a rebuttable presumption that its duration can't exceed half the length of the marriage. However, additional provisions allow short-term spousal support in order to:
  - Assist a spouse re-entering the workforce
  - Equalize a property settlement
  - Compensate a spouse who made substantial contributions to the other spouse's education during the marriage
- Maryland: The Maryland Court of Appeals has approved a trial judge's reference to the AAML alimony guidelines, meaning that Maryland judges may use that formula.[7]
- Massachusetts: A 2011 alimony statute set duration maximums for "general term alimony," according to 5 classes of marriage duration:[8]
  - Up to 5 years: up to 50% of the length of the marriage
  - 5 - 10 years: up to 60% of the length of the marriage
  - 10 - 15 years: up to 70% of the length of the marriage
  - 15 - 20 years: up to 80% of the length of the marriage
  - More than 20 years: indefinite term
- Michigan: Michigan judges can choose between two sets of unofficial guidelines . . . or they can choose to ignore them altogether.
- New Jersey: In marriages and civil unions of less than 20 years, the alimony term cannot exceed the length of the marriage or union. A rebuttable presumption ends alimony when the obligor becomes 67.
- New York: See http://www.nycourts.gov/divorce/legislationand courtrules.shtml for new formulas adopted in 2016.
- Pennsylvania: "*Pendente lite* alimony" and "temporary spousal support" are calculated as follows:
  - If there are no children, 40% of the difference between the obligor's net monthly income and the recipient's net income
  - If there are children, the income differential is reduced by the amount of child support and the result is multiplied by 30%.

---

7. *Boemio v. Boemio*, 914 A.2d 911 (Md. 2010)

8. As in many states, Massachusetts has additional provisions for short-term alimony in shorter marriages.

- Texas: With an exception relating to a history of family abuse, "maintenance" may not be ordered unless the marriage has lasted at least 10 years and the recipient lacks the ability to earn sufficient income to provide for his/her minimum reasonable needs. In longer marriages, the duration of maintenance may not exceed:
  - ○ 5 years for marriages of at least 10 but not more than 20 years
  - ○ 7 years for marriages of at least 20 years duration but not more than 30 years
  - ○ 10 years for marriages of at least 30 years
  - ○ The amount of maintenance may not exceed the lesser of $5,000 or 20% of the spouse's average monthly gross income.
- Northern Virginia: An unofficial formula used in some Virginia counties provides that if one spouse's earnings exceed the other's by at least 50%, alimony is calculated at 30% of the higher-earning spouse's gross income minus 50% of the other's gross income. If the alimony obligor is paying child support, the percentage of the obligor's income drops from 30% to 28% and the amount of the recipient's income to be subtracted rises from 50% to 58%.[9]

The Best and Worst Spousal Support States

A 2017 American Bar Association survey identified states that are among the least generous in their spousal support awards, and those that are among the most generous:[9]

- Least generous: Indiana, Louisiana, Texas and Wyoming
- Most generous: California, Connecticut, Nevada and Ohio.

Other Limitations on Spousal Support

Some state statutes that do not contain guidelines or presumptions, limit the circumstances in which spousal support can be awarded. For example, Kentucky and Montana share statutory language providing that spousal maintenance may only be awarded to spouses who:

- Lack sufficient property to provide for their reasonable needs; and

---

9.   Source: Vol. 51 *Family Law Quarterly* No. 1 (Spring 2017) a publication of The American Bar Association.

- Are unable to be self-supporting through appropriate employment or are custodians of a child whose condition or circumstances make employment outside the home inappropriate

The following states prohibit spousal support awards in specific situations:
- California: A spouse convicted of domestic violence within 5 years of the dissolution of marriage may be barred from receiving spousal support.
- Georgia: Marital infidelity that caused the divorce bars the unfaithful spouse from receiving spousal support unless the infidelity is forgiven by the other spouse, or the spouses continue to live together.
- North Carolina: A "dependent spouse" who commits adultery is barred from receiving spousal support unless the supporting spouse committed adultery as well.
- South Carolina: A spouse who commits adultery cannot be awarded spousal support. In addition, habitual drunkenness, physical cruelty, or desertion may prohibit spousal support if that conduct contributed to the breakdown of the marriage.

Other states limit spousal support duration:
- Indiana: Spousal support duration cannot exceed three years unless the recipient is disabled or caring for a disabled child.
- Delaware: In marriages of less than twenty years, the duration of spousal support cannot exceed 50% of the marriage length.

> **Lawglish lesson: What's a presumption?**
> A legal presumption allows a court to assume a fact to be true or requires a court to reach a certain conclusion until evidence disproves the fact or the reasonableness of the conclusion. For example, Maine has a statute containing a presumption that spousal support cannot last longer than half the length of the marriage. That presumption can be overcome or *rebutted* by evidence that it would be unreasonable or unfair under the circumstances of the case.

How to Calculate Spousal Support in Your Case

Whether or not your state is a formula state, you will still need to know more than what your state statutes say about spousal support in order to estimate the likely range of support in your case. You can start with the

state-by state information and forms available at http://family.findlaw
.com/divorce/spousal-support-alimony-forms-and-information-by-state
.html. If the link to your state has changed, search for information regarding alimony on your state's court system or bar association website.

An Old War (Horse) Story

In one of the first divorce cases I ever tried, I represented a husband who had won a Bronze Star as a helicopter pilot in Vietnam. We were assigned for trial to a traditional-thinking older judge whose chambers were ablaze with photos celebrating his own military experience in World War II.

I had not tried a case before this old war-horse judge. But I had learned that he never tired of telling, or hearing war stories. Accordingly, I elicited extensive testimony from my client about his military service. Such testimony would have served my client well with this judge under any circumstances … except maybe one.

Unfortunately, the judge's "traditional thinking" included an aversion to life styles that differed significantly from his. And my decorated veteran client was gay. Can you guess which one of the judge's partialities prevailed?

There's a lot more to learn about divorce in your state and county than the applicable law. A more veteran lawyer than I was at the time might have been able to predict how this judge would view my client. That kind of information can be important, and it can come only from local lawyers with substantial experience trying cases in your area.

State statutes, even if they do not include guidelines regarding amount or duration, typically provide the following guidance:

- The factors judges can consider in ordering spousal support. While most statutes include the factors listed below, there are still significant differences among them. Find out, for example, whether responsibility for the breakdown of the marriage or other "misconduct" affects alimony awards in your state.
- Definition of terms such as "length of marriage," which in some states ends upon commencement of the divorce action but in others, not until the final judgment of dissolution.
- Availability of the different types of support discussed above.

Remember that, in addition to your state's statutes and the case law interpreting them, support orders can be affected by:
- Customs in particular county or "judicial district" courthouses
- Particular judges' tendencies or biases

Finding Your State's Divorce Laws

For quick access to your state's laws regarding alimony and other divorce-related topics, visit The American Bar Association's hyperlinked directory of state and local bar associations at: http://shop.americanbar.org /ebus/ABAGroups/DivisionforBarServices/BarAssociationDirectories /StateLocalBarAssociations.aspx.

If selecting your state doesn't work, search in your browser:
- [Your state's] judicial "system," "branch" or "department;" or
- [Your state's] bar association

Once you get to your state, you should be able to access plain language pamphlets and information regarding your state's divorce laws via the following type of path:
- "For the public," "public resources," "Online help center," "Self-Help," or "FAQs; then ...
- "Family Law," Family Matters," "Divorce," "Alimony," "Child Support," and similar topics

Then ...
- An index of publications, videos, etc. or ...
- A link to the state bar's Family Law Section or ...
- A link to Lawyer Referral Services

Something Small in Texas

In Texas, where everything is supposed to be so big, spousal support isn't. Spousal support awards are often much less than in other states, and don't last as long. Texas law calls for 7 years of support after marriages of between 20 and 30 years, and 10 years for marriages of 30 years or more.

Factors Affecting Spousal Support

Local matrimonial lawyers are the best sources of information concerning the likely range of spousal support and of local judges' tendencies in your case. Because judges have a great deal of discretion even in states with stat-utory guidelines, predicting spousal support outcomes can be difficult, as discussed above. But you can find out what factors judges in your state are permitted to consider in making spousal support decisions. Those factors typically include some or all of the following:

- Length of marriage (the single most important factor affecting spousal support duration)
- Earnings and other sources of income
- Age and health of the parties
- The parties' respective needs
- Whether a spouse needs further education or training
- Future earnings prospects based on employment history, education, and professional qualifications
- How being a child's primary caregiving parent affects the feasibility and desirability of that parent's employment
- Standard of living during the marriage
- The parties' assets and liabilities
- Tax consequences of an alimony award
- Each party's financial and non-financial contributions to the mar-riage, including assistance with spouse's education or career
- Opportunities to acquire property in the future
- Marital misconduct by either spouse

Judges are not required to consider all of the factors enumerated in their state's spousal support statutes. Furthermore, they are usually free to give more weight to some factors than to others.[10] It can be valuable to learn whether your state laws contain any absolutes, such as circumstances that prohibit a spouse from paying or receiving spousal support.

Determining the Amount of Income on Which to Calculate Spousal Support

In most states, income is the most important factor affecting the amount of spousal support. In Chapter 11, we saw the importance of figuring out an obligor spouse's actual income when calculating his support obligation. We also saw how complicated it can be. If you skipped Chapter 11—or fell asleep reading it—you might want to take another look.

---

10. Most state statutes that list factors don't prioritize them. A notable exception is California, which emphasizes "the standard of living established during the marriage." California Family Code sec.s 4320(d), 4330(a), and 4332.

Using the Alimony Tax Deduction
(While You Can)

As mentioned in Chapter 9, the Tax Cuts and Jobs Act (TCJA) of 2017 eliminated the alimony tax deduction for payments made under "divorce instruments" that are "executed" (signed) after 2018. It did not change the tax rules for those who divorced or signed alimony agreements before 2019.

"Divorce instruments" are:
- Separation agreements
- Divorce judgments or decrees
- Any other court orders requiring a spouse to make payments for the support or "maintenance" of the other spouse

The TCJA's elimination of the alimony deduction reverses a 75-year-old rule by which alimony payments have been deductible by the payer and included in the recipient's taxable income. During that time, alimony has been used as a tax-saving device that has made divorces easier to settle. It works when the payer can deduct the alimony in a higher tax bracket than the recipient pays income taxes on it. The overall reduction in the couple's taxes makes more money available for spousal support. Skillful attorneys find a level of support that maximizes after-tax income for both spouses by increasing or "grossing up" the alimony amount to include some or all of the taxes the recipient must pay.

Under the new law, recipients of alimony pursuant to "divorce instruments" executed after December 31, 2018 will no longer pay taxes on it, and alimony payers will no longer be able to deduct it. (Note that the alimony changes take effect in 2019—a year later than most of the TCJA.) As a result, there will be less money available for the spouses and more for Uncle Sam—and a valuable tool used to settle divorces will be lost.

Which brings to mind a question Will Rogers, the cowboy philosopher once asked:
"If 'pro' is the opposite of 'con,' what is the opposite of progress?"

If your agreement or divorce was finalized after 2018, you may skip the next two sections as they do NOT apply to you.

Pre-TCJA Alimony Deduction Requirements

Not all pre-2019 spousal support "qualifies" for the alimony tax deduction. To qualify, the IRS requires that payments:

- Be made pursuant to a court order or written agreement signed by the spouses or their counsel
- Be made while the obligor and recipient occupy different residences
- End upon the recipient's death

Even if those requirements are met however, so-called "recapture rules" can nullify the tax deduction, leaving the payer with a sizeable tax bill, if:

- Alimony paid in the first post-separation year (the first calendar year in which the payer spouse pays alimony to the payee spouse and the parties live apart) exceeds the average of the payments in the second and third post-separation years by more than $15,000
- Alimony paid in the third post-separation year decrease by more than $15,000 from the preceding year

Recapture rules do not apply:

- To *pendente lite* alimony paid while divorce proceedings are pending
- Where the amount of alimony is tied to the payer's income, and that varies widely due to factors out of his/her control

Whaaaaaat?

I know! IRS's alimony rules are about as 'unSimply Stated' as it gets. The recapture rules in particular are traps for the unwary, and a good example of why you need the advice of a divorce lawyer, accountant or certified divorce planner or financial analyst. The elimination of the alimony deduction also eliminated this confusion; which may be as close as folks divorcing after 2018 get to a TCJA silver lining.

Protecting the Alimony Deduction

Pre-TCJA alimony can be a great tax-savings device. However, poor planning or poorly drafted alimony agreements can create a hefty back tax bill for the obligor. Use the following as a To-Do list to make sure your agreement complies with IRS regulations and maximizes the deduction benefits:

- Get help from qualified professionals (which includes CPAs, certified divorce planners, and matrimonial lawyers) in negotiating and drafting alimony agreements to avoid the alimony "recapture rules" mentioned above in the "Pre-TCJA Alimony Deduction Requirements" list. Under those rules, IRS can disallow the deduction and re-compute the obligor's taxes without it, plus interest and penalties. IRS Publication #502 provides a form for calculating whether and to what extent you risk recapture.
- If you have been paying or receiving *pendente lite* alimony during a year in which you and your spouse are still married on December 31, ask your tax advisor about filing separate tax returns. Normally, you should avoid using the "Married Filing Separately" tax filing status. However, tax savings from alimony, which cannot be claimed on a joint tax return, may outweigh the usual disadvantage of filing "Married Filing Separately."
- If you are the alimony obligor in circumstances where annual alimony amounts are expected to vary depending upon your income, acknowledge in your settlement agreement that you and your spouse expect that your income (and thus the alimony you pay) will vary, and why.
- Make sure that your alimony agreement is
  - In writing
  - Signed by each spouse or his/her counsel
  - Provides that alimony ends or "terminates" upon the recipient's death
- Be aware that if alimony is modified or terminated (other than because of remarriage or death), or pre-paid within the first three post-separation years, you must structure any such changes to avoid the recapture rules.
- In the event that alimony "recapture rules" do come into play, avoid the obligor getting hammered by IRS by using "safety net" language in your agreement that spreads the financial responsibility between the parties.
- Make sure that alimony is not reduced upon the occurrence of a "contingency related to a child," especially if you combine alimony and child support into a single "unallocated alimony" payment that is entirely deductible to the payer. Contingencies related to a child include the child attaining majority or a specified age, marrying,

dying or graduating from high school. If you have more than one child, consider whether unallocated alimony is worth the risk of running afoul of complex IRS regulations relating to overlapping "danger periods."

- Keep records of all payments made and retain them for at least 3 years in case of an IRS audit.
- Consider having alimony paid by automatic withdrawal and direct deposit. It simplifies record keeping and can alleviate both the obligor's pain and the recipient. Unsecured debts such as credit card and medical bills are obligations for which no security or "collateral" is given. They are treated differently under the Bankruptcy Code than "secured debts," such as home mortgages secured by real estate, or auto loans collateralized by a vehicle.

Premarital and Marital Agreements[11]

The material so far in this chapter assumes that the amount and duration of spousal support will be determined at the time of the divorce. However, those issues can be decided long beforehand—if the spouses have signed premarital or prenuptial ("prenup") agreements prior to the marriage, or marital agreements (sometimes called postnuptial agreements) during the marriage. These agreements, which often provide for little or no spousal support, are intended in part to make the financial issues of divorce more predictable. That's not always the case, however, because judges don't always uphold the agreements.

The Uniform Premarital Agreement Act

Enforceability of prenups varies among the states. However, 27 U.S. jurisdictions have passed some version of the 1983 Uniform Premarital Agreement Act (UPAA).[12] They are:

- Arizona, Arkansas, California, Connecticut, Delaware, District of Columbia, Florida, Hawaii, Idaho, Illinois, Indiana, Iowa, Kansas, Maine, Montana, Nebraska, Nevada, New Mexico, North Carolina,

---

11. In writing this section, the author relied heavily upon the work of a national expert on prenuptial and postnuptial agreements who many years ago sat just a few seats away from him in first year law school: Linda Ravdin, "The Uniform Premarital and Marital Agreements Act" (2015).

12. As discussed in Chapter 10, Uniform Law Commission acts are not binding unless and until the act, or some version of it, is passed by the relevant state legislature.

North Dakota, Oregon, Rhode Island, South Dakota, Texas, Utah, Virginia, and Wisconsin
- In UPAA states—and some others that have not adopted the UPAA—even an "unconscionable" (unreasonably unjust or one-sided) premarital agreement can be enforced so long as the spouse challenging its validity either received disclosure of the finances of his/her spouse-to-be or waived that disclosure. And in some states, that includes even agreements presented by one lovebird to the other within just a few days of The Big Day!
- Sounds like an awesome way to kick off that "til death do us part" thing, right?

The Uniform Premarital and Marital Agreements Act

The 2012 Uniform Premarital and Marital Agreements Act (UPMAA) is intended to be a more fair-minded replacement of the UPAA. Unlike the UPAA, the UPMAA covers marital agreements as well as prenups.[13] So far, only Colorado and North Dakota have adopted the UPMAA, but non-UPAA state lawyers and judges often look to the Act for guidance.

Under the UPMAA, judges may invalidate agreements if one of the following applies:
- The agreement was signed under duress or otherwise involuntarily
- The challenging spouse didn't receive (and did not waive in writing) adequate disclosure of the other spouse's property, liabilities and income
- The challenging spouse did not have access to independent counsel
- If the challenging spouse was unrepresented, the agreement did not contain a plain language explanation of what marital rights or obligations were being modified, and the challenging spouse did not waive, in a separate written statement, entitlement to that explanation

In addition, the UPMAA allows a judge to refuse to enforce the *term* of the agreement if:
- The agreement was unconscionable when signed; or

---

13. The great majority of states enforce agreements of married couples that provide for property division and support rights in the event of divorce. However, Ohio requires that such agreements be incident to an actual or imminent separation. And contradictory decisions by courts in Iowa, Oklahoma and Michigan raise questions about the enforcement of postnuptial agreements in those states.

- Enforcement would create a substantial hardship for a party due to a material change in circumstances arising after the agreement was signed
- State law defenses to contract enforcement, such as a lack of legal capacity, misrepresentation, undue influence ("duress"), and unconscionability, justify invalidating an agreement.

Invalidating prenups and marital agreements remains an uphill battle in most instances. That's true even where, for example, a spouse claims undue pressure to sign the agreement. Courts in the states below have found that the following situations of apparent duress are not sufficient—in and of themselves—to invalidate a prenup:

- Pregnancy (Rhode Island)
- Unequal bargaining power (West Virginia)
- Potential embarrassment over a canceled wedding (Wisconsin)
- Presentation of an agreement shortly before the wedding (Massachusetts, New Hampshire, and Missouri)

On the other hand, the following states have adopted statutes more protective of the less affluent spouse, such as the requirement that prenups, and in some cases marital agreements, must not be unconscionable at the time of divorce even if they were valid when signed:

Alaska, Connecticut, Georgia, Kentucky, Massachusetts, Michigan, Minnesota, Mississippi, New Hampshire, North Dakota, South Carolina, Vermont, West Virginia, and Wisconsin.

> ### What If the Tax Laws Change *Again?*
> In these unpredictable times, it's possible that the TCJA might be changed or rolled back entirely. If that happens, you will have 2 options:
> - If changes such as the elimination of the alimony deduction are reversed, be guided by the sections in this chapter relating to pre-TCJA law
> - If TCJA provisions are reversed or additional changes are made... or you can't figure out what in the world is going on, check for updates at divorcesimplystated.com

Protecting Your Rights Regarding Spousal Support

Nominal Support

In most states, if no spousal support is awarded at the time of the divorce, a party cannot return to court to ask for it in the future. Some settlement agreements provide for "nominal support" or "nominal alimony," usually in the amount of $1.00 per year. Those provisions preserve a spouse's rights to seek alimony in the future. They're often used when one spouse needs support but the other spouse, who historically has earned more, can't pay support at the time of the divorce. This happens, for example, in cases where the primary wage-earning spouse is:

- Unemployed
- Earning less than he/she has earned in the recent past or is capable of earning in the current job market (this applies especially to self-employed spouses)

If you're the spouse who'd be entitled to spousal support in such circumstances, make sure that you receive:

- Nominal support and/or
- Additional property settlement to compensate for the lack of support

Modification of Spousal Support

Generally, spousal support is modifiable if the parties' circumstances have substantially or "materially" changed since the original support award

or most recent post-judgment order. If you believe such a change has occurred, you must do the following:
- File a motion or application (check your state's judicial or bar website for forms) stating facts or reasonable belief of the existence of a ground for modification in your state.
- Request in the motion that any order be retroactive to the date of its filing, or (where state law permits) to the event, such as loss of employment, that triggered the modification claim.
- Prepare a financial disclosure statement (and file it with the motion, if required).
- Have the motion served in the same manner as the original divorce pleadings[14].
- If your ex-spouse requests a continuance, condition your consent upon a written agreement that any order entered will be effective retroactively
    - To the date of the originally scheduled hearing, or
    - If permitted by state law, to the date the motion was filed

What Changes in Circumstances Are Necessary For Modification?

A change in circumstances must be substantial in order to justify modification of support. Such changes can include:
- Loss of employment
- New employment
- Changes in either party's income
- Changes in either party's health
- Changes in either party's needs
- Cohabitation (see below)
- Change in custody
- Loss of child support
- Retirement

State law varies in defining the standard for modifying spousal support. For example:
- California is an exception to the general rule tying modification to changed circumstances. Instead, it is the lifestyle during the

---

14. Some states permit post-judgment motions or applications to be served on the opposing party or counsel by regular mail if filed within a certain period after entry of judgment.

marriage that determines whether alimony continues beyond the original term. An increase in the obligor's income cannot be the basis for an increase in support "except in unusual circumstances."[1]

- Connecticut falls between Kentucky's tough standard and North Carolina's broader one by requiring a "substantial change in circumstances." However, a 2014 decision changed Connecticut law, ruling that a substantial increase in the supporting spouse's income alone does not justify modification of spousal support.[2]
- Kentucky requires "a showing of changed circumstances so substantial and continuing as to make the terms unconscionable."[3]
- New Jersey differentiates between "durational" alimony of finite length and "permanent" alimony of indefinite length (usually after long-term marriages only). Substantial, continuous changed circumstances are grounds for modification of both amount and length of permanent alimony, but generally only the amount of durational alimony.
- North Carolina's statute simply requires "a showing of changed circumstances" by either party.
- Vermont requires that the changes in circumstances be both important and unanticipated.

The ability of a court to order, or parties to agree to, non-modifiable spousal support distinguishes it from child support, which is nearly always modifiable. Spouses can agree to prohibit or limit modification of spousal support in many ways, including the following:

- Prohibiting the obligor from seeking to reduce support below a specified dollar amount or percentage of the obligor's income
- Prohibiting the recipient from seeking more than a stated amount of support or percentage of income
- Prohibiting either party from seeking to modify the duration of support
- Prohibiting either party from seeking modification until after a certain date either party from seeking modification until after a certain date

---

1. N.J.S.A. 2A:34-23c.

2. *Dan v. Dan*, 315 Conn. 1 (2014). However, in *McKeon v. Lennon*, 321 Conn 323 (2016), the Connecticut Supreme Court ruled that a substantial increase in the income of a *child support paying* spouse alone still permits the recipient to ask for more child support.

3. Kentucky Revised Statutes sec. 403.250 (7/13/90)

So if you have an agreement that works for you and you'd like the security of knowing it will remain in effect, should you try to eliminate all possibility of future modification? Unfortunately, the answer is not a simple "yes." That's because:

- Courts scrutinize non-modification provisions carefully, so any ambiguity will be interpreted to allow modification
- A ban on modification could be disastrous if either spouse becomes disabled

The best approach to placing limitations on modification in your agreement is to add exceptions to cover the following situations:

- Either spouse encounters health issues that affect earnings
- Either spouse becomes disabled

 What to Do If You Cannot Fulfill Your Support Obligation

Losing your job or being out of work due to illness or disability does not automatically suspend your alimony obligation. If you cannot pay your support obligation, you must take steps to protect yourself:

- Ask your Ex to agree in writing that you are not obligated during the period of unemployment, disability, etc. and that your Ex won't oppose a court order incorporating that agreement. Then file a motion to amend or revise the judgment in accordance with that agreement (or "stipulation"), attaching the signed original. Don't delay, because until a court order is entered in accordance with such an agreement, the existing order remains in effect.
- If your Ex won't agree to any change in your obligation, immediately file a motion for modification that requests a reduction or suspension of alimony retroactive to the date of the filing of the motion.

The "Second Look"

Duration of spousal support can be one of the toughest issues to settle. Lawyers and mediators sometimes salvage a settlement by putting off resolution of the duration issue until sometime after the divorce. They accomplish that with a "second look" provision in a scenario such as the following:

- Settlement negotiations have stalled over the issue of spousal support. The obligor has made a final proposal regarding length of support. The recipient wants at least the possibility of receiving support for longer, without being required to prove the substantial change in circumstances required in modification proceedings.

- As a result, the parties craft a "second look" provision stating that at the end of the term to which the obligor has agreed, they will return to court (perhaps trying ADR first) to determine whether and for how long support will be paid thereafter, and in what amount.
- To avoid any "gap" in support, the provision also provides that any additional support will be retroactive to the end of the term stated in the original agreement.

The 2017 Tax Cut and Jobs Act may have created a new purpose for second look provisions. Because many TCJA tax breaks will "sunset" (disappear) in 2026, some obligors will suddenly have much less income from which to pay support.[4] A second look provision to anticipate this problem might be a good idea. If you include a second look in your agreement, consider adding a requirement that you and your Ex make a "good faith attempt to mediate" the issue before going to court.

Cohabitation

In all states, spousal support can be terminated, modified and/or suspended if the recipient cohabitates with another person.[5] However, there are numerous important differences among state cohabitation laws, including:

1. How cohabitation is defined, for example,

    ◦ Whether it must last more than a certain length of time

---

4. This will be especially true of spouses whose businesses are set up as so-called "pass-through entities." If you or your spouse is one of those business owners, see an accountant!

5. However, cohabitation at the time of the divorce doesn't necessarily preclude an award of spousal support. *In re Marriage of Vandenberg*, 229 P.3d 1187 (Kan. Ct. App. 2010)

○ The types of arrangements it covers; i.e., it must be more than spending weekends together but need not be full-time residence sharing

2. Whether the cohabitation alone is sufficient to justify termination, modification, etc., or whether the cohabitation must also change the alimony recipient's needs

3. Whether the statute gives judges alternatives to terminating support outright, such as modification or suspension while the cohabitation continues, so that

○ Judges are not forced to make "all-or-nothing" decisions
○ Recipients are not barred from future support

Statutory Definitions of Cohabitation

In most states, cohabitation sufficient to terminate or modify spousal support means more than simply sharing living space. It requires a relationship that resembles a marriage. Some states also require that the cohabitation must alter the recipient's financial needs or circumstances. Below is a sampling of statutory definitions of cohabitation:

• California: Unless the parties agree otherwise in writing, there is a rebuttable presumption that a supported party cohabiting with a person of the opposite sex has a decreased need for spousal support.[6]

• Connecticut: The support recipient must be "living with another person under circumstances which the court finds should result in the modification, suspension, reduction, or termination of alimony because the living arrangements cause such a change of circumstances as to alter the financial needs of that party."[7]

• Massachusetts: The spousal support recipient must have "maintained a common household" with another person for at least three continuous months.[8]

• North Carolina: ". . . the act of two adults dwelling together continuously and habitually in a private, heterosexual relationship, even if this relationship is not solemnized by marriage, or a private, homosexual relationship."[9]

• Virginia: "Habitual cohabitation" in a relationship analogous to a marriage for at least one year, unless (1) otherwise provided by

---

6. California Family Code §4323 (a)(1)
7. Conn. General Statutes §46b-86
8. Chapter 208 Massachusetts General Laws §49(d)
9. North Carolina General Statutes §50-16.9(b)

stipulation or contract or (2) the recipient proves by a preponderance of the evidence that termination of such support would be unconscionable.[10]

"Hard Cases Make Bad Law"

Lawyers and judges sometimes say, "hard cases make bad law." In other words, situations that tug at judges' heartstrings can lead to decisions based upon emotion rather than law.

Many settlement agreements create the potential for hard cases by providing that spousal support "terminates" upon cohabitation. Those provisions are a bad idea because they force judges into all-or-nothing choices: a "hard case." And that can lead to a finding of no cohabitation despite compelling evidence of it, if the judge feels that cutting off support forever could create a hardship for a recipient, especially one with children.

A much better idea is a provision giving the supporting spouse the right to ask the court for "suspension, modification or termination."

"Hard Time Makes Ridiculous Law."
If "hard cases" create bad law, "hard time" apparently leads to even worse law: In Florida, a judge terminated an incarcerated woman's alimony on the ground that she was cohabitating with her cellmate. *Craissati v. Craisatti,* 997 So. 2d 458 (Fla.Dist. Ct. App. 2008)

Cohabitation Statutes That Require Economic Impact

In many states, cohabitation that doesn't affect a spousal support recipient's needs, will not justify a change in the existing order. Those states include:
- California
- Colorado
- Connecticut
- Florida
- New Jersey
- Ohio

---

10. Code of Virginia §20-109

Cohabitation Statutes Containing Alternative Remedies

States with cohabitation statutes providing for less drastic remedies than termination, such as suspension or modification, include:

- California
- Connecticut
- Florida
- Massachusetts
- New York
- Virginia

Spousal Support by Automatic Direct Deposit

Consider providing for automatic deposit of spousal support in your settlement agreement. It offers benefits for both parties by:

- Creating reliable documentation of payments
- Allowing the recipient to count on receiving support payments on time
- Avoiding disputes over late payments, cash payments, etc.
- Relieving the obligor of the pain of writing monthly checks

---

Enforcing Obligations and Protecting Rights Under Spousal Support Orders

Spousal support recipients can use the following tools to protect their rights:

- The Uniform Interstate Family Support Act (UIFSA): UIFSA aids enforcement of out-of-state spousal and child support orders, as well as orders made by courts in your state against obligors who have left the state.[11] Enforcement is sometimes facilitated by judges from two states agreeing on a "home state" that will maintain authority or "jurisdiction" over the case. (See Chapter 11.) Note: UIFSA has been amended, so different states apply different versions of it.
- Wage orders or garnishment: Many states allow support recipients to elect a "wage garnishment" or "wage order" by which employers deduct support from the obligor's paycheck. If you are a recipient

---

11. While jurisdiction to modify *child support* orders can move to a "home state" that is more logical in view of ex-spouses moving away, UIFSA provides that only the court issuing a *spousal support order* may modify that order. UIFSA 2008 sec. 211.

and there has been a history of failure to comply with temporary orders, consider a wage order at the conclusion of the case.

- Life insurance provision: Require in your agreement that your Ex maintain life insurance naming you as beneficiary until spousal support terminates. You attorney, accountant, or an actuary can calculate the "present value" of the necessary amount of insurance. Your agreement can provide for one or more "step-downs" in the amount required as the years go by and the remaining support obligation is reduced.

- Security orders: Where there is reason to believe the obligor may not comply with a spousal support order, some states allow recipients to request that the court order the obligor to provide security for payments.

- Attorneys' fees provision: Most state statutes provide that attorneys' fees can be awarded in contempt proceedings. But those awards are usually up to the judge and require a finding that the obligor is in contempt of court. If you are a support recipient, provide in your settlement agreement that the obligor must pay your reasonable attorneys' fees if you are awarded past due support, even if the obligor is not held in contempt.

- Interest and penalties: Support recipients may seek language in their settlement agreements providing for interest and even an additional monetary penalty to be assessed for willful (and perhaps repeated) failure to honor the support obligation.

- Motions for contempt: Support orders, whether resulting from a judge's decision or a settlement agreement incorporated into a divorce decree, are enforceable by the court's contempt power. Motions for contempt get you speedy access to court to collect money that you are owed, or "arrearages." The contempt power includes the authority to assess attorneys' fees and ultimately to imprison obligors who are chronically and willfully in arrears.

- Obtaining a judgment regarding past due payments: If you are a support recipient and the obligor has run up a substantial arrearage, you can seek a judgment in the amount of the money past due, so that interest will accrue.

- Maintaining accurate records: Spousal support recipients and obligors should keep records of all payments made. Documentation will be necessary
  - In proceedings to collect past due support
  - If IRS audits you

Who Needs a Lawyer?

You do. Careful drafting of settlement agreements is crucial to avoid problems later on. If you're skeptical of a lawyer telling you that you need a lawyer, take a look at these examples of problems that poor drafting can create—and that skillful drafting can avoid:

- In Iowa, money paid to a support recipient to pay for health insurance was modifiable alimony, not non-modifiable property settlement.[12] SOLUTION: Make sure that any continuing payments in your settlement agreement are clearly designated as spousal support (or alimony), child support, or property settlement. Each of the three should be in separate provisions.

- A Virginia court has concluded that a husband's obligation to pay the wife's health insurance premiums did not constitute alimony and thus did not end upon her remarriage.[13] SOLUTION: Same as above.

- Where IRS disallows an obligor's alimony deduction (in pre-2019 divorces), the recipient receives a windfall of suddenly tax-free income and the obligor is socked with back taxes plus penalties and interest. SOLUTION: A "safety net" provision requiring renegotiation of the alimony amount in the event of changes in laws or regulations that cause unintended tax consequences.

- As a general rule, ambiguous language in a provision prohibiting modification will be construed as allowing it. Another general rule is that ambiguous language in an agreement is interpreted against the party who prepared the agreement. SOLUTION: If you or your lawyer are drafting a spousal support provision intended to prevent or limit modification, include language stating that no presumptions against the drafting party shall apply to that provision.

---

12. *In Re Marriage of Johnson*, 781 N.W.2d 553 (Iowa 2010)
13. *McKoy v. McKoy*, 687 S.E.2d 82 (Va. Ct. App. 2010)

Yes, there IS a quiz! Test what you have (or haven't) learned.

1. The term "cohabitate" is:
   A. Lawglish for the word "cohabit," lengthened by lawyers to make themselves sound important
   B. Lawglish for the word "cohabit," lengthened by lawyers who get paid by the letter
   C. A word like "co-dependency" that you find on AA meeting white boards
   D. A word to describe the relationship of unmarried individuals living together as married couples

2. The term "interest and penalties" can mean:
   A. How IRS punishes us for not understanding divorce tax rules that only a small number of accountants and an even smaller number of lawyers actually do understand
   B. The title you'd give to a timeline of your relationship with your spouse
   C. Incentives in a separation agreement to encourage timely payment of support

3. Pronounce out loud to a new friend, then unscramble the following key phrases from this chapter.
   A. laminon lamiyon
   B. necods kolo
   C. telatubber ternoppimus

CHAPTER 13

Understanding Property Distribution

"Sir, if you were my husband, I would poison your drink."
"Madam, if you were my wife, I would drink it."

— A conversation between
Lady Astor and Winston Churchill

The Split-Up Split Up

Property distribution is the process by which you (by agreement) or a court (by a divorce judgment or "decree") distributes between you and your spouse:
- What you own (property or "assets") and
- What you owe (debts or "liabilities")

In this chapter, we'll discuss what property gets divided up in divorce and how it all works.

The Difference Between "Marital" and "Non-Marital" Property

Nearly all states distinguish between "marital property," which is subject to distribution between divorcing spouses, and "separate property," which is usually not. State laws vary widely, of course, but the following definitions apply in most jurisdictions:
- "Marital property" is property acquired by one or both spouses during the marriage.
- Non-marital or "separate property" includes
  ○ Property acquired by one of the parties prior to the marriage which has not substantially changed in value during the marriage because of the efforts of one or both spouses such as renovating the marital residence or growing a small business

⚬ Property acquired with the proceeds of sale or trade of separate property
⚬ Property acquired by will, trust, or gift at any time

General Rules of Property Division

Many judges approach marital property distribution as follows, subject to state law[14] and (mostly in equitable distribution states) considerations of fairness or "equity":

- In longer marriages, judges often first consider dividing marital property equally. While most states don't include inherited property or assets owned before the marriage as marital property, the value of such assets can still be "in the pot" when it has been so "comingled" with marital property that there is no way to separate it.
- In short-term marriages (often considered to be approximately 5 years or less), especially 2nd marriages or those with no children, equitable distribution courts[15] often consider returning the parties to their situations prior to the marriage.
- Unless state law makes it impossible, judges often attempt to leave each party self-sufficient or at least in a position to become self-sufficient.

Types of Property Distributed in Divorce

Family courts have the authority or "jurisdiction" to divide up the following kinds of property upon divorce:

- Marital residence
- Second homes and other real estate interests including real estate investment trusts ("REITs")
- Bank, money market, and trade union accounts
- Investments, including securities such as stocks, bonds, and partnership interests
- Ownership of businesses including professional practices
- Automobiles, boats, RVs, and other vehicles

---

14. As discussed below, 3 of the 9 "community property states," require a 50/50 division of marital property.

15. See the discussion below of the differences between "community property jurisdictions" and the majority of states (and the District of Columbia) that are "equitable distribution jurisdictions."

- Personal property valuables such as antiques, collectibles, and artwork
- Retirement accounts, including pensions, savings plans (401(k) plans, IRAs, etc.)
- Vested stock options (and sometimes "unvested" options that an employee owns if he/she stays with the company for a certain period of time) and stock ownership plans ("ESOPs"), and other deferred compensation programs available through employment
- Trusts that a spouse controls or in which the spouse has a "legal interest"
- Higher education degrees and professional licenses
- Club memberships
- Debts owed to a spouse such as legal judgments
- Intellectual property such as inventions, books, and music that a spouse has written with some track record or realistic expectation of production or publication
- Income tax refunds
- Digital assets such as domain names, websites, and social media accounts
- Lottery, contest, and gambling winnings
- Miscellaneous assets (e.g., frequent flyer points, timeshares, etc.)

Types of Property Not Distributed in Divorce

Generally, the following are *not* divided in a divorce:
- As discussed above, separate, "non-marital" property owned by a spouse before the marriage which did not substantially change in value during the marriage due to the efforts of a spouse, such as renovating the marital residence or growing a small business. However, there are some exceptions, namely
  - Connecticut and Massachusetts, which don't recognize the distinction between separate and marital property
  - Indiana, in which the distinction is not determinative
  - New York and Ohio, in which judges have included property acquired before the marriage
- Property acquired after the "marriage termination date"—which is variously defined as one of the following
  - The date of legal separation
  - The date of physical separation
  - The date of filing for divorce

○ The date of entry of the divorce decree
- Mere "expectancies" such as revocable trusts and provisions naming a spouse as a beneficiary of a will of a person who is still alive and thus able to change the provision
- Children's assets, such as education accounts ("529 accounts," etc.), and Uniform Gifts to Minor Act (UGMA) accounts, and Uniform Transfers to Minor Act (UTMA) accounts
- Most unvested stock options and other employment benefits that employees don't own until after a certain number of years

---

Assisted Reproductive Technology

As assisted reproductive technology allows more couples to "freeze" sperm or eggs for possible future use, divorce cases sometimes now include disputes over who gets custody of this stored genetic material. Increasingly, the party who does not wish to reproduce gets to decide. But this is a developing area of law, so stay tuned! (See also Chapter 16.)

Factors Affecting Property Distribution

About two thirds of state statutes list the factors a judge may consider in dividing property. In the other states, those factors have been established by case law made by judges in deciding cases. Judges generally have broad discretion as to which of the following factors they wish to apply and how much importance or "weight" to give them.

- The parties' ages
- Health issues that might affect employability and cause post-divorce assets to be dissipated
- Length of marriage
- Whether the marriage is the parties' principal marriage that has produced children, as opposed to
    ○ A marriage subsequent to the principal marriage
    ○ A brief first marriage
- Lifestyle
- Amount and sources of income, including regular gifts or trust income
- Earning capacity based upon

- ○ Occupation
- ○ Education
- ○ Vocational skills
- ○ Employability including impact of long term absence from the work force
- Whether one spouse will receive child support
- The size of marital estates in exceptional circumstances such as
  - ○ Very substantial assets attributable principally to the efforts of one spouse, the other spouse receives less than 50% where 50% would substantially exceed the amount needed to maintain the life style established during the marriage
  - ○ Very insubstantial assets where the spouse with less earning capacity receives more than 50% of the property in order to "stay afloat"
- Contributions to the accumulation and preservation of assets
- Non-financial contributions such as raising children, managing the household, and "sweat-equity" in projects such as renovation of the family home
- Financial or non-financial contributions to the other spouse obtaining a professional license or degree
- Reasonable opportunity to acquire property in the future
- Contributions to the children's higher education
- The parties' respective liabilities
- The parties' needs
- "Economic misconduct" such as squandering assets or transferring them to family members, friends, or paramours
- Whether a spouse's "personal conduct" such as infidelity caused the breakdown of the marriage (except in some states where this factor applies only to alimony or in states such as Colorado where it is irrelevant to either alimony or property distribution)
- In some states, extraordinary value of non-marital property

> See Chapter 14 for a detailed discussion of how to negotiate property distribution whether yours is an ADR or traditional divorce, and whether or not you have a lawyer.

What You Need to Know About Your State's Property Distribution Laws

Matrimonial lawyers are experts on how your state's property distribution law applies to your case. Here are the questions to ask a local lawyer:

- Is your state a "community property state" or an "equitable distribution state"? (see below)
- When is your marriage considered to be over for purposes of determining ownership and valuation of property?
- Is property acquired during cohabitation prior to the marriage "in the pot" for purposes of property division at divorce?[16]
- Does "marital property" always exclude inheritances, gifts, or property acquired before the marriage?
- Can separate property be divided if it changes form or is comingled with marital property?
- Does your state presume a 50/50 division of marital assets?
- Can professional licenses and higher educational degrees be assigned a value for purposes of property division?
- Is there a state statute that lists factors to be used in property division?

You can learn more about your state's divorce laws using the resources provided in Chapter 18.

Ship Ahoy!

Be wary of online charts claiming to summarize state divorce laws. Charts are useful for sailors, but not so much for summarizing divorce rules. Too often, they ignore legal subtleties . . . or are just plain wrong.

---

16. In New York and Ohio, for example, there is case law for the proposition that portions of property acquired "in contemplation of marriage" may be treated as marital property.

Equitable Distribution States vs. Community Property States

The biggest difference among the states regarding property distribution is the distinction between the 41 "equitable distribution" jurisdictions and the remaining "community property" states listed in the section below on community property.

Equitable Distribution

In "equitable distribution" jurisdictions
- Judges generally have broader discretion to divide property than community property judges, who usually divide marital property equally.
- "Marital property" can sometimes include inherited property or property acquired before the marriage. (See "all-property states" below.)

When dealing with long-term marriages, lawyers and judges often start from a 50/50 division of marital assets and make adjustments as they feel the circumstances require. For example, a spouse who has been the primary earner but whose earnings have temporarily (or intentionally) declined at the time of the divorce, may be called upon to take less than 50% of the assets to make up for the reduced spousal support allowed by his/her decreased earnings. Such flexibility is considered part of the "equity" in equitable distribution.

However, even among equitable distribution states, there are significant differences in property distribution rules, exemplified by the following:
- Presumptions[17]
  - In Indiana and Ohio, marital assets are distributed equally unless an even split would be unfair.
  - New York, New Jersey, Connecticut, and Pennsylvania have no such "50/50 presumption."
- Legal title isn't controlling in "all-property states." In some equitable distribution states known as "all-property" or "kitchen sink" states, it doesn't matter which spouse is the legal owner of an item of property. These states include

---

17. Lawglish reminder: A legal presumption allows a court to assume a fact to be true or requires a court to reach a certain conclusion until evidence disproves the fact or the appropriateness of the conclusion.

- ○ Connecticut
- ○ Indiana
- ○ Kansas
- ○ Massachusetts
- ○ Michigan
- ○ Minnesota
- ○ Mississippi
- ○ Montana
- ○ New Hampshire
- ○ North Dakota
- ○ South Dakota
- ○ Oregon
- ○ Vermont
- ○ Washington
- ○ Wyoming
- Some states divide both marital and non-marital property. In several states, even non-marital property such as inherited property and property acquired prior to the marriage can be divided between spouses. These states include
  - ○ Connecticut
  - ○ Massachusetts
  - ○ North Dakota

  Courts in these states nevertheless typically award a larger portion of an inherited asset to the inheriting spouse, except in very long marriages (usually 30 years or more). Similarly, judges can take into consideration whether property was acquired by one spouse before the marriage and reduce the portion awarded to the other spouse in a manner that the court feels is equitable given the applicable property division criteria.

- "Comingling" (Lawglish for "mixing together") can convert non-marital property into marital property. Comingling occurs, for example, when money inherited by one spouse is deposited into a joint bank account. In order to establish that funds or other property that has been comingled with the other spouse's separate property or with marital property, it's necessary to use bank records, etc. to "trace" the property back to one spouse.

Equitable distribution state laws differ on the impact of comingling of marital and non-marital property. For example...

- In Florida, comingling non-marital property, such as inherited property or property acquired before the marriage, converts it into marital property.
- In Ohio, comingling converts separate property to marital property only if there is no way to identify the original separate property.
- In Connecticut, Massachusetts, and North Dakota where both marital and non-marital property can be divided, comingling is not an issue.

Note that the "equitable" in "equitable distribution" means "fair." It does not necessarily mean "equal." Equitable distribution judges have broad discretion in apportioning property and debt. For example, even in Connecticut where inheritances are "in the pot," a judge dividing the rest of a couple's property evenly might assign only 15 or 20% of a spouse's recent inheritance to the other spouse.

Note also that "equitable distribution" means different things in different states. In Ohio, it means that marital assets are distributed equally unless an even split would be unfair. New York, New Jersey, Connecticut, and Pennsylvania have no such "50/50 presumption." In fact, although Ohio is considered an equitable distribution state, many of its laws resemble more closely those of community property states.

Community Property States

Nine and a half states are known as "community property" states. Alaska is the "1/2"—an equitable distribution state that allows couples to elect community property treatment. The other community property states are:
- Arizona
- California
- Idaho
- Louisiana
- New Mexico
- Nevada
- Texas
- Washington
- Wisconsin

Community Property Principles

In community property states, there are two kinds of property—"separate" and "community" property. While state law varies even within community property states, some general principles apply:

- "Community property" includes earnings produced by the labor of the spouses, and property purchased with those earnings, between the date of the marriage and the end-date of the marriage. Gifts, inheritances, and certain trust assets are not considered community earnings or property.
- "Separate property" includes inheritances or gifts received by a spouse during the marriage, and assets owned by a spouse prior to the marriage, including the portion of retirement benefits that vested prior to the marriage.
- It can also include earnings from separate property and personal injury awards to one spouse. In some states, even if the asset has changed forms, such as cash used to buy a car, the car remains separate property. Spouses have no claim to each other's separate property.
- The "end-date" of the marriage after which property acquired is considered separate, is most often defined as the date of dissolution of the marriage. However in California, the marriage end-date occurs when the spouses physically separate.
- Community property is considered jointly owned, and it is divided in two basic ways.
  - ○ In California, Louisiana and New Mexico, community property is divided equally.
  - ○ Courts in Arizona, Idaho, Nevada, Texas, Washington, and Wisconsin are not quite as rigid; while an equal division is presumed or used as a starting point, a more equitable division can be considered.
- Some community property states adjust property division where
  - ○ A spouse is disabled
  - ○ Marital property is "wasted" by irresponsible spending
  - ○ Marital property is concealed
  - ○ There is disproportionate earning capacity between the spouses

  Note that in California, there is less "wiggle room" than in some other community property states for a judge to inject fairness.

- In community property states such as Arizona, Texas, and Wisconsin, it is presumed that property possessed by either spouse during the marriage is community property. Thus, a spouse claiming separate property bears the burden of proving it.

- Creditors can reach community property to pay debts that either spouse has incurred regardless of which spouse created the debt, or for whose benefit. However, the separate property of the spouse who did NOT incur the debt is generally NOT available to satisfy it.

> ## "Can't See There From Here!"
> Alaska is an equitable distribution state that nevertheless allows couples to elect community property treatment. That might be what comes from staring too long into the sun, trying to spot Russia.

Circumstances That Complicate Community Property Distribution

A number of circumstances can complicate property distribution in community property states:

- Separate property such as cash becomes community property when it is comingled with community property and can't be separated out or "traced" to its separate source.
- A portion of the increase in value (appreciation) of property such as a business owned by one spouse prior to the marriage, where the appreciation is the result of the efforts of both spouses during the marriage, can be considered community property.
- Determining the end-date of the marriage after which assets acquired and debts incurred by one spouse are no longer owned/owed by both. In states where the marriage end-date is defined as separation, that date can be disputed, especially if neither spouse moved out of the family home.
- Premarital agreements can negate the effect of a state's community property laws, but the validity of such agreements is often disputed.

Dealing With the Family Residence

Some property issues—covered in the remainder of this chapter—are common to both equitable distribution and community property states. They include how to deal with the "former marital residence."

Where there are no children, the home is often sold as soon as possible. However, a home with children requires balancing continuity in the children's lives with financial realities. The feasibility of keeping the home until older children leave the nest, should be considered.

Financial issues regarding the family home include:
- Whether the home expense can be afforded once the spouses have separated and have the cost of two households rather than one
- If the home is to be sold, whether it should be kept in joint names to preserve the full $500,000 capital gains tax exemption available to joint owners vs. $250,000 for a single owner
- What if any contributions the "out-spouse" must make, for example, to major repair and improvements necessary to preserve its value
- How long the out-spouse must wait for his/her share of the proceeds of sale
- Whether an overall tax savings can be realized by the out-spouse paying tax deductible property taxes and assessments
- Whether the out-spouse will be entitled to share in any appreciation in the residence's value after the divorce
- Whether the home can be refinanced in order to
  - Lower monthly payments
  - Remove the "out-spouse" from the mortgage and thus facilitate his/her purchase of another residence
  - Allow the resident spouse to buy out the other spouse's share in the house at market value established by a procedure spelled out in the settlement agreement

⚠ Protecting Your Interests Until the House is Sold

If the marital residence has not been sold by the time of the divorce, your settlement agreement should include protections for both parties by specifying the following:
- How the proceeds of sale will be divided
- A date by which the house must be listed for sale

- That the parties cooperate in marketing the house so as to sell quickly and upon the best possible terms
- Which ex-spouse is responsible for which house-related expenses
- How specific decisions will be made regarding
  - Setting the initial listing price
  - How often and by how much the listing price can be lowered
  - How the realtor and any successors will be chosen
  - What offers a spouse must accept (for example, offers within 5% of the listing price) if the other spouse wishes to accept
- That the court have "continuing jurisdiction" to resolve disputes regarding the marketing and sale of the house
- That a spouse who conveys title to the home at the time of the divorce will be protected by a mortgage note and deed, or other filing on the land records, establishing precedence over any subsequent claims or liens

Dealing With a Professional Practice or "Closely Held" Business

Two of the most difficult things to figure out in divorce are:
- The value of a spouse's small ("closely held") business or professional practice
- The actual earnings of a closely held business

A closely held business is often the largest marital asset in the divorce. So its value is critical to property distribution. Likewise, the business's actual earnings are crucial to determining the owner/spouse's earnings for support purposes.

Note that judges do not order that non-owner spouses become co-owners of the business. However, non-owner spouses can be entitled to additional property to offset the value of the business, or if there is more than one owner, the owner-spouse's interest in it.

Operating businesses have two main value components:
- "Tangible" assets such as
  - Equipment
  - Inventory
  - Buildings
  - Accounts receivable
  - "Intangible assets" (also referred to as "good will")

Good Will

"Good will" is the value of an operating business, over and above "tangible assets." Good will typically reflects the value of intangible assets such as:
- A well-regarded brand name or professional reputation
- Customer loyalty
- Advantageous location
- Proprietary information and technology
- Copyrights and trademarks

There are three kinds of good will:
- Enterprise Good Will: The business's intangible assets described above
- "Pure" Personal Good Will: Good will derived from skills, knowledge, and reputation of an individual member of the business that cannot be transferred to the entity or to other individuals
- "Transferrable" Good Will: Good will which is personal in nature but can be transferred to the entity or to another individual through training, etc.

Commercial Real Estate Appraisals

The appraisal of commercial real estate is based on its "highest and best use" and thus differs from that of other business interests such as an ownership interest of a company. The commercial real estate appraiser should:
- Be licensed as a "general" (not "residential") appraiser in the state where the property is located
- Be prepared to produce an appraisal report certifying that the appraisal complies with the Uniform Standards of Professional Appraisal Practice (USPAP)
- Preferably, have advanced credentials such as "MAI" or "SRPA" from the Appraisal Institute

---

Valuation

A business appraiser is usually needed to determine a small business's value. Appraisers can also determine the business's "real income" (as opposed to income reflected on tax returns) including non-cash "perks."

And as anyone who watches Shark Tank knows, income and value are related. That's how Mr. Wonderful instantly values a business. He simply "capitalizes" the company's annual earnings by multiplying them by ten.

If you or your lawyer wish to hire an appraiser (see below), find out the following before you do:

- The business appraiser's credentials such as certification as a business appraiser (CBA) or accredited senior appraiser (ASA)
- Whether the appraiser is familiar with the valuation methodology that has been approved by your state's family courts
- The appraiser's knowledge and experience valuing the same or similar type of business in your area
- How often the appraiser has given expert testimony and whether transcripts of that testimony are available to opposing counsel for use in cross-examination
- The number of articles and books the appraiser has written on the subject that can also be used against him on cross-examination

State laws differ (what a surprise!) on how to value a business's good will. Many courts use the fair market value (FMV) standard, which is the amount that an able and willing buyer would pay a willing seller when both have the necessary facts and neither is under any compulsion to make the deal.

As if that definition weren't complicated enough, applying the FMV standard adds more complications:

- In most states (California is an exception), only "enterprise good will" is marital property and it can be difficult to differentiate between "personal good will" and "enterprise good will."[18]
- Where a spouse does not control a company, the value of his/ her interest may be reduced by a "minority discount" due to the inability to control the company and a "marketability discount" due to the inability to sell a minority interest in it. Talk to a business professional about how all that stuff works.

Small Business: To Appraise or Not to Appraise

Before incurring the substantial expense of hiring a business appraiser, the following questions must be answered:

- Is the business likely to have enough value to justify the cost of an appraisal?

---

18. Many experts feel that only another valuation method, the capitalization of excess earnings method, can accurately separate out "personal good will" from entity or practice good will.

What Is a "Double Dip" and What's So Bad About Something That's So Good at Baskin Robbins?

A "double dip" can occur when one spouse receives assets in the property settlement based on the other spouse's solely owned business, and also receives support derived from the business's income. This happens most often with medical, law, and other professional practices as follows:

- Spouse A's sole practitioner law practice provides all of A's earned income
- The value of the practice, based entirely or nearly entirely upon A's earnings, is included in the total value of the assets to be divided between the spouses
- Spouse B receives assets in exchange for A keeping the practice
- But Spouse B also gets spousal support based on A's law income, thus giving B *both support and property in exchange for the same asset*

- Does the good will of the business (for example, a sole practitioner lawyer's practice) consist essentially of personal good will that is usually not considered marital property, thus rendering a valuation useless?
- Where the sole owner of a business is to pay alimony based on his/her income from the business, will that constitute an impermissible "double dip?"
- What standard of value should be used?
- Can the spouses agree on an appraiser to hire jointly (as is commonly done in mediation and collaborative divorce), rather than engage in a costly battle of "hired guns"?
- Is a Certified Business Appraiser (CBA) or Accredited Senior Appraiser (ASA) available?
- Is the owning spouse's interest a minority interest that will reduce its value?
- Does the fact of a minority interest or restrictive language in governing documents (such as the bylaws, operating agreement or partnership agreement) make it difficult or impossible to sell the interest? Does this then trigger a marketability discount that would further reduce its value?

An Appraisal Pearl

New tax breaks for certain businesses took effect in 2018 under the Tax Cut and Jobs Act. So if your spouse hires an expert who has used pre-2018 tax returns to appraise his/her business, it will likely *under-state* its value. And that will give you and your lawyer a great way to attack the appraisal.

Valuing Small Businesses in Community Property States

Even in community property states where a spouse owned a business prior to the marriage, the value of the business may nonetheless include marital property under these circumstances:

- Joint funds are invested in the business
- Joint contributions have increased the value of the business
- Non-financial contributions to the operation or growth of the business by the non-owning have increased the value of the business

---

Social Security Benefits: Not in the Pot

Occasionally a divorcing spouse will argue that the estimated value of the other spouse's future Social Security benefits are a marital asset that should be "in the pot" for purposes of property distribution. State courts that have ruled on the issue have rejected that argument. While Social Security benefits a spouse is receiving may figure into support calculations, they do *not* belong in the discussion of property distribution.

Dividing Retirement Plans

Another asset that is sometimes the largest in a divorce is the retirement plan. Although retirement plans are generally unavailable to creditors, federal law ("ERISA") permits the division of "qualified" retirement plans[19] in divorce proceedings. This is accomplished by a Qualified Domestic Relations Order or "QDRO" (pronounced "kwah-dro").

The portion of a retirement plan accumulated prior to marriage is usually excluded from the amount of the plan a family court can distribute.

---

19. Military, government, and many teachers' pensions are not "qualified" plans and are governed by other laws.

Appraisers determine the amount of benefits attributable to the marriage (and thus "in the pot") by using a *coverture fraction.*

Coverture fraction?!!

Don't ask. Let's get back to retirement plan basics. There are two main kinds of retirement plans:
- Defined contribution plans
- Defined benefit plans

From the Bizarro-World Law Dictionary

Intellectual Property—(1) The product of creative or intellectual endeavor that has value and/or income producing potential. (2) A house with a Smart Car parked in the driveway. (3) What they gave out the day your spouse's lawyer was absent. (4) An elitist egghead hang-out such as a library, museum, or Starbucks.

Defined Contribution Plans

These plans consist of
- Contributions by employees of a percentage of their compensation
- Matching contributions from employers
- Earnings and appreciation on those contributions

The most common types of defined contribution plans are
- 401(k) savings plans
- SEP IRA's
- Profit sharing plans
- Keogh Plans
- 401(3)(b) tax sheltered annuity plans ("TSAs")
- Stock ownership plans ("ESOPs")

Defined contribution plans have the following features:
- Their value is calculated simply by adding
  - The contributions of the employer that have vested
  - The employee's contributions, if any
  - Accrued earnings
- Some plans allow employees "hardship" borrowing against the plan.

- An employee leaving his/her company can "roll over" funds from a 401(k) plan into an IRA account. Care must be taken in such circumstances, however, that the funds move *directly from the 401(k) to the IRA* to avoid taxes and a 10% penalty.

Defined Benefit Plans

If you receive statements from your employer showing an estimated monthly benefit you will receive upon retirement, you have a defined benefit plan. Commonly known as "pensions," these plans are characterized by the following:

- Participants can depend upon receiving a known or at least calculable amount from retirement until death.
- Unlike defined contribution plans, employees become entitled to or "vested" in their benefits only after a specified number of years (often 5) of working for the employer.
- After a certain number of years of employment, employees also qualify for benefits at an "early" retirement age, commonly age 55. Electing early retirement trades receiving benefits sooner for receiving lower monthly amounts, similar to Social Security.
- The benefit amount is calculated according to
  - Length of "service" (employment)
  - Age at retirement
  - Level of earnings
- Unless otherwise elected, an employee's current spouse gets a death benefit when the employee dies. Divorcing spouses wishing to receive death or survivor's benefits must so provide in a QDRO.

Handling Defined Benefit Plans

Defined contribution plans are relatively simple to handle in divorce because the value on the account statement is the value of the plan.

Defined benefit plans are much more difficult to value. In property settlement, they can be handled in 1 of 3 ways:

- Each spouse retains his/her own pension/retirement plans and thus no division of retirement assets occurs.
- The spouses agree to evenly divide the future benefits when the pension goes into "pay status."
- A portion of one spouse's pension is assigned to the other spouse.

If the third option is chosen as to a substantial pension, an actuary should be hired to determine its "present value." This will allow the pension's value to be expressed in "today's dollars" and thus be comparable to the values of other retirement assets owned by the parties such as IRAs and 401(k) plans.

The present value of a pension is the amount that, if invested today at a reasonable investment rate of return, would produce the same benefit that the employee will receive under the plan. The calculation applies mortality rates and a "discount rate" (a kind of reverse interest rate) to the benefits to determine that value.[20]

Many employers and securities firms that administer retirement plans provide online forms and do-it-yourself instructions on preparing and submitting QDROs. Except with the simplest 401(k) savings plan, it is not a good idea to prepare a QDRO yourself (see below).

The Retirement Account No-No

Make sure that divorce-related transfers from IRAs or other retirement accounts go directly into another qualified retirement account. If retirement money is transferred to a non-retirement account, it can be taxed as income.

Steps to Dividing Non-IRA Retirement Plans[21]

If you settle your case on the basis of each spouse keeping his/her own retirement plans, you obviously don't have to be concerned about how to split them up. Otherwise, you do have to be concerned about it because there are strict requirements that must be followed. Here are the steps involved:
- Retain a lawyer or actuary with experience in QDRO preparation, to prepare the necessary QDRO(s).

---

20. Some employers provide defined contribution plan statements that include a present value. Online "pension calculators" are also available. Without knowing the discount rate and other assumptions used in the calculation, it is impossible to know if the values are valid. In addition, if you go to trial, you may need the actuary who has calculated the value to testify as an expert witness.

21. QDROs are not required for the transfer of funds in IRAs.

- The preparer will then read the retirement plan summary and determine what if any elections (e.g., survivor's benefits) must be made.
- Once agreement is reached regarding issues such as survivor's benefits, the preparer submits the QDRO to the plan administrator for "pre-approval." This avoids a judge signing an order that the plan administrator later rejects because it doesn't comply with the plan's rules.
- After the plan administrator pre-approves the QDRO, it is submitted to the court for signature.
- The preparer then sends the signed QDRO (which is now a court order) to the plan administrator who is required to distribute to the alternate payee according to its terms.

The Risks of Do-It-Yourself QDROs

Here are some reasons why you may not want to prepare your own QDRO, even if the plan administrator furnishes a form that seems easy to fill out.
- QDROs must strictly comply with often complex retirement plan rules.
- Many pension plans allow for participants to make choices or "elections" regarding matters such as
  - Whether the non-employee spouse (the "alternate payee") will be entitled to a survivor benefit upon the employee's death
  - What happens if the employee dies before retirement

A professional experienced in QDRO preparation can communicate knowledgeably with plan administrators regarding drafting questions, review procedures, elections, and valuation.

She's *Baaack!*

Remember this poor soul suffering from the alimony rules in Chapter 12? She just got rocked again by the retirement plan sections. And don't tell her that the tax stuff below is just as bad.

Keep in mind that I've included sophisticated material in this book to make you aware of issues that may need attention in your divorce. You aren't expected or required to understand it all. (I know a fair number of lawyers who don't.) If your case involves substantial assets or pre-TCJA alimony, get help from a lawyer, CDFA, CFDP or a CPA who can use the complicated rules to your benefit.

Saving Tax Dollars in Property Settlement

Taking Advantage of Special Divorce
Tax Rules Re: Property

Divorce property settlements present both tax-saving opportunities and tax pitfalls. First, the opportunities:

- Avoiding gift tax: Transfers of property exceeding the amount an individual can gift to another individual tax-free, called the "annual gift tax exemption," normally trigger gift tax. However, pursuant to Internal Revenue Code §1031, property transfers made "incident to a divorce" and within 6 years of it are not taxed.

- Avoiding retirement account penalties: Early withdrawals (prior to age 59 ½) from retirement plans normally trigger income taxes plus a 10% penalty. A withdrawal made in a divorce settlement does not incur the penalty, provided that it is made pursuant to a qualified domestic relations order ("QDRO").

- House sale benefits: A taxpayer can exclude up to $250,000 of capital gains from tax on the sale of a "principal residence." The taxpayer must have owned and used the property as a principal residence for 2 of the 5 years preceding sale. Taxpayers filing joint tax returns can exclude twice as much; $500,000 of capital gains on a principal residence owned by one or both of them if during the 5-year period preceding sale, each of them used it as a principal residence for at least 2 years. Because sales of principal residences often don't occur until years after the divorce, long after the ex-spouses are able to file joint tax returns, special rules allow each ex-spouse to exclude on their separate returns $250,000 of capital gains from tax if:
    - They continue to own the residence jointly
    - The ex-spouse granted use of the property by a divorce decree or agreement has used the property as a principal residence for 2 of the 5 years preceding the sale

Protecting Yourself Against Hidden Tax and Other Costs

You can lose the benefits of divorce tax breaks if you fail to adhere strictly to IRS requirements. Talk to your lawyer or a CPA about taking the following steps to protect yourself:

- Cover yourself in case of delays: Tax-free property transfers pursuant to IRC §1031 (tax-free transfers incident to divorce) must

occur within one year of your divorce. However, if your property settlement calls for a transfer that cannot occur within that period due to legal or business impediments such as restricted or minority stock, state those conditions in your agreement. You should still receive §1031 treatment if the transfer occurs
   ° Promptly after the impediment is removed, and
   ° Within six years of your divorce
- For non-citizens only: If you are a non-resident alien, IRC §1031 does not apply, and thus you will owe capital gain taxes on transfers even though they are "incident to divorce." So during settlement negotiations, you should reduce the value of assets you are receiving by any capital gain taxes you will owe.
- Avoid hidden tax costs: When dividing up stocks and bonds, find out the cost basis for each to determine their real "after-tax value." In this way, you can avoid receiving assets with "hidden tax" costs when you sell the security.
- Record improvements: Keep records regarding the cost basis of your home in case of an IRS audit. That includes documentation of improvements that increase the cost basis and thus decrease the amount of taxable capital gain.

 What Are Capital Gains Taxes, When Must I Pay Them, and How Are They Calculated?

Capital gains taxes are owed on the profit or "gain" you earn when you sell property or "capital assets." Capital gains taxes are associated most frequently with the sale of stock, bonds, mutual funds, art, collectibles and real estate. Gain is determined by subtracting the "cost basis" (the original purchase price plus transaction fees and commissions, and the cost of "capital improvements" to real estate) from the selling price. The difference is the "capital gain."

"Short-term capital gains" (for assets you have owned for 1 year or less) are taxed at regular federal income tax rates. However, "long-term capital gains" (relating to assets you sell after owning them for more than 1 year) are subject to federal tax at the more favorable rate of 15% except for higher income tax-payers who may pay 20% plus an additional 3.8% "net investment income tax." In addition, 41 states and The District of Columbia have their own capital gains taxes.

Capital gains taxes upon sale of a former marital residence that has grown substantially in value can be a major issue in divorce. Careful planning with a tax professional is necessary to take advantage of the special rules for divorcing spouses.

- Beware back-end fees: Find out whether any mutual funds or other securities funds you are to receive in your settlement contain penalties or "back-end fees" if you sell them prior to a specified date.
- Watch out for retirement plan penalties: In settlement negotiation, avoid trading non-retirement assets (e.g., your ownership interest in your home, savings accounts, etc.) for "pre-tax" retirement accounts [SEP IRAs, 401(k)s etc.] Income taxes are generally owed when you take money out of retirement accounts. Thus a $75,000 retirement account is worth less than a non-retirement account with $75,000 in it.

Allocation of Debts

The other (sometimes neglected) part of property division is the allocation of responsibility for debts or "liabilities." There are several things to keep in mind about splitting up your debts:

- Your settlement agreement will not stop creditors: The allocation of debts between spouses by a family court is not binding upon "third parties" such as mortgage lenders and taxing authorities. For example, even if your agreement provides that only one of you is responsible for the mortgage on the family home, the lender can still pursue either or both of you if the mortgage payments are not made.
- Debts in community property states: In community property states, creditors can go after a couple's community property regardless of which spouse actually incurred the debt. This may change if the couple moves from a community property state to a non-community property state, since generally the law in the place of "domicile" governs responsibility for debts.
- Don't forget those pesky liabilities! Make sure that your list of debts is complete, including things like unpaid real estate taxes for which you will not receive periodic bills. In fact, it's a good idea to have a "run-down of title" done regarding real estate you owe. That will ensure that you don't have any liens or other "encumbrances" that you've forgotten about. Also pay close attention to how much of what you and your spouse owe, will be your responsibility. The allocation to you of a substantial amount of debt can deprive you of the full value of the property settlement you thought you were getting.

> ⚠️ **Indemnification Provisions Regarding Debts**
> Make sure your settlement agreement provides:
> - That your spouse "indemnify" and "hold you harmless" in the event that he/she fails to pay a debt required by the agreement. The indemnification should cover anything you are required to pay toward the debt as well as all expenses you incur in connection with it including reasonable attorney's fees.
> - If you are a support recipient, state that the indemnification clause is in the nature of child (or spousal) support and thus not dischargeable if your Ex files for bankruptcy.

Pets

My dog Chuck would be unhappy to learn that state divorce laws generally do not distinguish pets from other personal property. Technically, that makes them subject to distribution in the same way as vehicles or furnishings. In practice, however, judges often consider special factors regarding pets.

For example, custody of pets usually follows that of the children. Where there are no children, judges are likely to consider the following factors:
- Whether one of the spouses owned the pet before the marriage
- Which spouse feeds and primarily cares for the pet
- Which spouse will have more time and resources to care for the pet and will be able to best provide for it

Modification of Property Distribution

Unlike spousal and child support—which can be modified after a substantial change in circumstances—property division is usually modifiable only if one of the following occurs:
- Modification is sought within a short period of time after the divorce, as specified by state law (for example, 4 months in Connecticut; 30 days in Illinois)
- The property distribution has been procured through fraud
- Both parties want to correct a "mutual mistake" such as a good faith omission, or erroneous valuation, of an asset or liability

And Last, But Not Least ... Bankruptcy!

If you, your spouse or both of you are considering bankruptcy, advice from a bankruptcy specialist is a must. If possible, get that advice before divorce proceedings begin, so you have the option of filing for bankruptcy first, based on the discussion below.

Joint Bankruptcy Filing

If your finances and those of your spouse are particularly dire, or if a bankruptcy filing by your spouse will likely force you into bankruptcy as well (due, for example, to joint debts for which you will become solely responsible) there's an opportunity for you to save money by filing jointly.

Separating spouses who remain on relatively good terms sometimes seek advice together from a bankruptcy lawyer. Some then go on to file jointly. Joint filing offers several benefits:
- It's cheaper: Joint filing saves on legal fees and expenses.
- It's easier: If you file before the divorce, it clarifies property division issues, streamlining their resolution in the divorce.
- More exempt property: The amount of marital property that is "exempt" (not available to creditors) increases.

However, be aware that some bankruptcy lawyers will not handle joint filings by divorcing spouses due to:
- Potential conflicts of interest
- Doubts about whether the spouses can continue to cooperate

> ### A Weighty Decision
>
> ⚠️ CAUTION: The decision to file for bankruptcy is a life decision that should not be made lightly or without a bankruptcy lawyer's advice.

Learning About Bankruptcy

Divorcing spouses considering bankruptcy should educate themselves about the matters below. At an initial consultation with a bankruptcy specialist, ask about:
- Whether you really need bankruptcy: A bankruptcy will have lasting repercussions for you, and thus should be pursued only as a last resort.

- Bankruptcy pros, cons, and alternatives: In particular, find out about the difference between filings under
  - Chapter 7 ("liquidation" or "straight bankruptcy") and
  - Chapter 13, a much lengthier process that "reorganizes" more manageable payments on tax obligations and "secured debts" such as mortgage and vehicle loans. Many lawyers advise divorcing spouses against Chapter 13 filings that will bind them together for 3 to 5 years while the debt repayment plan is being implemented. Chapter 7 bankruptcies, by contrast, are typically completed within 3 to 6 months.[1]
- Proper timing: You'll need to decide which you should seek first; divorce or bankruptcy. While filing for bankruptcy before divorce is sometimes preferred for the reasons above, it is not a good idea if you suspect that your spouse has hidden assets.
- Exemptions: Find out how much and what types of property may be exempt and thus unavailable to creditors under state law.
- Debts that remain: Learn which debts will not be erased ("discharged") under Chapter 7; e.g., tax bills and certain student loans.
- Do you qualify? You might be disqualified for a Chapter 7 bankruptcy if
  - Your income is too high
  - You are able to pay at least some of your debts
- The unsecured debt: Find out the extent to which "unsecured debts" will be discharged in Chapter 13. Unsecured debts (e.g., credit card and medical bills) are obligations for which no security or "collateral" is given. They are treated differently under the Bankruptcy Code than "secured debts" such as home mortgages "secured" by real estate, and auto loans "collateralized" by a vehicle.

Protecting Yourself Against Your Spouse's Bankruptcy During Your Divorce

Divorce being the funhouse that it is, bankruptcy—or the threat of it—is far more often initiated by one spouse than by two spouses cooperating.

The first result of a bankruptcy filing is to automatically "stay" or freeze most debt collection proceedings against the debtor. That includes most,

---

1. A filing under Chapter 11 is a third though rarely used option for individuals that is similar in many ways to a Chapter 13 filing.

but not all, of your divorce proceedings. Despite a bankruptcy filing, family courts can proceed to deal with:
- Child or spousal support
- Child custody
- Other child-related matters, such as visitation
- Enforcement of existing support orders

As you can see, property distribution (including debt allocation) isn't on that list. To protect your claims to marital property from creditors if your spouse has filed for bankruptcy, you must apply to the bankruptcy court to "lift" (get rid of) the partial stay of your divorce case. Bankruptcy judges routinely grant "relief from the automatic stay," but they have to be asked to do it.

Lifting the stay in bankruptcy accomplishes two things:
- Allows the family court to resolve all issues in your divorce including assigning property to you before the bankruptcy court can act with respect to it
- Makes the family court's resolution of issues binding on the bankruptcy court, so that you can get there before the creditors do

Protecting Yourself Against Your Spouse's Bankruptcy After Your Divorce Is Over

If your spouse files for bankruptcy after your divorce is over, a different set of problems can arise. You're no longer concerned about the automatic stay—since your divorce is over, there's nothing to stay. Instead, the focus shifts to how the bankruptcy will impact the terms of your divorce judgment.

As mentioned above, child and spousal support obligations are not dischargeable in bankruptcy. That means your ex-spouse's subsequent bankruptcy will not affect them.

Property settlement obligations also are not dischargeable in a Chapter 7 bankruptcy. However, they might be dischargeable in a Chapter 13 proceeding where the non-debtor spouse has failed to obtain relief from the automatic stay.

Problems arise most often when an agreement or court order requires a spouse to be solely responsible for specified joint debts. As mentioned above, such language does not bind "third-party" creditors.

For example, let's say your settlement agreement provides that your Ex is solely responsible, and will indemnify you for the balance owed on a joint Visa account. If your Ex misses payments, guess who the credit card company will come after?

You'll be on the hook because the credit card company's contract with you as a joint card owner is not affected by your agreement with your ex-spouse. And if your ex-spouse's obligation to pay the credit card balance is discharged in bankruptcy, that leaves you as the only collection target. Nice, right?

But don't despair. (*Never* despair!) The terms of your divorce settlement can be tailored to avoid some of that kind of damage by addressing the following:

- Get paid now: To the extent possible, provide that any joint debt for which your spouse is to be responsible under your agreement must be paid before or at the time of your divorce. Allowing your spouse to pay off the debt later could result in his/her responsibility for it being discharged in bankruptcy, leaving you vulnerable to collection by the creditor.
- Treat as support your spouse's obligation to pay the debt: If there are debts for which your spouse is responsible but which are not required to be paid at the time of the divorce, state in your agreement that
  - Your spouse's obligation to pay them is "in the nature of support" because . . .
  - The amount of spousal support provided for in the agreement is not sufficient to meet your needs

    Make sure to place this language in the spousal support section of your agreement, NOT in the property division or debt allocation sections. While bankruptcy judges are not bound by how you label or organize your agreement provisions, it's still worth locating these provisions in the sections that will do you the most good. As Grandma Sarezky used to say, "It couldn't hurt."

- Get indemnified: Provide further with respect to your spouse's obligation to pay off debt that
  - Your spouse will "indemnify" and "hold you harmless" as to any expense incurred by you resulting from your spouse's failure to pay the debt, including reasonable attorney's fees (see the sample separation agreement in Appendix 5)

° The indemnification provision itself is intended to be in the
nature of support and thus not dischargeable in bankruptcy.

 Yes, there IS a quiz! Test what you have (or haven't) learned.

1. "Equitable distribution" is

    A. The bonuses The Equitable Life Insurance Co. pays its fat-cat partners out
of your exorbitant life insurance premiums

    B. Just more Lawglish that makes a simple thing like "splitting stuff up" sound
complicated

    C. The division of marital property and allocation of debts between you and
your spouse in non-community property states

2. An "alternate payee" is

    A. The guy who cashed the paycheck he stole from your locker at Planet Fit-
ness

    B. A substitute juror who's on the jury because another juror got kicked off
for accepting a bribe, decides he'd like one too

    C. A former spouse who has received an assignment of benefits from your
pension

3. "Present value" is

    A. What you made on Stub Hub selling the opera tickets your Aunt Eunice
gave you for Christmas

    B. What the Buddhist guy at work tells you he gets out of meditating

    C. The amount by which your bonus exceeded last year's, after you gave your
boss an expensive Christmas gift

    D. A calculation of the current value of future payments, which allows you
to compare an alimony stream to property received at the time of the divorce; and a defined benefit pension's value with the value of other assets

CHAPTER 14

Negotiating Your Divorce Successfully

"Holding onto anger is like drinking poison and expecting the other person to die."

— Anonymous

Before Bargaining Begins

The great majority of divorces—including court-based ones—are resolved by settlement. Assuming your case will be as well, you'll want your settlement to be:

- Reached efficiently
- Favorable under all the circumstances
- Specific, clear and detailed enough to help keep you away from post-judgment court proceedings, and enforceable in the event you can't avoid court

Those kinds of settlement attributes usually result from sound negotiation and skilled drafting of the settlement agreement. But before you—or a lawyer working on your behalf—discuss settlement, a good deal of preparation is necessary. The good news is you've already done a fair amount of that preparation just by getting this far in this book.

The remaining work can be separated into three categories:

- Follow the money: Familiarize yourself with your spouse's financial circumstances
- Educate yourself: Learn your state's law and local courthouse rules and customs including judges' tendencies
- Strategize: Build a negotiation strategy

Familiarize Yourself with Your Spouse's Finances

It's essential that you thoroughly understand your spouse's financial situation. You began that process by exchanging disclosure statements with your spouse. But you also need to:

- Obtain documents and information to test the accuracy of your spouse's disclosures (Chapters 1, 8)
- Obtain more information and documents if there are discrepancies, inconsistencies, or omissions in your spouse's disclosure statement (Chapter 8)
- Have your spouse's disclosure statement analyzed by a divorce lawyer or certified divorce financial analyst (CDFA)

When Professional Help Is a Must

If your spouse owns all or a sizeable share of a business, get help from a divorce lawyer, accountant, or CDFA if you possibly can. Valuing the business, or your spouse's share in it, and determining what your spouse actually earns from the business is simply too complex a task for a non-professional.

Business valuation requires considerable financial expertise and experience. Likewise, finding cash and other benefits your spouse receives from the business can be extremely tricky. Even tax returns, for example, often omit things like:

- Employment "perks" such as rental cars and expense accounts
- Personal expenses paid by the business such as phone bills, gasoline, meals, etc.

It's highly unlikely that you'll find every bit of income your spouse has socked away or disguised. But give yourself a fighting chance to find the bulk of it with professional help.

Familiarize Yourself with Your State's Law and Local Courthouse Rules and Customs

Whether or not you have a lawyer, it's critical to learn how state law and local courthouse rules and customs might affect your case. If you do have a lawyer, discuss those matters with her. If you're unrepresented, meet with a lawyer if at all possible, to ask about the issues below. To be efficient, be sure to give the lawyer a summary of your case using the Statutory Criteria Summary (Appendix 1).

Pay particular attention to the following aspects of state law that might affect your case:

- How marital property is defined by law, and how it is customarily divided. This includes questions of whether inheritances and gifts received by a spouse are considered marital property—and if and how local family judges might divide them differently than other property.[2]
- The general definition of property, as compared to "mere expectancies" such as potential inheritances that are not considered property.
- Whether property acquired during pre-marriage cohabitation or after separation is deemed to be marital property.
- Whether your state has spousal support guidelines, and if so, how they will impact spousal support in your case.
- How income is defined for purposes of calculating support.

Be sure to also find out about local court procedures and customs that are not codified in state law but can be equally or even more important:

- "Rules of thumb" regarding amount and length of spousal support awards
- The availability of court assistance with settlement, such as "pre-trial conferences" (discussed below) and mediation, and how those procedures work
- Limitations on discovery

Finally, the predispositions of local family court judges can be a critical factor, even in cases that settle. Local lawyers often bargain by referring to what Judge So-and-So would likely do if the case went to trial.

Building Your Negotiation Strategy

You're now ready to put together a negotiation strategy—again with the help of a divorce professional, if at all possible. Later in this chapter, we'll talk about negotiating each of the "Big Three" divorce issues, which (in case your dog ate the first three-quarters of this book) are:

- Property division (including allocating responsibility for debts)
- Support (child and/or spousal)

---

2. In states where inheritances can be considered marital property, judges tend nonetheless to treat them as belonging mostly to the inheriting spouse, except in very long marriages (usually more than 30 years).

- Non-financial children's issues (decision-making and dividing time with the children)

Your goal is to decide on a game plan for achieving a fair and adequate overall settlement. In building that plan, consider the following:
- A general approach to finances: Decide on and prioritize your financial goals emphasizing your needs or "interests" rather than your positions (Chapters 1 and 7). Regarding marital property, it may be most helpful to think in terms of percentages. On the other hand, support is often best thought of primarily in terms of dollar amounts.[3]
- Reasonability test: Test whether your financial goals are achievable and your expectations are reasonable (see Chapter 1 and below) and if not, how best to adjust them.
- Child considerations: Consider whether your (non-financial) child-related goals
  - Are consistent with the best interests of your children
  - Are feasible in light of schedules and geography
  - Might be easier to achieve if you offered to help with things like transportation
- Impact of guidelines: Find out how child or spousal support guidelines (including "deviation criteria" that apply in unusual circumstances) might affect your case. (See Chapters 11 and 12.)
- What your spouse is thinking: Consider your spouse's motivations and priorities and think about how to use that knowledge to find areas in which she/he is most likely to be flexible. For example, ask yourself:
  - Might your spouse agree to pay/receive more/less support in return for receiving less or more in property settlement?
  - Are there items of property that for non-financial reasons are particularly important and thus worth more to your spouse than their monetary value?
  - Is your spouse more likely to agree to a higher amount of periodic support for a shorter period, or a smaller amount for a longer period?

---

3 If the income of the support-paying spouse varies substantially from year to year, it is sometimes best to decide upon a "base" amount of support premised on an income amount that is reasonably expected each year, plus a percentage of the income that exceeds the expected income.

Next, with legal advice, decide on your specific approach to each of the Big Three issues as follows:

- What if? Determine if you went to trial, what would be your:
  - Best reasonably achievable result
  - Worst result
  - Most likely result
- Your starting point: Identify an initial bargaining position that is a bit more than your goal and, ideally, either lower or only slightly higher than your best-case result. (Regarding support, make sure to factor in your expenses.) If you arrive at a goal that is substantially more than your best-case outcome, you may need to reconsider how reasonable that goal is.
- Your choke point: Decide on percentages or dollar amounts that are the least you can live with (your "must-haves" or "choke figures"). Choke figures are typically less than the likely result. How much below the likely result you are willing to set your choke figure depends partly on your needs and partly upon your "risk tolerance." If you have little hesitation about going to trial, your risk tolerance will be high, and as a result, your choke figure will be closer to the most likely result—and might even be higher. On the other hand, if you have a strong desire to avoid the uncertainties (risk) of a trial or its expense (attorney's fees can easily cancel out the improved results you might get at trial), your choke figure will be closer to your worst-case result.
- Your wiggle room: Determine where you have the most flexibility or "wiggle room" on a particular issue in circumstances where your goal (or needs) are lower, the same, or only slightly higher than the likely result.
- Your Plan B: Think about how you may be willing to revise goals–and reassess likely outcomes, wiggle room, and risk tolerance as the negotiation proceeds.

Using a Negotiation Chart

Recording on a spreadsheet the progress you've made toward your goals will help you stick to them. A "negotiation chart" also keeps track of how your and your spouse's positions at any point compare to earlier positions, as well as to to your

It's important to project strength and confidence as you negotiate.

best, worst, and most likely results. Appendix 4 is a sample negotiation chart. (Print one out at www.divorcesimplystated.com/.)

The chart has three main sections. The first summarizes (1) child support (child support guidelines amount plus any "extras" like contributions to extracurriculars and summer camp), (2) spousal support, and (3) property division (in percentages and amounts) split into retirement and non-retirement assets. The vertical column headings cover your best and worst case scenarios, your likely result, your "must-have" ("choke figures"), your goals, and both sides' initial and current positions.

Section 2 of the chart relates to property division only. It provides the details for assets (at the left) and debts (at the right) that add up to the totals in Section 1. Replace the sample assets and debts in Section 2 with your own, and put in amounts for each. At the beginning of the negotiation, put the amounts for each item in the column of the spouse who owns the asset or is responsible for the debt. For joint assets and debts, put half of the amount in each spouse's column. As you negotiate, move asset and debt amounts (or portions of them when dividing an asset or debt) between the "Wife" and "Husband" columns to reflect the current state of the negotiation. An Excel or similar spreadsheet will automatically adjust the totals as you move amounts.

Finally, Section 3 contains examples of assets that would be excluded from your negotiation, such as children's accounts and non-marital property as defined by your state's law.

Too Mad to Mediate

A few years ago, I mediated the divorce of a couple who had (barely) cleared my "too mad to mediate" threshold. During one particularly spirited session, the wife ("Susan") started adding the phrase, "so f*** you" at the end of her sentences.

Finally I said to her, "Susan, I'm wondering if ending your sentences, 'So f*** you!' is helping us get to yes;" something mediators don't often need to say.

Can you think of any other things *NOT* to say during mediation? Here are a few that I've seen do some serious damage:

- "You're just like your mother."
- "Just in case you might answer honestly by mistake ..."
- "*EVERYONE* warned me about you before we got married!"
- "... which is why you've been a failure all your life!"
- "Just what I need, advice from the parent of the year!"
- "Why don't you ask your new love interest?"
- "It's unbelievable that out of 100,000 sperm, you were the fastest!"

Negotiating Property Division

Once you've decided on your general negotiation strategy, you can focus on how to best put it into action for each of the Big Three issues. Let's begin with property division.

To negotiate property division, you must have a list that includes:
- Each item of marital property to be divided and each debt to be allocated between you and your spouse
- Agreed upon, accurate values for each asset
- Balances due on each debt
- Any accounts in your children's names, merely as a reminder to choose which parent will serve as guardian or trustee of the accounts (see Appendix 5)

Identifying Marital Property

As discussed in Chapter 13, most state divorce statutes provide definitions of "marital property."[4] In the majority of equitable distribution states and in all community property states, property that is acquired by inheritance or acquired before the marriage is not considered marital property and thus may not be distributed in divorce proceedings.

Be sure to familiarize yourself with exactly how marital property is defined in your state. After that, the process of identifying what's to be divided should be relatively simple . . . unless any of the following are in dispute:
- Whether a particular asset was acquired before the marriage or via inheritance or gift
- Whether property not acquired during the marriage, or acquired by inheritance or gift should be considered marital property
- Whether a particular asset was acquired after
  - Separation, or
  - Some other date on which state law cuts off marital rights
- Whether assets held in trust should be considered marital property

---

4. Connecticut is an exception to the rule because the concept of "marital property" has not been codified, leaving all property owned at the time of divorce available for distribution by a family court.

- Whether non-marital property has now been "comingled" (mixed in) with marital property and so should be considered marital property (see Chapter 13)[5]
- Whether items such as deferred compensation benefits or "unvested" stock options will be considered property in the property division "pot" as opposed to "mere expectancies" that aren't

Valuing Marital Property

After your marital property has been identified, you will need to agree with your spouse on the value of each significant item. That may require the following:

- Getting help: If the value of real estate cannot be agreed upon, obtain "opinion(s) of value" from experienced realtors, or an appraisal by an appraiser.[6]
- Handling loans: It's best to agree that mortgage balances (including home equity lines) will be deducted from or "netted out of" the value of your family home and other real estate to determine the property's "equity." That equity will then be used as the property's value.

Property division Step #1: Identify marital property.

However, be sure that those mortgages are not also listed as debts and thus "double-dipped." The only time a mortgage loan should be singled out for special attention is if it is
  - A "balloon" mortgage requiring repayment or refinancing after a certain period of time; or
  - An adjustable rate mortgage in which the interest rate increases after a certain period of time.
- Setting a date: Agree upon a "valuation date" (a date close to the signing of your settlement agreement or final hearing) for assets with significantly varying values, such as stock and mutual funds.

---

5. This "conversion" of non-marital property to marital property is called "transmutation" in many states including California, Mississippi, Missouri, New York, Oregon, and South Carolina.

6. Realtors' opinions are generally free, but you'll have to pay for an appraisal. Judges generally consider appraisals more reliable than opinions of value but if your case settles, that need not be a concern.

- Treating the working checking account differently: A "working checking account" used to pay monthly bills can be an exception to the "set a date" rule above. If the value of that account regularly sinks to a nominal amount after the bills are paid, you may want to simply assign it a value of $10 or so. This will keep your list of assets complete without skewing the total with a large amount that routinely disappears.
- Obtaining stock and bond cost bases: Get the "cost basis" of securities such as appreciated stocks and bonds so that you don't receive a disproportionate amount of assets with substantial "unrealized" capital gain that will be taxed when sold.
- Adjusting for future taxes? Discuss if and to what extent the value of the assets below should be reduced to factor in a projection of taxes that will be owed upon sale or withdrawal of funds:
  - "Pre-tax" retirement accounts in which withdrawals are taxed
  - Assets such as securities (stocks, bonds, etc.) whose value has "appreciated" (increased) and thus will be subject to capital gain tax when sold

---

Shelf Life

You're moving nicely toward an agreement on property division. Without warning, a roadblock appears. Your spouse insists that her/his retirement plan should not be included in the property division. The more you argue the retirement plan should be "in the pot," the more stubborn your spouse becomes.

What to do?

Shelve the retirement issue until the end of the negotiation. Moving on to something else will maintain the momentum of the negotiation and preserve progress made elsewhere.

By the time you return to the retirement issue, the momentum from resolving the rest of the issues may lead to a quick resolution!

Divorce Math Grad School:
Optimizing Your Property Settlement

Remember how you would have failed Algebra if you hadn't made those two mistakes on the final exam that canceled each other out to produce the correct answer?

No?

You mean that was just *me?*

Even if you hated high school math, you might want to buddy up with "divorce math." You (or your lawyer) can use divorce math to ensure that your property is valued accurately and in a way that is fair to you. To do that, the assets you will be receiving at least 50% of in your settlement must be valued as low as is permitted by law and custom. Reducing the value of those assets will require your spouse to give you additional dollars to bring your share of the overall property division up to the amount or percentage of the total that you've agreed upon.

You can accomplish all that (assuming your head hasn't exploded) by taking the steps below. But be forewarned. This gets a little . . . un-simple.

- Unless contrary to state law or local custom, if you will be receiving in your settlement more than 50%[7] of the securities such as stocks and bonds, reduce their value as follows . . .
    - Obtain from your financial institution the "cost basis" (essentially what you paid for the security) for each security; then . . .
    - Calculate "unrealized" capital gain (expected profit that you haven't received because you haven't sold the security yet) by subtracting the cost basis from the security's market price as of your valuation date; then . . .
    - Calculate a theoretical capital gain tax by multiplying the unrealized capital gain by the applicable tax rate (see a financial professional regarding the tax rate to use); then . . .
    - Subtract the resulting capital gain tax from the security's market value to yield a reduced value for the security.
- If you will be receiving or keeping more retirement ("pre-tax") accounts than your spouse, reduce their value by a percentage representing the rate at which a tax professional estimates you'll pay taxes when you begin withdrawing funds upon retirement.
- If your agreement requires that the marital residence be sold in the near future, and you are to receive more than 50% of the sale proceeds, reduce the residence value by deducting selling expenses

---

7. If you and your spouse are dividing an asset evenly, there's no advantage to reducing its value, because the reduction will benefit both of you equally. Reducing the value of an asset for future taxes or selling expenses becomes important only when you are receiving *more than half* of that asset.

including brokers' commissions, fix-up expenses, and conveyance taxes/fees (sometimes estimated at 6% in all).

Finally, use the "Divorce Math Pearl" in Chapter 3 to avoid being unfairly penalized if your spouse claims additional assets to compensate for money or other property you've already received. (This might apply, for example, if during the divorce proceedings you used marital funds to buy a car.)

> ## Not So Simple? Don't worry about it!
> You might be starting to wonder what happened to keeping things simple. This chapter includes some advanced material with which even some lawyers are not familiar. But as mentioned, one of the goals of this book is to expose you to a wide range of information and tips that you won't find elsewhere. So, don't worry if you don't understand some of the material here. Just make sure to ask an attorney or CDFA if you can somehow use the concepts to improve your negotiation result.

Negotiating Spousal and Child Support

Calculation of child support according to a state's child support guidelines (CSG) is relatively simple once the parents' incomes are accurately determined.[8] As explained in Chapter 11, you need a skilled lawyer's help to get to accurate income numbers. After that, the amount of child support (except in unusual circumstances that trigger "deviation" from the CSG) is a matter of filling out a CSG calculation worksheet and then referring to the CSG chart. The chart provides the child support amount usually based upon two factors; the number of children and the parents' incomes as calculated under the guidelines.

Child support duration is dictated by state statute, so it is even more straight forward than amount. Note however, that child support is usually terminated if a child marries, and is sometimes extended for students.

The negotiation of spousal support is more complex than child support. In fact, it's usually the most difficult of the Big Three issues to settle. This is especially true in the great majority of states that don't have spousal support guidelines. The amount and duration of spousal support often depends less upon state statutes and "case law" (court decisions) than on:

8. The only other complicating factor regarding child support can be whether "deviation criteria" exist that would make a state's child support guidelines inapplicable. See Chapter 11.

- The circumstances of your case
- The amount of support typically awarded in your county in similar cases

That's why it's so important to seek advice from an experienced local divorce lawyer. As I may have mentioned... countless times.

In most states, family law judges have broad discretion to determine spousal support (see Chapter 12). As a result, even veteran divorce lawyers sometimes have difficulty predicting what a judge will order. This uncertainty is an excellent reason to reach agreement on the issue if at all possible.

On the other hand, the complexity of spousal support offers some creative paths to agreement. As mentioned above for example, a spouse might be willing to pay more each month in return for a shorter duration ("term"). Likewise, a recipient spouse might be willing to accept a smaller monthly amount in exchange for the security of a longer term.

In addition, settlements are sometimes reached by trading less support for more property settlement or vice versa. Below, we'll discuss another divorce math concept, "present value," that allows you to compare the value of spousal support paid out over time, with property received at the time of the divorce.

Finally, keep in mind that negotiation strategies can be impacted by the spouses' expectations regarding the following questions:
- Is support likely to be cut off or modified due to the recipient's remarriage or cohabitation?
- Is it likely that the earnings of one or both spouses might substantially change, opening the door for a post-judgment motion for modification?
- Is it likely that a deteriorating health condition could reduce the supporting spouse's ability to pay, or increase the recipient's needs and lead to modification proceedings?

It's important to think about post-divorce changes in circumstances for another reason as well. You or your spouse might want to limit the extent to which spousal support can be modified. Ordinarily, spousal support modification can occur when the obligor's ability to pay or the recipient's need for support changes substantially (see Chapter 12). However, spouses can, by agreement place limitations on modification.[9] A spouse might be willing to pay more support if the agreement stipulates that:

- The duration cannot be extended
- The amount cannot exceed the original figure or some other specified amount
- In cases where support is calculated as a percentage of the supporting spouse's income, the total amount of support is "capped" and thus cannot exceed a certain amount [10][11]

⚠ One word of caution: A support obligation that's non-modifiable under any circumstances can be disastrous if either spouse becomes disabled. At the very least, always make disability an exception to limits on modification.

Paystub Pitfalls Revisited

If your spouse is a wage earner whose annual earnings exceed $130,000, his/her paystubs will understate net income until later in the year, when he/she reaches the income limit or "threshold" ($128,400 in 2018). At that point, 6.2% for Social Security will no longer be deducted, and your spouse's paystubs will show higher net pay.[1] If your settlement negotiations occur earlier in the year, avoid an understatement of your spouse's net income by calculating the *annual average* Social Security deduction. To do that:

- Divide the maximum Social Security deduction for the year (about $17,040 in 2018) by your spouse's total income
- Divide that number by 52 to get the weekly average, or by 12 for the monthly average
- Determine the correct amount of net income as of the valuation date

Similarly, if you earn more than $130,000 [2], your late year paystubs will overstate your net income. In that case, avoid unfairness to yourself by doing the same averaging calculation. (For more on "paystub pitfalls," see Chapter 8.)

---

9. Note that spouses are not permitted to limit modification of child support except in highly unusual circumstances.

10. The 1.45% Medicare deduction applies to all income, without a "cap."

11. Note: That income threshold increases slightly each year.

Present Value: The Last Piece of the Financial Puzzle

Support issues are typically negotiated separately from property division. However, there may come a time during your negotiation when you hit a wall on either spousal support or property settlement. The solution may be to trade "spousal support dollars" for "property division dollars," or vice versa.

However, that creates an "apples to oranges" problem. Fifty thousand dollars paid now as property settlement is worth more than fifty thousand dollars paid over time in support. That's because theoretically, property received in the present can appreciate or yield a "return" or "earnings" such as interest or dividends.

You can resolve this problem by calculating the "present value" of a stream of future support. That calculation converts the support stream into "today's dollars" that are equivalent to property settlement dollars. Present value is the amount that, if invested at a reasonable rate of return, would produce a specific regular payment (a particular amount of weekly or monthly spousal support) over a specified period of time (the number of weeks or months that the spousal support will be paid).

Whaaaat?

If that definition starts a countdown to your head exploding, don't worry about it. Divorce lawyers, CDFAs, and accountants have software to determine the present value of future payments. Again, the basic idea of present value is that $50,000 in property settlement paid today is worth more than $50,000 in support paid over a period of months or years.

Also keep in mind that $50,000 received today is a "bird-in-the-hand." Support obligations that extend into the future always involve some degree of uncertainty, which is not taken into account in present value calculations. You might have reason to worry about your spouse's ability or willingness to honor a support obligation in the future. If so, you might consider bargaining for more property settlement dollars and less in support.

You can also use present value in circumstances other than trading support for property dollars. Let's say you're the support recipient, and your spouse's goal is to pay for as short a period of time as possible. In return for a shorter term, your spouse may be willing to pay a higher amount. You can test whether a particular trade-off of duration for amount will result in you receiving less or more support overall by comparing the present value of

- A larger amount for a shorter time, with . . .
- A smaller amount for a longer time

Yet another use for present value is in valuing defined benefit pension benefits paid out over time. Don't try that at home, however. Unless you're dividing the benefits equally with your spouse, defined benefit pensions should always be valued by actuaries (see Chapter 13).

Negotiating Non-Financial Children's Issues

While support and property division may sometimes converge at the end of a negotiation, non-financial children's issues should never be negotiated at the same time as child support or other financial issues.

Parenting plans should always focus on the children's best interests, and maintaining a close and loving parent/child relationship. Throwing dollars into the mix can result in an outcome based on finances rather than what's best for the kids.

In Chapter 10, we looked at a path for resolving children's issues that begins with a Shared Parenting Goal Statement. Such statements can create momentum for agreement on a final parenting plan for sharing time with your children and making decisions about them.

At a minimum, your parenting plan negotiation should cover[1]:
- Legal custody: Who has decision-making power over the children?
- Physical custody, including
   - A parenting schedule that defines each parent's time with the children (see below)
   - Where applicable, a designation of the children's "primary residence"
   - A parenting schedule (see below)
- Obligations to parent cooperatively in the children's best interests, including
   - Sharing school, extracurricular, medical, and other information

---

1. See sample parenting plan provisions in Appendix 5.

- Being flexible in handling scheduling and other issues that might arise
- Nurturing the children's relationship with both parents
- Notifying the other parent of a child's illness or injury
- Relocation: What will happen in the event that the primary custodial parent wishes to move from the area with the child?
- Parental goals: If desired, statements of shared parenting goals or beliefs regarding matters such as
  - Religion
  - Health
  - Safety issues
  - Communication between parents (not using the children as messengers)

There are also some basics that should be included in your discussion of a parenting schedule:
- Weekend and/or mid-week time with the kids for the non-primary residential parent
- School year vacations
- Holidays and three-day weekends
- Summer vacations
- Special days: Mother's and Father's Days, parents' birthdays, children's birthdays, traditional family gatherings

Keep in mind that child psychologists and other family therapists, counselors, and divorce coaches can help you resolve children's issues. You can either name the professional or agree to cooperate in choosing one in the future, if it becomes necessary. Be sure that the provision (as with most provisions calling for future agreement) includes the words "which agreement shall not be unreasonably withheld." Your parenting plan can also provide that the professional be the first resort (before anyone runs to court) for resolving issues that arise in the future.

Another way to help resolve children's issues is to avoid all-or-nothing resolutions. Let's say you are the primary residential parent and you want your spouse's weekend time with the kids to begin Saturday morning. Your spouse wants the time to begin Friday evening. Negotiating parents sometimes forget that it doesn't have to be one or the other. For example, alternatives in this case could include one or more of the following:
- Alternating between two weekend pick-up schedules

- Adjusting the parenting time during three-day weekends, school-year vacations, or summer vacation to make up the difference
- Using one weekend schedule during the school year and another during summer vacations.

Also keep in mind that you can make your parenting plan subject to a future review provision, to take into account potential changes in the children's preferences, needs, and schedules as they get older. Again, consider involving a mental health professional, divorce coach, or a mediator to assist if you experience difficulty adapting your agreement to such changes.

Because life (especially life with teenagers) is full of surprises, include in your agreement language requiring both parents to act in good faith and in the children's best interests when:
- The parents' schedules or other circumstances force temporary adjustments to the parenting plan
- The need for more permanent changes arises due to the above-mentioned changes in the children's preferences, needs or schedules

Provisions requiring flexibility and good faith are difficult to enforce. However, in post-divorce hearings regarding children they can shed light on the parents' intent and what they felt was in their children's best interests at the time of the divorce.

Going It Alone:
Setting Ground-Rules and Creating Leverage

Much of the material in this chapter applies whether or not you have a lawyer. As mentioned, if you are self-represented you'll want to at least consult with a lawyer or financial analyst about formulating and presenting your settlement positions.

You can also hire a lawyer to conduct the negotiation for you under a limited scope representation arrangement as discussed in Chapter 4. A limited scope ("unbundled") arrangement allows a lawyer to handle only the negotiation of your settlement and follow-up work such as drafting and reviewing a settlement agreement. In this way, your settlement can be negotiated by an experienced professional without the emotion that often hampers spouses negotiating for themselves.

If there is no mediator or lawyer involved, you and your spouse will have to agree upon rules regarding your negotiation. To the extent possible, you want the circumstances of your negotiation to be favorable to you in order to give you "leverage," or at least to avoid giving your spouse leverage.

You can acquire the advantages leverage gives you, with:
- Expertise: Advice from divorce professionals.
- Risk tolerance: Belief that your positions are substantially closer to likely outcomes than your spouse's positions, making you more willing to risk going to trial.
- Self-confidence: Confidence in your ability to negotiate success-fully. This is especially critical if you have been intimidated by your spouse in the past.

Now let's turn to the ways in which the how and when of your negotiation can also affect leverage.

The "How"

You'll have enough to think about while you negotiate, without having to spend time figuring out the ground rules. So establish rules ahead of time covering:

Set negotiation ground rules and abide by them!

- Time: A negotiation session time limit
- Time-outs: Allow for breathers to handle stress or fatigue
- Agenda: An agenda for each session listing issues to be discussed
- Escape clause: An agreement that the session will end if either spouse becomes
  - Overwhelmed or unable to proceed for some other reason
  - Abusive, threatening or otherwise aggressive
- Documentation: Record partial agreements reached[2] (sometimes referred to as "consensuses") by, for example:
  - Putting the agreements in an email sent at the close of the session
  - Writing up, signing, and exchanging copies of agree-ments reached
  - Videotaping a recital of the agreements

---

2. Be aware that these partial agreements are neither binding nor admissible in court in the event that your negotiation breaks down. It is nevertheless very important to record them in order to avoid misunderstandings that can torpedo your negotiation.

The "When"

Let's say your spouse surprises you with a settlement proposal soon after your divorce begins. Not to be paranoid, but if that happens, be a little . . . paranoid.

Unfair leverage in negotiation can result from one spouse having information the other doesn't. The discovery process in traditional divorce and the gathering of information and documents in ADR are intended to eliminate that kind of leverage. So before starting to bargain, make sure you have all the information you need, including the following documents:

- Your spouse's sworn financial disclosure statement
- The most recent two to three years of income and business entity tax returns, plus
  - The most recent W-2s or other year-to-date income summaries
  - Year-to-date financials or other documentation of the entities
- The most recent year-end statements of
  - Pensions and retirement accounts (including IRAs)
  - Mortgage interest and property taxes paid by you and/or your spouse
- Two to three years of
  - Checkbook registers
  - Bank account statements
  - Major credit card statements
- Summaries of retirement plans, deferred compensation programs, stock ownership and stock option programs, and other employment-related "perks"
- The most recent statements of balances owed on debts
- Year-end statements and other summaries of
  - Amazon.com
  - PayPal
  - Other frequently used online stores and payment resources
- Appraisals of real estate and other significant property items for which you and your spouse can't agree on value.
- Documentation of expensive personal property values such as appraisals and insurance policy schedules
- The most recent statements regarding "529" or other education expense accounts
- Current information regarding trusts in which your spouse has an interest, which should include trust documents (to the extent that trust assets may be includible in the "marital estate") and the last

two year-end account statements plus the most recent statement as to trust accounts

One more word about a spouse in a hurry to settle. You can use that urgency to create leverage for yourself.

I once represented a woman whose husband not only had a girlfriend but a pregnant girlfriend. The demands of this guy's unexpected new family were pressuring him to extricate himself from his old one, ASAP. As a result, he was willing to make concessions he wouldn't otherwise have made. Understanding the husband's motivations to settle quickly, my client dug in her heels and came away with a very favorable settlement.

Don't Tip the Boat

Trying to arrange the end of a very *un*business-like relationship in a business-like way is hard enough. Don't make it harder with inappropriate or counterproductive behavior. Your divorce negotiation is NOT the time to:

- Rehash old arguments
- Get stuck on unimportant details
- Discuss your spouse's previous conduct
- Demand apologies
- Lose your cool

Clients sometimes ask me how to keep their cool during negotiations. I've suggested to some to act as if their kids were in the room: that is, to behave in a courteous and dignified way. I've advised others to treat spouses and opposing counsel as they would folks sharing their table at a wedding reception: with attentiveness and courtesy . . . even if neither applies.

Try to keep your feelings about the *issues* separate from your feelings about *your spouse*. I know . . . that's easy for me to say. But do your best. If you feel emotion creeping in, take a break for a short walk, some deep breathing, or a chat with your lawyer.

Keep in mind that negotiations can begin too late as well as too early. Settlement agreements worked out "on the courthouse steps" on the day of trial are magnets for misunderstandings and mistakes. That's due, in part, to the fact that agreements require careful drafting in order to:

- Faithfully record the resolution of issues
- Include all necessary details
- Provide appropriate protections for each party in the event of the other's noncompliance

Hastily prepared agreements often fail at one or more of the above. And that can lead to serious problems later on. So once you and your spouse have exchanged the necessary information and documents, and you have received the necessary advice, get the negotiation process going without delay. If, despite your best efforts, you do wind up settling your case on the eve or day of your trial, be sure to refer to your negotiation chart or some other checklist to make sure you haven't forgotten anything essential.

Non-Verbal Cues: "Body Language"

You will be more successful in your negotiation if you are:
- Confident of the reasonableness of your positions
- Productively "engaged" in the discussion
- Flexible enough, when appropriate, to consider changing your negotiation plan

Of course, you can demonstrate those attitudes verbally. But your actions may speak louder. Here are some examples of important nonverbal cues or "body language" that you will want to use ... and avoid:
- Project confidence by
  - Maintaining eye contact
  - Keeping your body relaxed (avoiding fidgeting, foot tapping, etc.)
- Show "engagement" (involvement in the process) by
  - Leaning toward the conversation
  - Nodding slightly to indicate empathy or a shared belief or interest
  - Waiting before responding to a statement from the other side, to indicate that you have listened carefully and wish to respond thoughtfully
  - "Mirroring" (copying) engaging body language of your spouse
- Show flexibility by keeping your hands apart and your arms uncrossed.
- Avoid body language that suggests disengagement, hostility, or inflexibility such as:
  - Leaning back
  - Frowning
  - Looking away
  - Rolling your eyes
- Avoid body language suggesting that you may be untruthful or are hiding something such as:

ᵒ Crossing your arms in front of you
ᵒ Fidgeting
ᵒ Putting your hands over your mouth or eyes
ᵒ Touching your throat

Court-Sponsored Settlement Conferences and Mediations

Typically, cases that have been pending in the courthouse for several months are scheduled for court-sponsored settlement conferences (sometimes referred to as pre-trials). Pre-trials occur in the courthouse and are usually presided over by neutral third parties such as mediators appointed or employed by the court, or volunteer attorneys (called "special masters" in some jurisdictions) who sometimes work in teams of two.

Judges also sometimes conduct pre-trials. However, that can be a mixed blessing. A judge who pre-tries a case will often recuse herself from trying it if the parties fail to settle. That can deprive you of a good judge and extend your case as you wait for another judge to become available.

At the pre-trial, each side provides a financial disclosure statement and often a summary of the case. The summary is typically made up of a brief recital of the facts, and proposed orders or "claims for relief." The pre-trier(s) ask questions and give each side an opportunity to provide a mini-presentation. Then the pre-triers recommend a settlement based on the law, facts, and often most importantly, what the likely result would be if the case went to trial.

Pre-trials can be extremely useful in settling cases because they provide the opinions of experienced, neutral divorce professionals. They can help jump-start the settlement process, and a pre-trier's recommendation can reign in an unreasonable spouse's unrealistic expectations.

In some court systems, couples whose unresolved cases are nearing a trial date are asked to participate in a mediated settlement session. Such sessions can last for several hours. Like pre-trials, they offer the assistance of experienced matrimonial lawyers in settling your case. This type of mediation is called "evaluative mediation" and differs from the "facilitative mediation" discussed in Chapter 5 because the mediator is proactive in recommending a specific settlement of your case. However, like facilitative mediation, you cannot be required to accept any particular settlement.

Nevertheless, spouses sitting in a courthouse conference room with a trial imminent sometimes feel pressured to settle. A mediator overly intent on resolving cases can add to this pressure. Mediators with that mind-set sometimes try to extract concessions from the spouse who seems more flexible. While flexibility usually helps "get to yes," a spouse perceived by the mediator to be weaker or "more reasonable" may face more pressure than a less reasonable spouse. This can happen even if you have a lawyer present.

As a result, in courthouse mediations, it's very important to:
- Project confidence and relaxation, as discussed above.
- Have clearly in mind what is, and what is not, acceptable to you. (Bringing along your negotiation chart or a checklist will help with that.)
- Ask for a break if you feel overwhelmed.
- Remember that you will not be forced to agree to a settlement recommendation. And if you need more time to think about it, tell the mediator that you are considering the proposal but cannot agree to it without having additional time.

 Yes, there IS a quiz! Test what you have (or haven't) learned.

1. Non-verbal communication ("body language") is important in negotiation because:
   A. Certain bodily noises signal the removal of obstructions
   B. Leaning forward makes it easier to bite your spouse's head off
   C. Body language can project confidence and engagement
2. Assign the terms "wiggle room," "risk tolerance" and "engagement" to one of the following definitions:
   A. What you won't have as much of if you ever consider getting married again
   B. The name of the strip joint in which you caught your Ex on a supposed "working late" evening
   C. Being productively involved in good-faith negotiation
3. The next time a telemarketer calls your cell, identify yourself as one of the "names" below and ask them to send their literature to you c/o The Boom Boom Massage Parlor in the Tatra Mountains of Slovakia. Then unscramble to find key concepts discussed in this chapter:
   Ganionettio Thrac
   Rimalat Ryterpop
   Rovecid Tham

CHAPTER 15

Scared Witless to Star Witness: A Testimony Primer

"I was gratified to be able to answer promptly, and I did. I said I didn't know."

— Mark Twain, *Life on the Mississippi*

Will I Have to Testify?

One of the best things about alternative dispute resolution (ADR) is that you don't have to go to court, except for a brief "uncontested hearing" at the end of your case. So if your divorce is on track to be resolved through ADR, you won't have to testify. And you can skip this chapter![3]

If your case is court-based, it too will most likely settle. Even if it does however, you may have to testify along the way at:
- Temporary (*"pendente lite"*) court proceedings to obtain court orders that remain in effect until your divorce is final. *Pendente lite* hearings cover matters such as
  - ° Temporary spousal support, child support, or child custody/access
  - ° Other matters such as requests for attorneys' fees or exclusive possession of the family home

  Note that *pendente lite* proceedings are limited not only as to how long the orders last, but also as to the evidence that can be introduced. For example, *pendente lite* support hearings focus primarily on current income and spending rather future earnings prospects or the marital assets. Hearings on temporary custody or access to children usually exclude financial matters altogether.

---

3. As discussed in Chapter 5, one form of ADR—arbitration—resembles a trial at which the parties testify. If you are headed for arbitration, you do need to read the material in this chapter.

- Depositions during which opposing counsel questions you at his office. Depositions are part of the discovery process through which a party to a lawsuit obtains information and documents from the other party. A court stenographer records the questions, answers, and lawyers' objections, and prepares a transcript of the proceedings. Questions about any matter that might lead to admissible evidence are permitted at depositions, so the questioning can cover a broad range of topics.

Conquering Courtophobia: Road Trip!

If you're like most people, you might feel just a bit anxious at the prospect of answering questions from a potentially hostile lawyer under oath in front of your STBX, a judge, a couple of lawyers, various courthouse personnel and an assortment of other folks awaiting their turn in the Legal Funhouse. A great way to bring down your anxiety level is to take a road trip to your local courthouse before you testify.

When you get there, do the following:

- Find out at the Clerk's Office where family cases are being heard.
- If possible, choose a courtroom with a hearing similar to what yours will be, or at least where a "contested" hearing or trial is taking place so that you can observe witnesses testifying on both direct and cross-examination.
- Locate the "Family" or "Court Services" Office. Many courts require a meeting with a Court Services Counselor to try to resolve *pendente lite* matters before a judge will hear them.
- Ask an assistant clerk, bailiff or dozing lawyer about the best places to park so that you don't kick off your Big Day in Court panhandling for parking meter quarters.

Of course, if your case doesn't settle, you'll have to testify at trial.[4] There, you can be questioned regarding all financial or child-related issues. We'll discuss trial testimony in more detail later in the chapter. But one thing to keep in mind throughout your case is that at trial you'll be asked about previous "statements," such as

- Your previous testimony at a deposition or *pendente lite* hearing
- Documents that you produced during discovery

---

4. Occasionally a case settles even after trial has begun. That happened in one of my cases when opposing counsel, surprised by how skilled a witness my client was on the first day of trial, decided not to risk an unfavorable decision. Instead, he called me that night to make an offer that basically mirrored our last demand, and we settled the case.

- Your financial disclosure statement
- Other documents that you prepared, received, or were responsible for such as
  - Tax returns
  - Loan applications
  - Emails, online posts and other correspondence

What Should I Wear to Court?

Court attire should be neat, conservative and reflect respect for the court. Wear what you would wear to a job interview. Leave the chewing gum home and wear only the most modest jewelry. Martha Stewart went to jail after showing up in court with a $20,000 handbag. Enough said.

Your appearance should also match your case "story-line." If you are reentering the workforce but claiming you're too old for your former field, let your age show. If your spouse accuses you of serial infidelity, avoid your most flattering outfits.

Your Star Witness Makeover

Your performance as a witness can substantially impact how quickly and favorably your case is resolved. Effective testimony at a pretrial hearing or deposition can dampen the other side's enthusiasm for a trial and thus increase your leverage during settlement negotiation. Effective testimony at trial earns points with the judge that can translate into favorable court orders.

That's why we're spending a whole chapter on your star witness makeover.

Types of Examination of Witnesses

There are essentially 4 types of questioning or "examination" of witnesses:
- Direct examination: Questions asked by the attorney who calls a witness in court. In divorce trials, the parties typically answer questions from their own lawyer on "direct."
- Cross-examination:
  - In court, examination of opposing parties or other "hostile" or "adversary" witnesses, such as experts retained by the opposing

party. "Cross" is used to test the witness's credibility, reliability and the accuracy of his/her testimony on direct examination.

    ◦ At a deposition, examination of the opposing party or adversary witness for the purpose of gathering information in preparation for settlement negotiation and/or court proceedings.

- Redirect examination: Questions asked in court by the initial examiner regarding matters covered on cross-examination. Redirect is used to "rehabilitate" a witness's credibility and/or to revise inaccurate, damaging or confusing testimony. The "scope" of redirect examination is limited to matters about which the witness has testified on cross-examination.
- Re-cross-examination: Additional cross-examination by opposing counsel, limited to the scope of redirect.

The Four Commandments of Testimony

The "Four Commandments" of testimony discussed below are the building blocks of success as a witness. Memorize them!

I. Listen Carefully to Each Question in Its Entirety and Be Sure That You Fully Understand It.

Listening carefully is a MUST when you testify, whether on direct or cross-examination. That means, first of all, listen to the entire question.

Next, be sure you understand the question fully. If you don't, say so! You won't be required to answer questions you don't hear or understand.

You might not hear or fully understand a question because:
- Your attention might stray due to emotion or fatigue
- The question is incomprehensible. (Lawyers are asking the questions, so confusion is always just around the corner.)

Don't get rattled if you didn't hear or understand a question. Instead:
- Ask that the question be repeated or rephrased.
- State that you don't understand the question. Again, you won't be required to answer a question you genuinely don't understand.

II. Answer Each Question Accurately, Concisely, Responsively, and in a Way That Is Fair to You.

Nothing angers judges more than a dishonest witness. Running a close second, however, is a witness who gives long, unresponsive answers. Unfocused, rambling testimony can hurt your case in several ways:

- On direct examination, that kind of testimony
  - ° Disrupts the flow of your story
  - ° Drives the judge—and your lawyer—nuts
  - ° Gives opposing counsel additional cross-examination opportunities
- On cross-examination, such testimony provides the cross-examiner
  - ° New areas of questioning
  - ° Additional opportunities to find inconsistencies in your testimony and question your credibility and reliability as a witness

---

⚠ **Pearls of Witness Wisdom: Questions About Documents**

If you are asked about a document, ask to see it *before* answering the question. Take as much time as you need to carefully review the document.

Documents most frequently asked about are:
- Your financial disclosure statement
- Tax returns
- Business records if you own or operate a business
- Documents regarding spending such as bank, credit card and online account records for PayPal, Amazon.com, etc.
- Statements for pension benefit and other employment related benefits and "perks"
- Employment agreements
- Loan applications
- Emails, texts, social media posts, etc. especially where child-related issues or reason for the breakdown of the marriage are in dispute

The "Fairness Exception"

Note the phrase, "in a way that is fair to you" at the end of Commandment II. I call this the "fairness exception." It applies when a concise response without explanation creates a misimpression that is damaging or "prejudicial" to your case.

The fairness exception most often applies to questions that lack a time period or other context. If you are asked a question without the necessary context

- Ask for a time period, geographic location or other circumstance that's needed to avoid confusion or a misimpression; or
- State in your response when or where you said or did what you've been asked about, and if necessary, explain why that context matters

Placing Questions in Context

Below is an example of how the "fairness exception" works. Consider the following exchange at a *pendente lite* hearing between the husband and Attorney Fox, the wife's lawyer:

ATTORNEY FOX: Mr. Sherwood, you feel that your wife should be employed at least part time, correct?

MR. SUREWOOD: Yes, I do.

ATTORNEY FOX: But that's now that you're divorcing her. Before the divorce began, you told her that she didn't have to work, correct?

MR. SUREWOOD: Yes, but that was before Nicky, our second child was born and our expenses went up. At that point, I asked her to consider working part time.

Attorney Fox's 2ⁿᵈ question relates to a statement Mr. Sherwood made sometime in the past. Answering that question "yes" would have been concise and responsive, but would have left a misimpression. Realizing that, Mr. Sherwood had the choice of:

- Asking that the question be rephrased to include a time period, or
- Adding an explanation to his "yes" answer

He chose the 2ⁿᵈ option, a "Yes, but" answer that explained the yes by supplying the necessary context.

III. Don't Be Argumentative, Sarcastic or Witty, or Try to Outsmart the Examining Lawyer.

Losing your cool at a deposition suggests to opposing counsel that you'd make a poor witness at trial. That can increase counsel's willingness to go to trial and thus make it more difficult to negotiate settlement.

Losing your cool at trial can accomplish several other things, none of which are good, namely:
- Presenting you in a bad light to the judge
- Causing you to lose the focus necessary to follow the testimony commandments
- Strengthening your spouse's case. For example, if your spouse contends that your bad temper helped destroy the marriage, arguing with opposing counsel:
  - Makes that contention more believable
  - Bolsters your spouse's credibility

Staying Out of the Judge's Dog House

Judges particularly dislike seeing the following in the courtroom:

- Witnesses who lie
- Witnesses who give rambling, unresponsive answers
- Witnesses who quibble with the attorneys questioning them
- Witnesses who chew gum, slouch or "lounge" on the witness stand or otherwise show disrespect for the court
- Witnesses who wear overly casual or revealing clothing such as T-shirts, flip-flops, low-rise pants or mini-skirts.
- Non-testifying parties who react out loud to their spouse's testimony
- Non-testifying parties whom the judge can hear talking to their lawyers
- Anyone with a cell phone!

The Argumentative Witness

You have the right as a witness to insist upon clear, unambiguous, and understandable questions. But don't argue unnecessarily with your cross-examiner. The methods above allow you to obtain clarification of the question or explain a "yes" or "no" answer without being contentious.

As mentioned, it's particularly important to keep your cool in court. Judges do not want to listen to bickering witnesses and lawyers. What they do want is testimony that is:
- Presented in an efficient and understandable way on direct examination.
- Tested in a meaningful way on cross-examination, despite the fact that it may annoy or antagonize you as the witness. If you have a lawyer, ask her to grill you ahead of time on topics that make you feel uncomfortable or vulnerable, in order to help you remain calm when answering difficult questions. If you're self-represented, make a list of the same type of questions for a friend to fire at you. You might even try videotaping your answers and then grading yourself on how well you followed the Four Commandments.

IV. Prepare Effectively for Your Testimony.

Witness preparation is one of the most important—and neglected—aspects of effective testimony. To help you remember how to prepare yourself to testify, try using an acronym that's so tasteless, it'll be hard to forget:

The Key to Effective Testimony: B.U.R.P.

- Breathe: Practice relaxation techniques once or twice a day during the weeks preceding—and including—the day of your testimony.
- Update: Avoid difficulties on the witness stand relating to your financial disclosure statement by periodically updating and checking it for accuracy.
- Road Trip! Visit the courthouse prior to testifying to watch contested hearings and to familiarize yourself with the terrain (see below).
- Prepare by:
  - Going over your prior "statements" regarding your finances, including your financial disclosure statement (don't forget earlier versions that opposing counsel has), interrogatory responses,

transcripts of your testimony and documents such as loan applications and tax returns.

- ○ Meeting with your lawyer to go over both your direct testimony and the cross-examination you should expect. Ask your lawyer to focus on issues on which you feel vulnerable or uncertain.

- ○ Periodically reviewing the testimony commandments as your hearing or deposition approaches.

Be a Proactive Client!

Busy lawyers too often neglect to prepare their clients to testify. If your lawyer hasn't arranged to meet with you regarding testimony you are expecting to give at a hearing or deposition, take the initiative and schedule the meeting yourself. And tell your lawyer you want to do more than *discuss* your testimony: You want to

If your lawyer hasn't prepared you to testify, take the wheel!

practice it by having her fire questions at you and evaluate your responses to them.

Dealing with the Cross-Examining Attorney

The testimony commandments apply both to direct and cross-examination. Concise, responsive answers on direct will help present your story in a methodical way that's easy for the judge to follow. Similar responses on cross will portray you as credible and reasonable, and will avoid giving opposing counsel additional material about which to cross-examine you.

However, cross-examination in court can be very different from cross at a deposition. Understanding the differences between the two can help you testify more effectively.

The Cross-Examiner's Goals in Court

In court, cross-examination typically comes after your lawyer questions you on direct exam. It is used to:

- Try to make you acknowledge facts unfavorable to you or favorable to your spouse

- Cast doubt on your testimony by challenging your memory and understanding ("reliability") or your honesty ("credibility")
- Cast doubt on your entitlement to the financial and other orders ("relief") that you are seeking

> ## Pearls of Witness Wisdom: "Prior Statements"
> ⚠️ If you are asked about a statement you made in the past (including statements contained in documents), you can request that the question be rephrased to locate your statement in time and place. This is crucial, especially if you have said different things about a topic at different times.

The Cross-Examiner's Goals at a Deposition

Lawyers use depositions to prepare for trial and settlement negotiations. Their goals at depositions are to:
- Gather relevant information
- Ask questions designed to learn what you will say at trial, and to "lock in" testimony that might be helpful to your spouse at trial
- Authenticate documents that you have authored or that relate to you
- Size up your skills as a witness

Avoiding "Yes" and "No" Responses

In court, skilled cross-examiners use "leading questions" nearly exclusively. Leading questions contain the cross-examiner's version of facts or conclusions with which the witness is simply asked to agree or disagree. They are actually more in the nature of statements than questions. As a result, cross-examiners using leading questions are actually the ones testifying.

The following are common types of leading questions:
- "So you didn't tell your husband that you got a bonus, did you?"
- "You quit your job to try to get more support, didn't you?"
- "The cash your father gave you was never intended to be a loan that had to be repaid; isn't that a fact?"
- "The fact is you have another savings account that you opened to try to hide money from your wife, correct?"

Responding "yes" to, or otherwise agreeing with a leading question is often the least desirable response to give. That's because once you give it, the version of the facts that the cross-examiner includes in his question becomes your testimony. The trick is to be sure that everything in a question is accurate before answering "yes."

Your cross-examiner may try to insist upon "yes or no" answers to leading questions. You don't have to go along. When a "yes" or "no" response would be incomplete or misleading, respond with one of the following:
- "No, I can't answer that yes or no."
- "I can't answer yes or no without an explanation."
- "That question can't be answered that simply."
- "I can't answer simply yes or no, the way you've phrased the question."

Taking Advantage of "Why?" Questions

In law school, baby lawyers are taught 3 rules of cross-examination:
- Don't (meaning, don't cross-examine unless there's something valuable to be gained)
- Don't ask a question to which you don't already know the answer.
- Never ask "why?"

These rules are intended to avoid harmful testimony in response to questions a lawyer does not have to ask . . . other than to show off what a master cross-examiner he is. As you might imagine, lawyers routinely ignore the rules.

If you are lucky enough to be asked "why" you said, did or thought something, be ready to respond with your version of the relevant facts. You might even prepare an answer to a couple of questions you anticipate concerning something particularly important that you've said or done. If the reasons you said, did or thought something are important and responsive, don't hold back. You might not get another chance to "load up the record" with your version of the facts.

Standing Up to the Cross-Examiner

You can stand your ground on cross-examination in ways other than refusing to answer ambiguous questions "yes" or "no." For example:
- Refuse to give an unqualified answer when you are almost, but not completely, sure of the answer. Instead, being careful not to overuse them, respond with one of the following ways to qualify your answer:
  - "I think so, but I'm not completely sure."

- ○ "That sounds right, but I can't swear to it."
- ○ "I don't believe so, but I'd have to check [specify a document] to be sure."
- ○ "I believe so, but I'm not 100% sure."
- ○ "I don't know."
- ○ "I don't remember."
- ○ "I'm not [exactly] sure."
- ○ "I don't recall that specifically."
- If you're being questioned about a document, ask to see it and review it carefully before responding. After you do that, ask for the question to be "read back" by the court reporter (or played back on a tape recorder) so that you can see whether the question described the contents of the document accurately and fairly.
- Take advantage of the "witness's magic word" that stops cross-examiners in their tracks. That word is "speculation." For example, responding, "I'd just be speculating if I answered that question," will force counsel to move on. Judges prohibit speculation because it doesn't prove anything; or translated into Lawglish, it has no "probative value."

What Lawyers "Cannot" Ask You

There are—believe it or not—some limitations on what lawyers can ask:

"SPECULATION": The Witness's Magic Word!

- At a deposition: harassing or overly burdensome questions. Any question that might lead to admissible evidence is permissible at a deposition. Because financial orders are based upon a wide range of factors, there's very little that's irrelevant. Note that relevance is narrowed somewhat at trial where judges generally don't allow "fishing expeditions" for minor scraps of information.
- In court: questions that are impermissible under the rules of evidence. Each state has complex rules of evidence designed to enhance the reliability of testimony and other evidence. For example, most statements made by a witness who is not a party and who is not present in the courtroom is considered "hearsay" and cannot be quoted or referred to by a witness in his/her court testimony. Similarly, witnesses who are not experts in the field

about which they are testifying are generally not permitted to offer opinions. There are also numerous exceptions to evidentiary rules that complicate their application. That's one reason why you need experienced trial counsel in a court-based case.

Courtroom Decorum

Above, we noted behavior that can land you in the judge's doghouse.[1] Below are a few more things you should know about what to do, and not do, in the courtroom.

When You Are Testifying in Court

Keep in mind the following when you testify:
- Speak loudly enough to be heard by the lawyers, the court stenographer and the judge. Courtroom microphones are generally for recording, not amplification. You have to supply the volume yourself. Glance at the judge occasionally. If she's straining to hear you, dial up the volume.
- During your testimony, a lawyer may ask you a question to which the other lawyer objects. When that happens, don't answer unless the judge "overrules" the objection. If the judge "sustains" an objection to a question, you may not answer it. Simply wait for the next question. (This differs from depositions where no judge is present, and you must answer even questions to which an objection has been made—unless your lawyer advises you not to.)
- If there's no drinking water on the witness stand, ask for some.
- If you start to feel overwhelmed to the extent that you can't concentrate on the questions, say so. Judges are generally sensitive to the emotional nature of family cases, and will give you an opportunity to regroup.
- The witness stand is located beside the judge, though usually at a slightly lower elevation. You'll spend the great majority of your time

---

1. Judges nearly always decide financial and child-related issues in divorces. However, in Georgia and Texas, juries can decide all issues in a divorce case, though the cost of jury trials, which last much longer than cases tried before a judge, is quite often prohibitive. Colorado, Illinois, Louisiana, Maine, Nevada, New York, North Carolina, Tennessee, and Wisconsin permit juries to decide limited issues such as grounds for, or entitlement to divorce, but those issues are rarely litigated in this era of no-fault divorce.

facing the lawyer who is questioning you. However, it's not a bad idea to make brief, occasional eye contact with the judge especially to emphasize important testimony.

- ⚠️ Take your time! Skilled cross-examiners sometimes use a fast-paced rhythm to try to unnerve witnesses and keep them from giving sufficient thought to their answers. If that happens, you can slow the pace by doing one of the following:
    ○ Saying something to the effect of:
        ▪ "Let me think about that for a moment."
        ▪ "I have to think—I want to make sure I'm being accurate."
        ▪ "Give me a moment; I'm trying to recall."
    ○ Asking if you can refer to a document in evidence that will help you answer the question
    ○ Asking that the question be repeated
    ○ Taking a drink of water

When You Aren't Testifying in Court

During testimony by your spouse or other witnesses, you can provide valuable assistance to your lawyer, as follows:

- Pay close attention and take plenty of (legible) notes. You know more about your marriage than your lawyer, so you may pick up on something that she doesn't.
- If you wish to bring something to your lawyer's attention, communicate with her in writing, not verbally, so that she doesn't miss important testimony.
- If you've maintained a divorce binder as discussed in Chapter 7, keep it at the ready for quick access to key documents.
- Don't let emotion prevent you from performing the tasks above. And don't react to testimony beyond an understated shake of the head, no matter how provocative it is.

Talking to the Judge

Judges sometimes ask witnesses questions. If your judge does that, don't feel intimidated. Answer the questions as thoroughly as you can. Make eye contact and convey respect, both verbally and with body language. As with any questions you are asked in court, if you don't understand them, say so.

If the judge appears dissatisfied or confused by an answer you give, try to remedy the situation. Encourage the judge to ask you for clarification with something like:

- "I may not be understanding your question."
- "Am I being clear?"
- "I feel like I'm not helping you."

In certain situations such as uncontested hearings (see page 27), a judge may speak directly to parties while they are seated at counsel table. If that happens and a response is called for, be sure to stand up when "addressing the court."

Getting Through a Courthouse Day

A typical court day begins between 9:00 and 10:00 A.M., suspends for lunch at 1:00 P.M., resumes at 2:00 and ends at 5:00. Many judges take mid-morning and mid-afternoon recesses.

Of course, your day will be much longer than the court's hours—starting with the moment you wake up thinking, "Oh, ===! Today's the day!" Leave yourself extra time in the morning to be sure that you can get to court on time without having to rush. Pace yourself through the day to avoid fatigue, because testifying in the highly focused manner described in this chapter burns a lot of energy.

Try your best to get a good night's sleep the night before. Avoid insomnia triggers like alcohol, caffeinated beverages, sugary snacks, and glowing electronics. If all else fails, choose something incredibly boring to read. Like the pension material in Chapter 13.

On the Road to Witness Stardom

You'll be far better prepared than the vast majority of witnesses if you:

- Master the testimony commandments
- Visit the courthouse ahead of time to observe contested family hearings
- Practice before you testify[2]

---

2. If you don't have a lawyer to help you prepare, write out questions about the matters that concern you the most, and have a friend fire them at you. Then grade yourself (and have your friend grade you as well) according to how well you followed the testimony commandments. Repeat, until you get it right.

So, relax. Or at least try to. No one is perfect and you won't need to be as a witness. Don't worry if you make a mistake here or there while testifying. If you do, and realize it while still being questioned, state that you'd like to add something to, or change an earlier answer.

The bottom line is that concise, thoughtful testimony will impress a judge in court, and render an attorney who takes your deposition more eager to settle your case.

 Yes, there IS a quiz! Test what you have (or haven't) learned.

1. You can begin conquering courtophobia by:
   A. Embracing a tiger
   B. Taking a tiger by the tail
   C. Getting trashed at a karaoke bar and singing "Eye of the Tiger"
   D. Getting over this thing you have about tigers, and visiting a local court-house prior to your court date

2. You can tell that you are watching cross-examination when:
   A. The witness begins speaking in tongues.
   B. The lawyer is more obnoxious than any of the Real Housewives of New Jersey. Except maybe Teresa.
   C. A lawyer wearing a tuxedo concludes his cross-examination with, "I'm through with dis guy!"
   D. Mostly "leading questions" are being asked, which allows the lawyer to be the one actually testifying and simply asking the witness to agree or disagree with the fact or conclusion contained in the question.

3. Rate the texter below who's texting from the courtroom, for compli-ance with the testimony commandments:

CHAPTER 16

Same-Sex Marriage and Divorce

The Supreme Court has rejected what some call "traditional values."

> *"At his best, man is the noblest of all animals; separated from law and justice he is the worst."*
>
> — Aristotle

Same-Sex Marriage

On June 26, 2015, the United States Supreme Court ruled that all states must recognize same-sex marriages, and that same-sex spouses are entitled to the same rights as heterosexual spouses. Writing for a 5-4 majority in the case of *Obergefell v. Hodges,*[3] Justice Anthony M. Kennedy based his ruling on the entitlement of same-sex spouses to "equal dignity in the eyes of the law."[4]

The *Obergefell* decision will have far-reaching consequences, particularly in the 13 states that had not recognized same-sex marriage. Those consequences include the right of same-sex couples to divorce in each state, whether or not same-sex marriage was previously permitted there.

Same-Sex Divorce

Under the *Obergefell* decision, same-sex divorces will work the same as opposite-sex divorces. Nonetheless, certain issues and fact patterns will occur more often in same-sex divorces. And at least while state laws are evolving in the wake of *Obergefell*, resolution of those issues is likely to be more complicated.

---

3. 576 U.S. ___ (2015)

4. Two years earlier in the case of *United States v. Windsor,* 570 U.S. 12 (2013), the Supreme Court had invalidated key provisions of the Defense of Marriage Act (DOMA) and granted to same-sex spouses the same rights enjoyed by opposite-sex spouses under federal law.

Same-Sex Property and Spousal Maintenance Issues

Because same-sex marriages didn't exist a mere dozen years before *Obergefell* (and were never sanctioned in 13 states), many same-sex couples lived together for long periods before they were able to marry. Before their marriages, many of those couples acquired substantial assets that they considered to belong to both of them.

Unfortunately, such circumstances could complicate property division issues at the time of divorce.

Most of the 42 equitable distribution jurisdictions in the U.S. consider property acquired before marriage to be non-marital property that upon divorce remains with the spouse that acquired it. In all 9 community property states, such property is also considered non-marital. (See Chapter 13 for details and exceptions.)

Issues in divorce relating to property acquired before marriage are not new. Certainly, heterosexual couples cohabit before marriage as well. But that cohabitation is by choice.

Pre-marital cohabitation for many same-sex couples has been due at least in part to prohibitions against marriage. Those prohibitions also led to quite lengthy periods of cohabitation, especially in states that never sanctioned same-sex marriage, or did so only shortly before June 2015. As a result, limiting marital property to that acquired after marriage creates significant potential for unfairness in same-sex divorces.

Consider 2 partners that have lived together for 15 years, then marry when their state law changes to permit same-sex marriage. Three years later, the couple decides to divorce. A court that limits marital property to what was acquired during the last 3 years of an 18-year relationship could create a devastating injustice for one of the spouses.

Similar considerations apply to spousal maintenance. Let's say the same couple lives in a state where maintenance is typically awarded for half the length of marriages that exceed 10 years. A judge who ignores the 15-year cohabitation would award 1 or 2 years of maintenance at the most.

Using Prenuptial Agreements to Avoid Unfairness

Prenuptial agreements (also known as "premarital agreements") have traditionally been used to protect wealthier spouses from financial claims during divorce by their less well-off partners.

But "prenups" can also be used to try to avoid unfair results such as those discussed above. Long-term same-sex partners who weren't permitted to marry during part or all of their pre-marriage relationships can use prenups to

- Expand their state's definition of marital property
- Provide for spousal maintenance awards based on the length of the entire relationship

Keep in mind that prenups need not be one-sided. By way of example, let's consider again the couple that lived together for 15 years prior to a 3-year marriage that ended in divorce. The more affluent spouse may be willing to agree to spousal maintenance for longer than state law would allow after a 3-year marriage in exchange for a limitation on claims for property acquired by that spouse that became marital property due to comingling during the long relationship.

Of course, a prenup must be able to hold up in court. While it has become increasingly difficult to invalidate prenups in recent years, some courts still refuse to honor them when at least 1 of the following factors is present:

1. The more well-to-do partner fails to fully disclose his/her finances
2. The less affluent partner doesn't have access to professional advice
3. The agreement is obtained through "duress" or "undue influence"
4. The agreement is essentially unfair or "unconscionable"

A combination of good will and good planning can avoid the first two factors. And partners drafting a prenup to be more rather than less fair generally needn't worry about #3 or 4.

Broaching the subject of a prenuptial agreement can be a dicey matter, to say the least. It's difficult even for long-time partners to predict what reaction to expect. But those who are able to discuss—frankly and dispassionately—ways to avoid unfair results upon divorce may find it well worth their while to do so.

Child-Related Issues: Adoption and ART

While issues relating to adopted children and those conceived through assisted reproduction technology ("ART") arise in heterosexual divorces, they will come up more regularly for same-sex spouses with children. And controversies regarding those children are likely to be more complex in many same-sex divorces.

For example, let's say a same-sex couple decided to adopt a child in 2012 in a state in which same-sex marriage was not allowed. Though both partners wished to adopt, only one of them was permitted to do so under that state's law. Will the adopting parent be entitled to greater rights regarding the child if the couple later marries and then, following years of co-parenting, files for divorce?

Similar issues will arise regarding ART. Here's another example:

A lesbian couple marries in Massachusetts in 2004, the year in which that state became the first to allow same-sex marriage. Several months later, the couple moves to a state that doesn't recognize their marriage. In 2005, one of the spouses conceives through *in vitro* fertilization, and gives birth. In 2015, after 10 years of loving and nurturing their child equally, the spouses decide to divorce. Unfortunately, they are unable to agree on custody.

The family court is confronted with a number of thorny legal issues:
- Should the birth spouse have superior legal rights regarding custody and access solely because under the law of a state that didn't recognize same-sex marriage, she alone is listed on the birth certificate?
- Should the court apply by analogy the Uniform Status of Children of Assisted Conception Act under which a woman who bears a child (other than as a surrogate) is the child's mother, and the woman's husband is the father?
- Should the court apply by analogy the legal presumption that the husband of a woman who gives birth during marriage is the father?
- Should the court ignore birth certificates, common-law presumptions, and non-binding uniform acts, and instead base its decision solely on the best interests of the child ("BIC") standard?

Same-sex couples that marry and subsequently adopt, or conceive through ART after June 2015 will no longer be victimized by discriminatory laws. But they will still be forced to confront the issues faced by all couples where only one spouse is an adoptive or natural parent. And those issues can be further complicated in "blended families" where children of previous marriages are raised together by a parent and that parent's new spouse.

Unfortunately, prenuptial agreements are not as helpful in dealing with child-related issues as they can be with financial matters. That's because courts in every jurisdiction reserve the right to determine "ultimate" child-related issues such as custody, regardless of agreements the parents may reach. Thus, judges are free to ignore prenuptial agreement provisions that they consider to be inconsistent with BIC.[1]

Nevertheless, prenup provisions can affect custody and access determinations. For example, language acknowledging that both spouses have in the past, and expect in the future to participate equally in child-rearing can have an impact. The same is true of an acknowledgment of a child's close and loving relationship with both spouses and/or a statement of intention to continue to nurture the child's relationship with both spouses in the event of divorce.[2]

Moving Forward

As demonstrated by the above examples, state laws will need to be changed to avoid same-sex divorce's potential for unfairness. Those changes are likely to emerge slowly as judges struggle to resolve novel issues in the wake of the *Obergefell* decision.

In the meantime, same-sex spouses who can resolve matters themselves or through alternative dispute resolution will be able to avoid the uncertainties that will loom particularly large for them while the law develops.

My hope for those couples is the same as my hope for all divorcing couples: a divorce that resolves issues fairly and efficiently, and allows ex-partners to move forward with dignity toward a new, happier life.

---

1. See Chapter 10 for more on BIC.
2. If the agreement contains additional provisions that affect "ultimate" child-related issues, make sure that it also contains a "severability" clause that preserves the remainder of the agreement in the event that such provisions are invalidated.

Yes, there IS a quiz! Test what you have (or haven't) learned.

1. A main idea in this chapter is:
   A. Civil unions encourage employees to be polite.
   B. Same-old, same-old, same-sex marriages get boring after a while.
   C. The U.S. Supreme Court has eliminated distinctions between opposite-sex and same-sex marriage and divorce.

2. Some same-sex couples have lived together for many years before marriage because:
   A. They could share wardrobes more easily
   B. Breaking up is so hard on the cats
   C. Judges won't distribute property acquired before same-sex marriages because dividing up shoes is too emotional.
   D. Legal marriage wasn't available to them

3. Mention these "prominent climate change scientists" in a question for your Congressperson at a Town Hall meeting, then unscramble them!
   A. Udenu eclenifun
   B. Gella Stuppormine
   C. Flul Cludossire

CHAPTER 17

Your Divorce Afterlife

*"Life is not a matter of holding
good cards, but of playing a
poor hand well."*

— Robert Louis Stevenson

Your Post-Divorce TBD List

You walk from the courthouse, free at last of the clutches of the divorce process. After all is said and done, you've reached the finish line in one piece.

Except all is not quite "said and done." Most likely, there are still some things for you to do. Try to take care of the matters below at or before your final hearing. But if you can't, address them as soon as possible afterwards. Keep copies of all correspondence regarding these tasks and make sure that all snail-mailed official documents go via certified mail or other trackable means. Use the following as a check-list for your post-divorce TBD list:

- Sign documents to transfer real estate, vehicles, etc. in accordance with your settlement agreement.
- Divide any savings or securities accounts per your settlement agreement.
- After cancelling any automatic withdrawals and making sure there are no outstanding checks, close all
  - ⁰ Joint bank accounts,
  - ⁰ Joint investment accounts
  - ⁰ Joint credit cards (including accounts in your name for which your Ex had charging privileges)
  - ⁰ Home equity and other loan accounts
- Change beneficiaries and survivor's rights per your settlement agreement for
  - ⁰ Pension and other retirement plans including IRAs
  - ⁰ Life insurance
- Make sure that any life insurance policies required to insure child or spousal support have been obtained or amended in accordance with your agreement and are in full force and effect. (If you are the

recipient of support insured by a policy insuring your Ex's life, your settlement agreement should require notice to you of any lapses or beneficiary changes.)

- Revise or revoke any of the following in which your Ex has an interest or power to act on your behalf.
  - ° Revocable trusts
  - ° Living wills
  - ° Powers of attorney
- Change email and other online passwords even if you don't think your Ex knows them because . . . you just never know.
- Obtain a certified copy of your divorce decree from the Clerk of Court to keep on hand in case you need it.
- If retirement assets are to be transferred by QDRO (see Chapter 13), make sure that the QDRO is
  - ° Prepared by a qualified lawyer, actuary or financial planner
  - ° Submitted to the plan administrator for pre-approval
  - ° Submitted to the court for a judge's signature
  - ° Received back from the court containing a judge's signature
  - ° Forwarded to the plan administrator (via certified mail)
  - ° Acknowledged in writing by the plan administrator as being received, approved, and in effect
- If you will be obtaining COBRA health insurance through your Ex's employer, notify the employer of that election in writing within 30 days of the divorce.
- Make sure any other documents required by your agreement are signed and delivered to the appropriate entities.
- If your birth name has been restored, do the following.
  - ° Download, fill out and submit a Form SS5, "Application for Social Security Card" at http://www.socialsecurity.gov to obtain a new card bearing your birth name
  - ° Notify your employer, bank(s), insurance companies, the Post Office, retirement plan administrators, credit card companies, and utility companies
  - ° Contact the U.S. Passport Office for a new passport
  - ° Change car titles and registrations
- If you don't decide until after your final hearing to have your birth name restored, find out if you can file a post-judgment motion for restoration in your dissolution case. Otherwise, you can make the change through your local Probate Court (known as "Surrogate's Courts" in New York and New Jersey).

- Obtain any personal property belonging to you that is in your Ex's possession, ASAP.
- Set up automatic withdrawal and direct deposit for support payments.
- Obtain from your lawyer any of your documents that you wish to have.
- Obtain a copy of your credit report (available free at www .AnnualCreditReport.com) to resolve any problems and to make sure the information used for your credit rating is accurate.

Taking Care of Your Children

Keep in mind that your divorce after-life will be a new world not only for you but for your children as well. Assistance in guiding your children's transition is available from numerous sources (see lists in Chapter 18), including:

- www.ourfamilywizard.com 2houses.com and custodyxchange.com (online tools to avoid co-parenting conflict that traumatizes children, using online calendars, message boards, etc.)
- www.helpguide.org/mental/children_divorce.htm
- www.sesamestreet.org/parents/topicsandactivities/toolkits/divorce (for children through the age of 8)

A good deal of the parenting advice in this book applies both during and after the divorce. Start by telling your children that you love them. Then *show* them that you love them by following these rules:

- Be positive and reassuring.
- Keep involved in your children's lives—attending programs and games (or better still, coaching). This is more important than ever, especially for the parent not living with the children.
- Revise your Parenting Goal Statement with your Ex. If you didn't do one, it's never too late. (See Chapter 10.)
- Avoid criticizing your Ex especially to or in your children's presence.
- Avoid arguments with your Ex, especially in the presence of the children, who often believe disputes are their fault.
- Never use the children to exchange messages with your Ex.
- Encourage your children to ask questions about the new state of things. Ideally, this should happen after you've agreed with your co-parent how to handle such questions.

- Don't contribute to children's "reconciliation fantasies" by implying that there might be one.
- Have your child see a professional if you notice signs of distress.
- Provide stability for your kids by maintaining routines that are as consistent with those of your co-parent as possible. Prepare schedules so they will know when they will be with each parent.
- Review your parenting plan to make sure you and your Ex are fulfilling your respective responsibilities including
  ○ Requesting that all notices and bulletins are sent to both parents
  ○ Adhering to your parenting plan details such as consistent bedtime, homework, and curfew rules
- Get your post-divorce co-parenting off to a good start with amiable communication and constructive discussions about the items on this list.
- Read more on conflict management and cooperative problem-solving in "The *Talk to Strangers* Pocket Guide for Parents" at: www.ChildCustodyFilm.com.

Child Distress Warning Signs

Your children may experience lingering difficulties adjusting to their changed lives after your divorce. Be on the lookout for behavioral changes that can indicate anxiety, stress, insecurity, or depression, such as:
- Altered sleep patterns or eating habits
- Declining performance in academics, athletics, or other activities
- Frequent and/or broad mood changes
- Acting out through anger, aggression, defiance, or other misbehavior with peers, teachers, or family members
- Withdrawal from family and friends
- Lethargy or disinterest
- Regression
- Becoming accident prone
- Excessive catering to parents that may signal a child's self-blame for the divorce

Taking Care of Yourself

If you possibly can, take some "R and R" time to help achieve closure on your marriage and the divorce process. Reflect upon how you are functioning and relating to those around you. To improve or "maintain," consider the following:

- Counseling to help you adjust to the new realities of your life
- Continued work on joint parenting with your Ex (as discussed in Chapter 10) in order to
  - Provide your children with a good model for dealing with conflict
  - Maintain consistency for your children regarding their routines and rules for bedtimes/curfews, homework, etc.
- Keeping stress and guilt levels down, and your wellbeing and self-esteem up by
  - Joining meditation group or yoga class that you felt too busy to join during the divorce (See Chapter 18 for resources.) There's likely to be a meditation community ("sangha") near you with regularly scheduled meditation sittings. You can show up (unannounced) even if you know little or nothing about meditation. The sittings are usually followed by short "dharma talks" on Buddhist philosophy that you may also find helpful.
  - Maintaining nutrition with a balanced diet including plenty of fresh fruits and vegetables, and staying away from soda and other sugar-laden products
  - Exercising regularly for cardio, core, etc.
  - Getting sufficient sleep (See the sleep tips in Chapter 7.)
  - Joining a post-divorce support group locally or online (See Chapter 18 for resources to help you locate support groups.)
- If you are reentering the job market, look into
  - Taking a computer class (at a local library, college, etc.) to acquire or sharpen your skills
  - Catching up on developments in your field

Try something new to get the juices going again!

  - Modernizing your resume and learning about key words and other techniques to get yourself past online "screening robots," to an actual person
- Get/Stay organized by
  - Checking out personal finance software such as MoneyDance or Quicken. Besides helping you organize, personal finance software can save you lots of fun-time paying bills and organizing tax information.

- ○ Managing your time efficiently with electronic "To Be Done Lists" synched to your phone, iPad, etc.
- ○ Handling paperwork with "one-touch" paper management techniques.
- ○ If you're comfortable with electronics, consider apps and hardware that scan and organize documents. If you're not so comfortable, organize your correspondence, bills, and account statements in color-coded folders.
- Try something new, and at long last, have some fun. Remember, laughing is actually healthy for you!

Take a Moment and Breathe

When you arrive at the end of your divorce journey, don't forget to congratulate yourself for reaching the finish line of an obstacle course no one wants to run. If you have children, congratulate yourself again for everything you did to make the divorce easier for them.

Then, take a little time to . . . breathe. Reflect upon things you've learned that can be useful as you move forward. While you may have some wistful "the-way-we-were" moments now and again, be

Kemba

thankful for the opportunity to continue along your path free of a dysfunctional relationship from which some people are unable to escape.

Because you never know what new and exciting experience is just around the corner.

Yes, there IS a quiz! Test what you have (or haven't) learned.

1. The main idea of this chapter is:
   A. It's not over 'til the Fat Lady sings, which will be me if I don't start getting to the gym.
   B. Soon I can forget I ever knew what COBRA and QDRO stand for.
   C. There are numerous details to take care of after divorce.

2. Say out loud at your Nearly Single Again Party and unscramble the following key phrases from this chapter!
   A. Stop-coverdi granpetin
   B. Nonile prutops prugos
   C. Mininangati tinnitruo

CHAPTER 18

More Divorce Resources

Come in out of the rain—there's plenty of help available!

"It is never too late to be the person you might have been."

— George Eliot

It would be impossible to list all, or even most of the worthwhile divorce resources available online and in book form, so this chapter does not attempt to do that. Instead, the sites and resources here represent a sampling of high quality general divorce resources plus others that relate to specific issues and demographic groups.

Remember, to learn more about divorce law and practice in your state, always begin with your state's judicial branch or bar association site.

Finding Divorce Professionals

Matrimonial Lawyers

Chapter 4 provides resources for locating matrimonial lawyers including additional details about the following:
- National Professional Organizations:
  - The American Bar Association Division for Bar Services/ Resources offers a database of state and local bar associations at http://www.americanbar.org/aba.html
  - The American Academy of Matrimonial Lawyers at www.aaml .org offers a searchable database of AAML members by location
  - The National Board of Trial Advocacy, a non-profit body accredited by the ABA to certify lawyers in family law trial advocacy: http://www.nblsc.us/

○ The International Academy of Collaborative
Professionals maintains a member directory: http://
www.collaborativepractice.com/

- State Judiciary Websites: These state court sites provide lists of
lawyers certified in matrimonial law in those states that offer
certification. They also can confirm that a lawyer's bar membership
is in good standing, and some provide the lawyer's bar disciplinary
history, if any. You can also check out a lawyer's disciplinary history
at http://hirealawyer.findlaw.com/choosing-the-right-lawyer/
researching-attorney-discipline.html.

You can access your state's website with the links provided by
The National Center for State Courts at http://www.ncsc.
org/Information-and-Resources/Browse-by-State/State-Court-
Websites.aspx.

- Lawyer Referral Services: The American Bar Association website,
www.abanet.org, provides access to lawyer referral services.
Generally, these services provide contact information for attorneys
who are more moderately priced than, for example, the top-notch
but usually top-dollar lawyers you'd find through The American
Academy of Matrimonial Lawyers.

Lawyer referral services are maintained or authorized by state,
county, and city bar associations in each state and U.S. territory. To
find one nearby, select "Public Resource," then "Lawyer Referral
Services," followed by the name of your state.

- Lawyer Rating Services: The most reliable of the rating services is
Martindale Hubbell. Hard copies of the multi-volume set containing detailed information should be available in libraries and some
local law offices. More limited information is available at www
.martindale.com.
- Law School Legal Clinics: Most law schools maintain clinics
offering free or nominal-cost help from law students supervised by
faculty members. A list of your state's law schools can be found at
https://www.martindale.com/. Select "law schools" in the "search
tools" drop-down box.
- Special Interest Bar Associations:
○ American Association of Jewish Lawyers and Jurists: http://
www.jewishlawyers.org
○ Hispanic National Bar Association: www.hnba.com

- ○ National Asian Pacific American Bar Association: http://www
  .napaba.org/
- ○ National Bar Association: www.nationalbar.org (an association
  of African American lawyers and judges)
- ○ National LGBT Bar Association: https://lgbtbar.org/
- ○ National Native American Bar Association:
  http://www.nativeamericanbar.org/
- State Licensing Boards and Professional Organizations: If you are
  unable to access these entities through the national associations at
  the top of this list, search online using the key words below that are
  applicable to your inquiry:
  - ○ Your state's name, plus
  - ○ "State bar association," "unified bar," "county bar association,"
    "judicial department," "courts," "lawyer referral," "licensing
    board" "psychiatrist," "psychologist," "psychotherapist," "family
    therapist," "accountant" or "financial planner," plus
  - ○ "Association," "state," "board," and/or "licensing"

States With Private Bar Associations in Addition to State Bars

A majority of jurisdictions have a single "unified bar" to which all licensed lawyers must belong. Seventeen jurisdictions, however, have both

- A bar administered by the state government to which all practicing attorneys must belong (search the "judicial branch" of your
  state), and:
- A private bar association to which most attorneys belong though
  they are not required to (search your state's "bar association")

If you live in one of the states listed below, you can find authoritative information about divorce in your state on websites maintained by both the state judicial branch and the private state bar association.

Arkansas, Colorado, Connecticut, Delaware, Illinois,
Indiana, Iowa, Kansas, Maine, Maryland, Massachusetts,
Minnesota, New York, Ohio, Pennsylvania, Tennessee, Vermont

Mediators, Collaborative Divorce Practitioners, Mental Health Professionals, Divorce Coaches, Analysts and Planners

The following national professional organization websites can help you locate qualified mediators, mental health professionals, divorce coaches, and divorce financial analysts and planners:

- Academy of Family Mediators: www.mediate.com (contains state directory of family mediators and mediation standards)
- Academy of Professional Family Mediators: https://apfmnet.org/
- Association of Family and Conciliation Courts: http://www.afccnet.org/ (offers resources for divorcing families)
- American Psychological Association: http://www.afccnet.org/
- American Psychological Association - State, Provincial & Territorial Psychological Association Directory: http://www.apa.org/about/apa/organizations/associations.aspx
- Association for Conflict Resolution: http://www.acrnet.org/ (mediators and other ADR practitioners)
- Association of Divorce Financial Planners: http://www.divorceandfinance.org/
- Institute for Divorce Financial Analysts: http://www.institutedfa.com
- International Academy of Collaborative Professionals (IACP): http://www.collaborativepractice.com/
- International Christian Coaching Association: http://iccaonline.net/courses/divorce-coaching

Information on Self-Representation and Legal Aid

- Celebrity divorce lawyer Laura Wasser who shares the author's concern for divorcing spouses, has established www.itsovereasy.com/ an on-line DIY for folks in uncontested divorces.
- Resources for self-represented litigants are available at http://www.srln.org
- Lawhelp.org offers resources for your divorce in your area, including legal aid referrals: http://www.lawhelp.org/
- At https://www.martindale.com/ select "law schools" in the "search tools" drop-down box to find a law school nearby offering free or nominal cost divorce help.

Resources For Federal and State Family Law, and For Making Sound Divorce Decisions

- http://family.findlaw.com/divorce
- Cornell University's Legal Information Institute provides links to federal, state and uniform divorce-related laws: http://www.law.cornell.edu/states
- The Children's Rights Council website contains resources for parents as well as links to state government sites on which you can search your state's law: http://www.crckids.org/
- National Center for State Courts website contains links to your particular state's court website to find pertinent forms and information:
  http://www.ncsc.org
- Lawhelp.org offers resources for your divorce in your area, including legal aid referrals: http://www.lawhelp.org/
- http://public.findlaw.com/bookshelf-mdf/
- The American Bar Association Guide to Marriage, Divorce & Families: a general guide to many of the major issues and options in a divorce, for general background information
- A Judge's Guide to Divorce: Uncommon Advice from the Bench by Judge Roderic Duncan http://www.amazon.com/Judges-Guide-Divorce-Uncommon-Advice/dp/1413305687
- *Picture Your Divorce to See the Right Decisions* by Terry McNiff, Esq.: http://pictureyourdivorce.com/
- See parenting resources below

Parenting And Parenting Education Resources

There's plenty of online help for divorcing parents. The list below contains resources for all parents as well as for particular demographics or parenting issues. The second site is authorized in some jurisdictions to fulfill state parenting education requirements for divorcing parents.

- http://www.divorcedmoms.com—A wide range of articles for divorced and divorcing mothers
- https://www.onlineparentingprograms.com/—An online parenting education program
- http://a.co/d/diYnzdh—Putting Kids First in Divorce: How to Reduce Conflict, Preserve Relationships and Protect Children During and After Divorce by Jeremy Kossen and Mark Baer

- http://www.overcomingbarriers.org/—Overcoming Barriers High-Conflict Divorce Family Camps
- http://iamachildofdivorce.com/what-is-custody-and-visitation/
- http://www.goodreads.com/book/show/8598798-don-t-alienate-the-kids-raising-resilient-children-while-avoiding-high—*Don't Alienate the Kids! Raising Resilient Children While Avoiding High Conflict Divorce* by Bill Eddy
- http://shop.americanbar.org/ebus/store—Enter "My Parents Are Getting Divorced" in the ABA bookstore search box
- www.sesameworkshop.org/—Resources for parents and children ages 2 to 8 to help children understand and cope with divorce
- http://www.childcentereddivorce.com/kids/—Unique approach to breaking the news about the divorce to the children
- www.childcustodyfilm.com—Film and resource site for Larry Sarezky's short film, *Talk to Strangers,* accompanying Parents' Guide and other resources for divorce professionals and parents
- http://www.amazon.com/exec/obidos/ASIN/1886230269/divorcecenter-20—*Parenting After Divorce: A Guide to Resolving Conflicts and Meeting Your Children's Needs* by Philip Stahl, Ph.D.
- www.familysupportamerica.org—Parenting advice, and information regarding child abuse, alcoholism, disciplining children, divorce, and other topics related to families
- www.Familyequality.org—An organization dedicated to family equality for lesbian, gay, bisexual and transgender parents, guardians, and allies

Appraisals and Valuation

The types of property appraised in divorce generally fall into 3 categories:
- "Personal property" such as collectibles, antiques, and artwork
- Real estate
- Business interests

In court-based cases in which valuation may be contested, an appraisal by a qualified expert may be necessary. Using such experts is preferable even in ADR cases or court-based cases on a settlement track. You can learn about the certification and training of experts from these organizations:
- American Society of Appraisers: http://www.appraisers.org/ (search site for appraisers of particular types of property such as jewelry and machinery and technical specialties)

- Appraisal Institute: http://www.appraisalinstitute.org/ (worldwide real estate appraisals)
- Appraisers Association of America: http://appraisersassociation .org/ (for appraisals of collectibles, antiques, artwork, and other personal property)
- Institute of Business Appraisers: http://go-iba.org/
- International Society of Appraisers: http://www.isa-appraisers.org/

Locating More Experts and Consultants

Information about potential expert witnesses such as accountants, actuaries, appraisers and computer experts can be found on national organization websites:

- American Academy of Actuaries: http://actuary.org/
- American Board of Forensic Psychology: http://abfp.com/
- American Board of Vocational Experts: http://abve.net
- American Institute of Certified Public Accountants: www.aicpa.com
- ASIS International (computer forensics): www.asisonline.org
- International Association of Computer Investigative Specialists (IACIS): www.iacis.com
- International Society of Forensic Computer Examiners (ISFCE): www.isfce.com
- National Association of State Boards of Accountancy: http://nasba .org/stateboards/
- National Association of State Mental Health Program Directors (division roster page for Children, Youth and Family Division Members):
  http://www.nasmhpd.org/content/children-youth-and-families-division

If you are unable to access an association or board through the resources above, search online using key words applicable to your inquiry. For example, search:

- Your state's name, plus
- "State bar association," "unified bar," "county bar association," "judicial department," "courts," "lawyer referral," "licensing board" "psychiatrist," "psychologist," "psychotherapist," "family therapist," "accountant" or "financial planner," plus
- Association, state, board, or licensing agency

Relaxation and Meditation

- One of the simplest ways to calm down and find the rhythm that will foster health, awareness and all that good stuff is through breathing meditation. Jon Kabat-Zinn's meditation CD/MP3 downloads are a good place to start. Zinn teaches and guides meditation practice that can take as little as ten minutes a couple of times a day: http://www.mindfulnesscds.com/
- For a more intensive experience, try a retreat at the Insight Meditation Society's terrific facility in Barre, MA: http://www.dharma.org/ or at Spirit Rock in Woodacre, CA https://www.SpiritRock.org
- Learn meditation technique via "Headspace": https://www.headspace.com
- WebMD offers 10 relaxation techniques: http://www.webmd.com/balance/guide/blissing-out-10-relaxation-techniques-reduce-stress-spot
- To learn more about meditation and the Buddhist philosophy underlying it, check out *Listening to the Heart: A Contemplative Journey to Engaged Buddhism* by Kittisaro and Thanissara: https://www.goodreads.com/book/show/22856368-listening-to-the-heart

Dealing With Domestic Violence and Impaired Spouses

In addition to the resources below, you can find local help for domestic violence by searching: [Your state, or your state and county] domestic violence resources. Depending upon your circumstances, you might want to do those searches outside the home. If you do use a home computer, delete the recent search history that your search engine keeps on your computer. And remember, at the very first sign that you or children may be in jeopardy, get to a safe place.

- http://www.womenshealth.gov U.S. Department of Health and Human Services site offering safety planning for abusive situations including safety packing lists, hotline resources, etc.
- The National Domestic Violence Hotline at 800-799-SAFE (7233) or TDD 800-787-3224. If you are concerned that your computer use is being monitored, you can call the hotline numbers for assistance.

- https://www.childwelfare.gov/ Resources on child abuse prevention, protecting children from risk of abuse, and strengthening families.
- http://www.goodreads.com/book/show/9996542-splitting *Splitting: Protecting Yourself While Divorcing Someone with Borderline or Narcissistic Personality Disorder* by Bill Eddy & Randi Kreger.

Support Groups and Post-Divorce Assistance

- *Chicken Soup for the Soul: Divorce and Recovery* by Jack Canfield, Mark Victor Hansen and Patty Hansen
- http://www.divorcedmoms.com Extensive resources for dealing with both divorce and post-divorce issues
- http://divorcesupport.meetup.com locates support groups in your area
- About.com's blogs re post-divorce co-parenting: http://divorcesupport.about.com/od/relationshipwithyourex/?nl=1
- The National Association for Divorced Women & Children; and Post-Divorce Boot Camp for Women: http://www.freshstartafterdivorce.com/
- Faith-based support groups: http://www.divorcecare.org/
- Miscellaneous resources: http://www.thedivorceforum.com/

Yes, there IS a quiz! Test what you have (or haven't) learned.

1. Which of the following are not mentioned in this chapter?
   A. Lawyer Rating Services
   B. Lawyer Dating Services
   C. Lawyer Baiting Services
   D. United States Center for Disease Control
   E. United States Center for Lawyer Control

2. Go to the nearest hill or mountaintop and scream the following key phrases from this chapter. Then unscramble them.
   A. onatarilex dna onatedimit
   B. wrelay gitarn revecis
   C. dienufi rab
   D. on rome dwor semjulb!

Appendix 1

STATUTORY CRITERIA SUMMARY

Note: You can download and print this Summary at https://divorcesimplystated. com/updates-materials/

Date of marriage: _____ /_____/_____

Marriage # for Wife (1st, 2nd, etc.):_____

Marriage # for Husband (1st, 2nd, etc.): _____

Wife's date of birth: _____/_____/_____

Husband's date of birth:_____ /_____/_____

Wife's occupation: _____

Husband's occupation: _____

Ages of children:_____

Children's special needs: _____

Value of property currently in Wife's name: $_____

Property (with values) in Wife's name at time of marriage: $_____

_____

_____

Value of property currently in Husband's name: $_____

Property (with values) in Husband's name at time of marriage: $_____

_____

_____

Value of jointly owned assets: $_____

Wife's employer: _____

Wife's current total annual compensation (salary/wages/commissions/bonus): $_____

Wife's current total annual compensation over the past three calendar years: $_____

If Wife is self-employed, business's gross revenue/net profit from last filed tax return:

$ _____(gross revenue) /$ _____(net revenue)

Husband's employer: _____

Husband's current total annual compensation (salary/wages/commissions/bonus):

$_____

Husband's current total annual compensation over the past three calendar years:

$_____

If Husband is self-employed, business's gross revenue/net profit from last filed tax return: $_____ (gross revenue) /$_____ (net revenue)

Combined annual unearned income (interest, dividends, etc.)

$ _____/yr.

Other expected future sources of income or property such as trusts (source and est. amount):

Wife: $_____

Husband: $_____

Property (with estimated values) received by inheritance or gift during marriage:

Husband: $_____; Wife: $_____

Significant health issues:

Wife:_____

_____

Husband: _____

_____

Educational level, including degrees and dates: _____

Wife: _____

Husband: _____

If applicable, length of time currently out of the workforce:

Wife: _____ Husband:_____

Do you have a prenuptial agreement?_____

If so, when was it signed?_____ /_____/_____

Which, if either, spouse has been primarily responsible for child-raising? _____

Reasons for breakdown of marriage: _____

_____

Appendix 2

Initial Consultation Checklist

[Note: The following is a menu of questions from which to choose a few that are most important to you. To maximize the usefulness of your consultation, bring 3 years of tax returns, a net worth statement, and your Statutory Criteria Summary. You can download this Checklist at http://divorcesimplystated.com/updates-materials/.]

Attorney/Client Relationship and Handling of the Case

1. Are you supportive of ADR? If I decided to mediate, would you act as my review counsel? What do you understand the role of review counsel to be?

2. Do you offer "unbundled legal services" and if so, how might that work most productively in my case?

3. How many of your divorce cases go to trial each year?

4. Do you have a policy of returning calls within a certain amount of time?

5. Will you be available to meet with me before any court proceedings or "four-way" negotiation session?

6. Do you prepare clients prior to depositions or court hearings by cross-examining them as you expect the other lawyer would?

7. How would you try to minimize the impact of the divorce on my children?

8. Is there anything I should do right away to protect my interests (for example, regarding joint bank accounts and credit cards, pending loan applications, upcoming pension elections, etc.)?

9. Are there things that I can get started on (financial affidavit, gathering documents, etc.) that will expedite my case?

10. Are there things that I shouldn't talk to my spouse about?

Attorney's Experience

11. How long have you been practicing family law?

12. What percentage of your practice is devoted to divorces?

13. Besides family law, what other types of law have you practiced?

14. What kind of relationship do you have with my spouse's attorney?

15. Are there any attorneys with whom you would prefer not to work?

Others Who May Become Involved in Your Case

16. In the event a lawyer or guardian is to be appointed for my child, will I be able to participate in the decisions regarding who you would recommend and what role such a representative would play?

17. What other members of the firm will be involved in my case? What experience do they have and what work will they be doing on my case?

18. Is your support staff experienced in family cases? What tasks do they perform?

⚠19. Might an actuary, accountant, or lawyer outside your firm render services such as preparing qualified domestic relations orders? If so, who and what tasks do you envision them performing?

⚠20. Will you personally handle all substantive court proceedings and settlement negotiations?

Fees and Disbursements

⚠21. What is your hourly billing rate and the hourly rates of other lawyers who may work on my case?

⚠22. Will I be charged for non-legal clerical work such as bill preparation and scheduling of appointments?

⚠23. Will you be sending me a letter regarding your fees?

24. Do you charge by the minute, increments (of .1/hour or more), or charge in some other way?

Range of Likely Outcomes

25. Based on my tax returns, net worth statement, and statutory criteria summary, what can you tell me about the range of likely outcomes in my case regarding child custody/access, property settlement, child support, and alimony?

Miscellaneous

26. Do you use software to run alimony scenarios, calculate present value, etc.?

Appendix 3

CHILDREN'S BILL OF RIGHTS
WHEN PARENTS ARE NOT TOGETHER ...

Every child has rights, particularly when mom and dad are splitting up. Below are some things parents shouldn't forget—and kids shouldn't let them—when the family is in the midst of a break-up.

You have the right to love both your parents. You also have the right to be loved by both of them. That means you shouldn't feel guilty about wanting to see your dad or your mom at any time. It's important for you to have both parents in your life, particularly during difficult times such as a break-up of your parents.

You do not have to choose one parent over the other. If you have an opinion about which parent you want to live with, let it be known. But nobody can force you to make that choice. If your parents can't work it out, a judge may make the decision for them.

You're entitled to all the feelings you're having. Don't be embarrassed by what you're feeling. It is scary when your parents break up, and you're allowed to be scared. Or angry. Or sad. Or whatever.

You have the right to be in a safe environment. This means that nobody is allowed to put you in danger, either physically or emotionally. If one of your parents is hurting you, tell someone—either your other parent or a trusted adult like a teacher.

You don't belong in the middle of your parents' break-up. Sometimes your parents may get so caught up in their own problems that they forget that you're just a kid, and that you can't handle their adult worries. If they start putting you in the middle of their dispute, remind them that it's their fight, not yours.

Grandparents, aunts, uncles and cousins are still part of your life. Even if you're living with one parent, you can still see relatives on your other parent's side. You'll always be a part of their lives, even if your parents aren't together anymore.

You have the right to be a child. Kids shouldn't worry about adult problems. Concentrate on your school work, your friends, activities, etc. Your mom and dad just need your love. They can handle the rest.

IT IS NOT YOUR FAULT AND DON'T BLAME YOURSELF.

© 2005 American Academy of Matrimonial Lawyers

Appendix 4

Negotiation Chart

FINANCIAL ISSUES NEGOTIATION CHART— page 1

	Best Case	Worst Case	Likely Result	Support Must-have	Property Must-have	GOAL	Initial offer (Us)	Initial Offer (Them)	Last offer (Us)
SUPPORT									
Guidelines Child Support									
Child Support Extras									
Spousal Support									
TOTAL SUPPORT									
PROPERTY DIVISION (expressed in dollars)									
Non-retirement assets									
Retirement asset									
TOTAL ASSETS									
Debts (subtract fr. Assets)									
TOTAL NET ASSETS									
PROPERTY DIVISION (expressed in percentages)									
Non-retirement assets %									
Retirement assets %									
Debt allocation %									
TOTAL PROPERTY DIV. %									

MOST RECENT PROPERTY DIVISION PROPOSAL DETAILS

Asset Details

	John	Lisa	Total
Fam. Res. (Equity)			
W's Wells Fargo Checking			
H's Bnk America checking			

Liability Details

	John	Lisa	Total
H's Visa cc			
H's M/C cc			

FINANCIAL ISSUES NEGOTIATION CHART — page 2

MOST RECENT PROPERTY DIVISION PROPOSAL DETAILS (cont.)

H's Merrill Lynch stock fund			
W's Merrill Lynch bond fund		W's AmEx cc	
H's collectibles			
Jointly owned condo		W's WF cc	
H's Nissan (Equity)			
W's Acura (Equity)		Orthodontist	
Total Non-Retirement Assets			
W's 401(k) acct.		H's atty. fee	
H's IRA			
W's annuity		W's atty. fee	
Total Retirement Assets			
GRAND TOTAL ASSETS	$	$	$
		TOTAL DEBT	$ $ $

OTHER PROPERTY (not included in amounts above)

Children's 529 accounts			
W's non-marital property			
(Inheritance)			
H's non-marital property			
(Owned before marriage)			
Household furnishings (not valued)			
Term Life Insurance (not valued)			
W'S PERSONAL EFFECTS (NOT VALUED)			
H'S PERSONAL EFFECTS (NOT VALUED)			

Appendix 5

SAMPLE SEPARATION AGREEMENT[3]

AGREEMENT

THIS AGREEMENT, made and entered into as of June ___, 20___ by and between ============, of ============, Connecticut, hereinafter referred to as the WIFE, and ========, of =============, Connecticut, hereinafter referred to as the HUSBAND;

WITNESSETH:

WHEREAS, the parties hereto are HUSBAND and WIFE, having intermarried on ======== in ============, Connecticut; and

WHEREAS, the parties have two children, issue of their marriage, to wit: ========== ======== ========, born on ========; and ========= ========, born on ========, hereinafter referred to as the "children", or the "minor children"; and

WHEREAS, the HUSBAND has instituted an action for a dissolution of marriage against the WIFE, which action is pending in the Superior Court for the Judicial District of Stamford/Norwalk at Stamford, Connecticut and bears Docket No. FA ============ S; and

WHEREAS, irreconcilable differences have arisen between the parties as a result of which their marriage has broken down irretrievably and they have separated and desire to live separate and apart and will continue to live separate and apart; and

WHEREAS, the parties are desirous of entering into an agreement under which reasonable provisions will be made for, among other things, the care, custody, maintenance and support of the wife and the parties' children and for the settlement, adjustment and compromise of all property rights in question; and

WHEREAS, the parties have made a full and fair disclosure of all income and property, as set forth in their financial affidavits and other documents delivered and exchanged between them.

---

[3] **NOTE:** This agreement conforms to the applicable law of the State of Connecticut. Just as the law and customs vary widely among jurisdictions, so to do the form and substance of settlement agreements. This agreement should not be used or adapted for use outside of the State of Connecticut, or anywhere without the advice of a matrimonial lawyer

NOW, THEREFORE, in consideration of the premises and the mutual promises and undertakings herein contained and set forth and for good and valuable consideration made over by each party to the other, the receipt and sufficiency of which is hereby acknowledged, it is covenanted and agreed as follows:

ARTICLE I - SEPARATION

1.1 The parties may and shall at all times hereafter live and continue to live separate and apart for the rest of their natural lives. Except as is otherwise provided herein, each party shall be free from interference, authority and control, direct or indirect, by the other as fully as if he or she were single and unmarried. Each may reside at such place or places as he or she may select. The parties shall not molest each other or compel or endeavor to compel the other to cohabit or dwell with him or her, by any legal or other proceedings for the restitution of conjugal rights or otherwise.

ARTICLE II - SPOUSAL AND CHILD SUPPORT

2.1 Effective July 1, =====, the HUSBAND shall pay to the WIFE as alimony, during her lifetime to, or on behalf of, the WIFE, until the sooner of her death or her remarriage, or June 30, =====, whichever shall first occur, the sum of $============ per month, payable on the first day of each month. Subject to paragraph 2.2 below, the duration of alimony hereunder shall be non-modifiable, except in the event that either of the parties shall qualify for SSI benefits as a result of disability.

2.2 Notwithstanding anything contained herein to the contrary, in the event that the WIFE shall cohabitate with another person in the manner contemplated by Connecticut General Statutes sec. 46b-86(b), the HUSBAND shall have available to him the rights to seek termination, modification or suspension of alimony as set forth in said statute.

2.3 Effective July 1, =====, the HUSBAND shall pay to the WIFE as child support on the first day of each month the sum of $============ per month per child for the period set forth in CGS §46b-84.

2.4 It is the desire of both parties that their children be afforded the opportunity to obtain a higher education. The parties agree that notwithstanding any rights they might have to terminate support of the child pursuant to CGS §46b-84, that had their marriage remained intact, they would have provided support to their children for higher education. Accordingly, the parties agree that they shall contribute in proportion to their respective abilities at the time, as may be necessary, to the cost of each child's tuition, room & board, dues, fees, registration and application expense relating to each child's undergraduate education provided however, that such obligation shall terminate when the child attains the age of twenty-three (23) years. These provisions shall specifically survive the attainment of majority by any child and shall be enforceable by any means available to enforce awards of support for minor children as well as any other legal or equitable remedies.

2.5 In addition to the foregoing, the HUSBAND shall reimburse the WIFE as additional child support until the younger of the children attains the age of nineteen (19), up to a total of $==== per year of the expense the WIFE has incurred during such year for each child's "extraordinary expenses". The term "extraordinary expenses" shall be defined as the cost of summer camp, tutoring, lessons and activities related to athletics and the arts (and related equipment and accessories.

OR:

2.5 In addition to the foregoing, the parties shall divide evenly the cost of the "extraordinary expenses" [provided however that the HUSBAND's total annual obligation pursuant to this paragraph shall not exceed the total of $=========. The term "extraordinary expenses" shall be defined as the cost of summer camp, tutoring, lessons and activities related to athletics and the arts (and related equipment and accessories.

ARTICLE III - CUSTODY AND VISITATION

3.1 Legal Custody; Primary Residence. The parties shall have joint legal custody of their children, until each said child attains her majority, with the children having their primary residence with the WIFE, subject to the HUSBAND's rights to a reasonable and substantial amount of time with the children pursuant to the parenting plan set forth below.

3.2 Parenting Decisions. The parties shall confer with each other on all important matters pertaining to the children's health, education, religion, welfare and upbringing, with the view to arriving at a harmonious policy, and shall make joint decisions calculated to promote the children's best interests. All communications regarding such decisions will be between the parties directly, without interference or participation by either party's new spouse, paramour or any other third parties except those whom both the HUSBAND and the WIFE have specifically agreed may so participate. Each party shall have sole decision making authority with respect to the routine, day to day decisions affecting the children, when the child is with that party, subject to the children's activities upon which the parties have previously agreed.

3.3 Maintaining Relationship; Access. The parties shall exert every reasonable effort to maintain free access and unhampered contact between the children and both parents, and to foster a feeling of affection between the children and both of their parents. Neither party shall do anything, which may estrange the children from the other party nor injure the opinion of the children as to their mother or father nor act in such a way as to hamper the free and natural development of the children's love and respect for the other party.

3.4 Information. The parties shall keep each other reasonably informed as to all important matters pertaining to the children's health, education, religion, welfare and upbringing. Both parties shall be entitled to obtain full information from any physician, therapist counselor, etc. attending any of the children for any reason whatsoever and from any teacher, tutor or school giving instruction to any of the children. The parties shall share in a timely manner all notices and information relating to school meetings & events as well as the children's extracurricular activities, so as to enable both parties to attend such meetings and events.

3.5 Illness of Children. In the event of the illness or personal injury of any of the children, the first party to learn of such illness or injury shall notify the other immediately and each party shall keep the other informed at all times of the whereabouts and condition of said child. For purposes of this paragraph, the word "illness" shall mean any sickness or ailment, which requires the services of a physician; and the word "injury" shall mean any harm to a child as a result of which the services of a physician are reasonably required. During any illness or injury, each party shall have access to the ill or injured child in addition to the other rights provided for herein.

3.6 Parenting Plan. The parties shall speak weekly to address issues relating to the children. In addition, the parties shall confer at the beginning of the third month of each calendar quarter to decide upon matters relating to the children including but not limited to scheduling the HUSBAND's weekend and other time with the children, which parent shall have the children with him/her during holidays and extended weekends, plans for the children's birthdays, travel plans that involve the children and the like. In making such decisions, the parties shall be guided by the following principles:

A. The HUSBAND shall have the children with him on alternate weekends.

B. The parties shall share as equally as is possible given the HUSBAND's work schedule, the children's school vacations during the school year.

C. During the summer, the HUSBAND shall have the right to have the children with him (and to take them away on vacation) for up to three periods of a week each, subject to his work schedule and the WIFE shall have the right to have the children with her (and to take them away on vacation) for up to three periods of a week each.

D. Neither parent shall be entitled, without the other parent's prior agreement, to take the children away prior to December 26th during the Christmas school vacation, in order to afford each of the parents the opportunity to celebrate Christmas holiday with the children as they agree during their preceding quarterly conference.

E. The parties acknowledge that circumstances, including but not limited to the children's ages, the children's school & activity schedules, and the parties' work schedules will change from time to time requiring the parties to alter the manner in which they implement the above recited principles set forth in subparagraphs A – C of this paragraph 3.6. In addition, the parties acknowledge that unforeseen events may upon occasion make it difficult or impossible for them to fulfill their obligations or exercise their rights pursuant to this ARTICLE III. Accordingly, the parties agree to exert their best efforts to be flexible in implementing their parenting plan so as to foster the spirit of cooperation inherent in their parenting plan in a manner calculated to avoid conflict.

F. The WIFE shall have the children with her on Mother's Day. The HUSBAND shall have the children with him on Father's Day. The parties shall both have access to the children on the children's birthdays and shall be entitled to attend the children's birthday parties.

G. Miscellaneous

1) Upon occasion, if the HUSBAND encounters difficulties in transporting the children pursuant to the parenting plan, the WIFE shall exert her best efforts to assist with such transportation.

2) In the event that either parent wishes to take the children or any of them out of the country, that parent must obtain the other parent's prior consent, which consent shall not be unreasonably withheld.

3) The parties may by mutual agreement arrange for the children to spend time with the HUSBAND in addition to that which is set forth in this parenting plan, so long as such arrangements do not conflict with the children's pre-scheduled activities.

3.7 Relocation.

A. The parties acknowledge that it is in the best interests of their children to have both parents living in proximity to them. Accordingly, the parties agree that in the event that the WIFE shall consider moving with the children more than fifteen miles from her current residence in ====== CT, she shall immediately notify the HUSBAND of such possibility. Thereupon the parties shall confer without delay to determine in good faith to what extent their parenting plan can be revised so as to accommodate the WIFE's contemplated move without substantially reducing the amount of time that the HUSBAND spends with the children or otherwise adversely affecting the HUSBAND's relationship with the children. Nothing contained in this subparagraph shall be deemed to abridge the HUSBAND's right to seek appropriate judicial remedies including but not limited to injunctive relief should the circumstances so warrant.

B. If such relocation does occur, the parties agree and understand that special efforts shall be required of both of them to implement a revised parenting plan that is as consistent with the parenting plan provided for herein as possible. In the event that such relocation does occur and it substantially increases the cost to be incurred by the nonresidential parent in spending time with the children, the parties will attempt to agree on what if any allocation of this increase in cost between the parties would be appropriate. The Superior Court for the Judicial District of Stamford/ Norwalk at Stamford shall retain jurisdiction to determine the issues set forth in this paragraph.

C. In the event that one of the parties decides to move to a new residence that is not outside the geographical area set forth in subparagraph 3.7A above, such party shall inform the other party of such decision as soon as is reasonably possible. Thereafter, the parties shall attempt to agree upon such changes to the parenting plan as the new circumstances reasonably require, preserving as much of the existing plan as is possible.

3.8 Assistance with Future Disputes. In the event that disputes arise between the parents with respect to the interpretation, implementation and/or enforcement of this Article III, the parents shall attempt to resolve all such disputes other than those related to relocation, with the assistance of Dr. ==========, or a mutually agreeable mediator or mental health professional. Nothing in this Agreement however shall be deemed to abridge either party's right to seek immediate judicial relief including injunctive relief, where such party believes in good faith that such relief is necessary to avoid imminent and substantial harm to the children, or to either of them.

ARTICLE IV - HEALTH RELATED EXPENSES

4.1 The HUSBAND represents to the WIFE that he presently has a health insurance program through his employer. The HUSBAND agrees that he will, at his own cost and expense, maintain said program or its equivalent for each of the children for so long as he is able to cover them under said policy (including his rights to COBRA coverage), with his current or any subsequent employer, including such period of time after the children reach the age of majority, as may be permitted by such plan or such subsequent plan under which the HUSBAND becomes insured.

4.2 The parties shall divide evenly the cost of any uninsured medical, vision care, surgical, hospital, physical therapy and nursing costs, as well as costs of prescriptive drugs, dental expenses and orthodontia expenses for each of the minor children. The HUSBAND's obligations hereunder however shall be conditioned upon his agreement that such expenses are necessary, which agreement shall not be unreasonably withheld. The parties shall divide the children's reasonable psychiatric and psychological expenses evenly. The parties' obligations pursuant to the preceding sentence however shall be conditioned upon their agreement that such expenses are necessary, which agreement shall not be unreasonably withheld.

4.3 The HUSBAND agrees to cooperate with the WIFE in the event of any claims made pursuant to the insurance program above provided and the WIFE shall have all rights, including the right to process any claims in the HUSBAND'S name and to receive direct payment from the insurer, to which she is entitled pursuant to Conn. Gen. Stat. §46b-84(e). The Superior Court shall retain jurisdiction of the pending dissolution action for the purpose of entering orders in accordance with this paragraph.

4.4 Until the marriage of the parties is terminated, the HUSBAND shall continue to have the WIFE as the beneficiary on any health insurance plan he has available through his present employer or which is in existence at this time. When the marriage of the parties is dissolved, the HUSBAND shall assist the continuation of the WIFE coverage thereunder for so long as is permitted by law, provided the same can be continued without additional cost or expense to the HUSBAND. If such coverage can be continued only with additional cost or expense, the WIFE shall have the option of paying for such additional cost and expense and remaining a beneficiary of said insurance plan. The HUSBAND shall promptly process any of the WIFE'S health insurance claims which have accrued prior to the date of judgment in the pending dissolution action, for the benefit of the WIFE.

ARTICLE V - PAST AND FUTURE DEBTS

5.1 It is the intention of the parties that, except as otherwise provided in this Agreement, all liability of whatsoever nature, on the part of each to the other, past, present and future, actual or potential, whether arising from their relationship as husband and wife, or otherwise, shall cease and terminate absolutely and forever.

A. The HUSBAND shall pay and be solely responsible for all those debts (whether they be joint debts of the parties or otherwise) designated as "HUSBAND'S Sole Debts and Obligations" on Schedule "A" attached hereto. As to all such debts, (as well as any other debts not enumerated on Schedules A or B incurred by the HUSBAND solely in his name during the course of the marriage) the HUSBAND shall hold the WIFE free, harmless and shall indemnify her from any and all liability, including reasonable attorney's fees arising from, or in connection, with said liabilities.

B. The WIFE shall pay and be solely responsible for all those debts designated as "WIFE'S Sole Debts and Obligations" which appear on Schedule "B" attached hereto. As to all such debts (as well as any other debts not enumerated on Schedules A or B incurred solely by the WIFE during the course of the marriage) the WIFE shall hold the HUSBAND free, harmless and shall indemnify him from any and all liability, including reasonable attorney's fees arising from, or in connection with, said debts.

5.2 Except as provided herein, the parties covenant and agree that neither of them will at any time hereafter contract any debt or debts, charges or liabilities whatsoever for which the other party hereto, or his or her property or estate, shall or may be or become liable or answerable, nor use nor pledge the credit of the other party, and each agrees that he or she will at all times keep the other party free, harmless, and indemnified from any and all such liabilities, including reasonable attorney's fees and any expenses incurred as a result of a breach of the provisions of this paragraph, arising after the date hereof. Notwithstanding anything herein to the contrary, the WIFE shall be solely responsible for, and shall keep the HUSBAND free, harmless and shall indemnify him from any and all liability, including attorney's fees arising from, the payment of the mortgage note and real estate taxes with respect to the former marital residence; except as to those payments the HUSBAND elects to pay directly pursuant to paragraph 2.2 above.

ARTICLE VI - DIVISION OF PROPERTY

6.1 The WIFE shall be entitled to exclusive possession of the former marital residence (hereinafter sometimes referred to as "the Residence") until such time as the WIFE elects to sell it. Notwithstanding the foregoing, the parties agree that the WIFE shall list the Residence for sale no later than March 1 ======, after which time she shall in good faith take all steps to sell the Residence as are reasonable and customary under the circumstances. The parties agree that the net proceeds of such sale (i.e. gross sales price less the balance due of the presently existing mortgages and other encumbrances, property taxes due, closing fees and expenses including, but not limited to, conveyance taxes, broker's commissions, attorney's fees, recording fees and adjustments normally made to the purchase price at the time of closing) shall be divided between them equally at the time of closing. Notwithstanding the foregoing, the parties shall have the following rights:

A. The WIFE shall have the option in lieu of selling the marital residence, to pay to the HUSBAND 50% of the "net market value" of The Residence. "Net market value" shall be calculated in the same way as "net proceeds" of sale as defined above except that the gross sales price shall be determined (in the event that the parties cannot agree on a gross sales price) by realtors in the following manner. The WIFE shall designate a realtor or appraiser to determine a fair market value for the marital residence. If the HUSBAND does not agree to such value, he shall also appoint a realtor or appraiser to make a determination as to fair market value. In the event that the two said realtors are not able to agree upon a fair market value, the two realtors so appointed shall choose a third realtor or appraiser, whose determination of fair market value shall be binding upon the parties. The HUSBAND'S entitlement shall then be calculated as if The Residence had been sold and the gross sales proceeds had been equal to the fair market value so determined, less 5% brokers' commissions.

B. In the event that the WIFE decides to sell the Residence, The HUSBAND shall have a right of first refusal to purchase the WIFE'S share of the Residence at 50% of the fair market value mutually agreed upon by the parties (or failing agreement, as determined by Realtors as set forth in sub-paragraph A above), or on the terms of any bona fide offer received to purchase it. The HUSBAND shall exercise his rights pursuant to this sub-paragraph B within seven (7) days of the parties agreeing on a listing price, or the WIFE notifying him of an offer to purchase, whichever shall apply. Notwithstanding the foregoing, in any conveyance of the WIFE's interest to the HUSBAND pursuant to this paragraph B, the fair market value or bona fide offer price shall be reduced by 5%; i.e., the likely amount of brokers' commissions had the Residence been sold on the open market. The parties shall stipulate as part of any listing agreement for the sale of the Residence that no commissions shall be owed if the Residence is conveyed to the HUSBAND pursuant to this paragraph.

6.2 The parties acknowledge and agree that despite the fact that the HUSBAND shall continue to be a legal owner of the marital residence, he hereby relinquishes and waives any and all rights to occupy said residence, or to require any person to vacate the premises under any circumstances whatsoever. Subject to paragraph 6.3 below, the WIFE shall have the sole responsibility for the upkeep and maintenance of the marital residence. The WIFE shall hold the HUSBAND free, harmless and shall indemnify him from any and all liability, including attorney's fees arising from, or in connection with the mortgages, real estate taxes and insurance relating to the marital residence, as of the date of execution of this Agreement.

6.3 With respect to any capital replacements or improvements, or repairs costing in excess of $_____, that are necessary to the normal and customary use and continued structural integrirty of the Residence, the parties shall divide the cost of same ==% to be paid by the WIFE, and ==% to be paid by the HUSBAND. The HUSBAND'S responsibilities pursuant to this paragraph 6.3 shall terminate once he has received or is entitled to receive his share of the net proceeds of sale of The Residence; or alternatively, until he has received 50% of the net market value pursuant to paragraph 6.1 above.

6.4 As to any capital gain that may be realized upon the sale of the marital residence, the parties agree that each shall be solely responsible for his/her share, respectively, of any taxes which may be levied as a result of said sale and that each shall satisfy his/her liability for such taxes respectively at their respective options, by qualifying for a deferment or exemption or by paying the tax due. The parties hereby acknowledge the WIFE'S equal contribution to the purchase and maintenance of said real estate and it is agreed that the tax basis shall be equally divided between the parties hereto. It is further acknowledged that the marital residence has been maintained as the principal residence of both parties prior to the date of this Agreement.

6.5 The parties shall divide the remainder of their assets as reflected on Schedule "C" annexed hereto.

6.6 With respect to the parties' personal property not otherwise specifically provided for in this Agreement, the parties shall divide such items as reflected on Schedule "D" annexed hereto.

6.7 Except as expressly provided for herein, the WIFE waives and relinquishes any and all claim of right title or interest to the HUSBAND's Wells Fargo Index Fund 401(k) plan and IRA account currently located at Fidelity Investments. The HUSBAND represents that he has no interest or entitlement, vested or non-vested, in any other pension, retirement or similar plans other than said IRA and said Wells Fargo Index Fund 401(k) plan, whether through his present or any past employment.

6.8 Except as expressly provided for herein, the HUSBAND waives and relinquishes any and all claim of right title or interest to the WIFE's IRA account currently located at Fidelity Investments. The WIFE represents that She has no interest or entitlement, vested or non-vested, in any other pension, retirement or similar plans other than said IRA, whether through his present or any past employment.

6.9 The parties shall make available to each other all documents regarding the acquisition and improvement of The Residence, for the purpose of determining the cost basis and the capital gain upon sale.

6.10 The WIFE shall continue to have sole possession of the silver ======== automobile leased by the parties. In addition, the WIFE shall have sole possession of the ============ which the parties are leasing. The WIFE shall hold the HUSBAND harmless and shall indemnify him as to the lease payments, taxes, insurance and any other expense incurred pursuant to said automobile leases.

6.11 The HUSBAND has redeemed for the WIFE's benefit certain Frequent Flyer mileage points. The WIFE waives any claim whatsoever to any additional Frequent Flyer mileage points owned by the HUSBAND.

ARTICLE VII - LIFE AND DISABILITY INSURANCE

7.1 The HUSBAND represents, warrants and acknowledges that his life is insured under a life insurance policy set forth on Schedule "E" annexed hereto, which policy is hereinafter referred to as the "Policy" and has a total of death benefits of approximately $===========. The Policy shall be dealt with as hereinafter stated.

7.2 The HUSBAND represents and warrants that the Policy is now in full force and effect; that he is the sole owner thereof, and that he has not borrowed against, pledged or hypothecated the same, nor shall he in the future borrow on, or encumber the same.

7.3 The HUSBAND has designated the WIFE in the capacity as trustee for the benefit of the minor children, as beneficiary to the extent of ========= of life insurance which amount shall be payable to the WIFE for the benefit of the minor children in a lump sum upon the death of the HUSBAND, provided however that the HUSBAND'S obligation pursuant to this paragraph shall terminate upon the termination of his child support (including college education expense) obligation hereunder.

7.4 The HUSBAND has designated the WIFE as beneficiary to the extent of ======== of life insurance, which amount shall be payable to the WIFE for her benefit in a lump sum upon the death of the HUSBAND, provided however that the HUSBAND'S obligation pursuant to this paragraph shall terminate upon the termination of his spousal support obligation hereunder.

7.5 The HUSBAND shall, at all times during the above specified periods, maintain life insurance in the above amounts for the benefit of the WIFE in her capacity as trustee for the benefit of the minor children, and for the benefit of herself as hereinabove provided, and shall pay all premiums, dues and assessments due thereon required to be paid by him to maintain said insurance in full force and effect and shall make arrangements for all premium notices and premium receipts to be sent to the WIFE at her request. Notwithstanding the foregoing, the HUSBAND shall have the right to reduce the amounts of life insurance coverage as follows:

A. As to the insurance for the benefit of the minor children, the HUSBAND may reduce such coverage by $_____ on or after _____20__ .

B. As to the insurance for the benefit of the WIFE, the HUSBAND may reduce such coverage by $_____ on or after _____20__

Said payment of premiums by the HUSBAND shall not be construed as alimony includable in the income of the WIFE.

In the event that any insurance policy required by this Article is not in full force and effect as provided for herein, or for any other reason the intended beneficiary does not receive the full benefits contemplated in this Article, the intended beneficiary will be a creditor of the HUSBAND'S estate for the full amount that would otherwise have been received, and the intended beneficiary shall be entitled to be paid by the estate as a charge against said estate, having priority over all heirs, beneficiaries, legatees and devisees in the full amount (plus the amount of any unpaid premiums), and not charged with or reduced by any taxes.

7.6 The WIFE hereby renounces for herself and in her capacity as trustee or guardian of the minor children any right, title or interest in the life insurance proceeds provided for in this Article; provided however, that such renunciation shall become effective on the dates that the HUSBAND's applicable insurance obligations terminate pursuant to this Agreement. Said renunciation shall be self-effectuating, and neither the WIFE nor any agent, representative or other person acting on her behalf will make any claim to such proceeds after the dates mentioned in the preceding sentence. To the extent that the WIFE remains a beneficiary on any such policy beyond the dates on which the HUSBAND's applicable insurance obligations terminate, this Agreement shall be deemed a directive to the applicable insurance company to distribute the proceeds as instructed by the HUSBAND's personal representative with respect to his estate

7.7 The HUSBAND shall have the right to substitute comparable new insurance for the policies set forth in Schedule "D" provided that prior to such substitution, the HUSBAND shall notify the WIFE in writing of the name of the insurance company, the policy number, the amount, the name and address of the broker, and appropriate endorsements, but no substitution shall in any way permit the HUSBAND to provide less than the death benefits required under this Article.

7.8 In the event that the HUSBAND shall fail to pay any premiums necessary to maintain the insurance coverage required above, the WIFE shall have the option to pay such premiums and the HUSBAND shall be indebted to the WIFE in the amount of the sums so paid by the WIFE. If the WIFE pays any such premiums in accordance with the provisions of this Paragraph, the HUSBAND shall reimburse her in the amount so paid on or before the first day of the first month following any such payment made by the WIFE.

7.9 The HUSBAND shall, upon request, provide satisfactory evidence to the WIFE showing his compliance with the provisions of this Article. The HUSBAND shall also exert his best efforts to cause the insurance companies to notify the WIFE in the event of a premium default, or any request for a beneficiary change, or in the event of any requests for a loan against said insurance.

7.10 The HUSBAND shall maintain in full force and effect the disability insurance available to him through his current employment or subsequent employment so long as it continues to be available to the HUSBAND at no cost, for so long as he is obligated to maintenance and/or pay child support pursuant to this Agreement. The HUSBAND represents that the amount of the disability insurance benefit which he presently has available to him is ======== per month. The HUSBAND agrees that he shall not voluntarily reduce the present amount, percentage or term of disability insurance available to him.

ARTICLE VIII - TAXES

8.1 The parties shall file joint federal and state income tax returns for the calendar year ====.

8.2 The HUSBAND shall pay any and all taxes due on said ====== returns, and shall be entitled to any refunds thereon. The HUSBAND estimates that there will be a federal income tax refund of approximately $==========.

8.3 In the event of any future claims, demands and/or suits with respect to foreign, federal, state or municipal income taxes (and/or penalties and interest) for any year in which the parties filed a joint income tax return the HUSBAND shall be responsible for ====%, and the WIFE shall be responsible for ====% of any amounts determined to be due. If either party receives notice of any audit or tax proceeding involving any such joint tax return, he/she shall immediately notify the other or his/her representative of such proceedings.

8.4 The parties agree that this Agreement has been negotiated and entered into with the understanding that the only payments to be made by the HUSBAND to the WIFE pursuant to Article II above intended to be alimony are the $======= per month payments provided for in paragraph 2.1 above. Thus the HUSBAND shall have no right to deduct, and the WIFE shall not declare as income for federal and state income tax purposes any payments made hereunder except those provided for in said paragraph 2.1.

8.5 For income tax purposes, the WIFE shall be considered the custodial parent of the minor children in any taxable year in which the custody arrangement provided for in Article III of this Agreement is in effect. Accordingly, the WIFE shall be entitled to the dependency exemptions and child tax credits for the children to the extent permitted by applicable law, if and when said exemptions again become available to claim. If the HUSBAND claims an exemption or child tax credits in violation of the terms hereof, he shall reimburse the WIFE the amount of any additional income tax liability including interest and penalties, as well as attorneys' fees that result from his claiming such exemptions and/or tax credits.

8.6 The HUSBAND shall be entitled to the income tax deductions for mortgage interest and property taxes related to the residence for the year 2018. The HUSBAND shall be entitled to the property tax deductions in future years to the extent permitted by applicable law; provided however, that in the event that the HUSBAND cannot deduct any portion of said property taxes due to deduction caps, the parties shall allocate to the WIFE that excess portion of property taxes which the WIFE may be entitled to deduct under applicable law. The parties acknowledge and agree that the implementation of this paragraph may require advance planning, and that they will cooperate in such planning in order to maximize the benefits of the property tax deduction.

ARTICLE IX - LEGAL COUNSEL

9.1 The parties hereto declare and acknowledge that each has received advice from independent legal review or consulting counsel of his or her own selection, in connection with the mediation of their divorce. The WIFE has been represented by Attorney ============== of ==========, Connecticut and the HUSBAND has been represented by Attorney ============== of =========, Connecticut.

9.2 Each party shall pay his/her own attorney's fees in connection with the execution of this Agreement and the pending dissolution action.

9.3 In the event that it shall be determined by a Court of competent jurisdiction that either party shall have breached any of the provisions of this Agreement or of any judgment or decree incorporating by reference or otherwise this Agreement or portions thereof, the offending party shall pay to the other party reasonable attorney's fees, Court costs and other expenses incurred in the enforcement of the provisions of this Agreement and/or judgment or decree incorporating any or all of the provisions hereof. The parties agree that no adjudication of contempt will be necessary to invoke the provisions of this paragraph regarding payment of attorney's fees.

ARTICLE X - RELEASES

10.1 Except as to the obligations created hereunder, and reserving to the parties hereto the rights set forth in this Agreement and the right to bring and/or maintain any action for dissolution of marriage for any reason or cause heretofore or hereafter occurring, including the right of the parties to prosecute the action now pending, each party hereby releases and relinquishes to the other party, and to his or her heirs, executors, administrators or assigns, any and all claims or rights which the parties hereto have with respect to any property whether real, personal or mixed, belonging to such other party, and without limiting the foregoing, each party hereby waives and releases to the other party and to his or her heirs, executors, administrators and assigns, all rights to share in any of the property or Estate of such other party, which has arisen or may hereafter arise by operation of law or otherwise, and hereby specifically waives and releases all right of dower or courtesy and all rights to share in the estate of the other party under the intestacy laws of any jurisdiction and all right of election to take against any last will and testament of such other party, whether executed prior to or subsequent to the execution of this Agreement, and all rights to secure administration of the estate of such other party.

10.2 Notwithstanding the provisions of the preceding paragraph, the parties agree and acknowledge that all obligations of both parties to effectuate property transfers; support obligations of the HUSBAND; and obligations of the HUSBAND to keep in full force and effect life insurance and medical insurance for the benefit of the WIFE and/or the parties' children, shall survive the death of the respective party, and shall constitute a charge upon such party's estate.

ARTICLE XI - REPRESENTATIONS

11.1 The HUSBAND represents to the WIFE that an affidavit dated June ___, 20===
setting forth a true and accurate statement under oath of his income, expenses, assets and liabilities has been delivered to the WIFE and will be filed in Court in connection with the final hearing in the pending action. The HUSBAND represents that he has no other assets or income except those set forth in said Affidavit.

11.2 The WIFE represents to the HUSBAND that an affidavit dated June ___, 20====
setting forth a true and accurate statement under oath of her income, expenses, assets, and liabilities has been delivered to the HUSBAND and will be filed in Court in connection with the final hearing in the pending action. The WIFE represents that she has no other assets or income except those set forth in said affidavit.

11.3 Each party hereto agrees that no representations of any kind whatsoever have been made to him or her as an inducement to enter into this Agreement other than the said affidavits and the provisions of this Agreement.

ARTICLE XII - DECREE AND BINDING EFFECT

12.1 The parties covenant and agree with each other that this Agreement shall be submitted to the Superior Court, J.D. of Stamford/Norwalk at Stamford, Connecticut, for approval and for incorporation of the substantive provisions hereof. The parties agree that neither will ask for any different or greater rights than those specified herein at the time of said submission and that they will abide with and be bound by the provisions of this Agreement whether or not incorporated in such judgment. This Agreement shall not merge with any judgment but shall survive any such judgment and remain in full force and effect, but shall be subject to modification as hereinafter provided.

ARTICLE XIII - MODIFICATION OF AGREEMENT

13.1 Subject to Article II above, in the event either of the parties to this Agreement shall undergo any substantial change in circumstances, either party may petition a court of competent jurisdiction to seek modification of any support provisions of any judgment for divorce or dissolution of the marriage of the parties which incorporates the terms of this Agreement, which modification shall be based upon a substantial change in circumstances of one or both of the parties, or one or more of the parties' minor children. In the event such Judgment shall be modified neither party shall seek to interpose any of the terms of this Agreement which shall differ from the Judgment as modified, and this Agreement shall be automatically deemed modified in the same manner and to the same extent as the Judgment.

13.2 No change shall be made in the foregoing covenants and agreements except by instrument in writing duly executed by the parties hereto, or except by virtue of a modification of any judgment for divorce or dissolution of the marriage of the parties which incorporates the terms of this Agreement.

13.3 Notwithstanding anything herein to the contrary, the parties hereby acknowledge that should the WIFE become employed, the first $======= in annual income earned by the WIFE shall not be deemed to be a substantial change in her circumstances, or to entitle the HUSBAND to modification. Any court in adjudicating any modification motion which either party might file in the future shall deem the WIFE to have been earning such amount of income at the time of the judgment of dissolution of the parties' marriage.

ARTICLE XIV - ENTIRE AGREEMENT

14.1 Both the legal and practical effect of this Agreement in each and every respect and the financial status of the parties have been fully explained to both parties by their respective counsel, and they both acknowledge that it is a fair agreement and is not the result of any fraud, duress or undue influence exercised by either party upon the other or by any other person or persons upon either, and they further agree that this Agreement contains the entire understanding of the parties.

ARTICLE XV - SEVERABILITY

15.1 In the event that any provision of this Agreement is deemed to be unenforceable or contrary to law by any court of competent jurisdiction, the remaining provisions shall remain in full force and effect, and be binding upon the parties.

ARTICLE XVI - DOCUMENTS

16.1 The parties agree that each shall execute and deliver any and all documents reasonably necessary to effectuate the provisions of this Agreement.

ARTICLE XVII - ORIGINAL COPY

17.1 This Agreement may be executed in any number of counterparts, any one of which, executed by both parties, shall be deemed to be the original, although the others are not produced.

ARTICLE XVIII - NOTICES

18.1 Each party shall at all times keep the other informed of his or her place of residence and business and shall promptly notify the other party of any change, giving the address of any new place of residence or business. All notices or other communications given or made hereunder shall, unless expressly provided herein to the contrary, be given by certified or registered mail to the other party at such party's principal residence.

ARTICLE XIX - LAW APPLICATION

19.1 All questions as to the validity, construction or effect of any provisions of this Agreement, or of this Agreement as a whole, shall be determined with reference to and in accordance with the laws of the State of Connecticut.

ARTICLE XX - HEADINGS

20.1 The paragraph headings herein are for convenience only and shall not be construed to limit or affect any provisions of this Agreement.

ARTICLE XXI - MEDIATION

21.1 The parties have reached the agreements contained herein by way of mediation, with the assistance of =============== who has acted as mediator. The parties understand and acknowledge that Mr. ======== has not represented either of them but has acted solely as a neutral mediator. The parties further understand and acknowledge that Mr. ======== has not consulted with either party out of the presence of the other, except with the prior permission of the other party. Finally, the parties agree and acknowledge that their communications in such mediation are, and shall remain, privileged and confidential.

21.2 The parties shall be jointly and severally liable for any fees remaining due to Mr. ========.

21.3 The parties agree to submit to a mutually agreeable mediator any issues, which may arise with respect to the implementation, enforcement or interpretation of this Agreement. Mediation shall be defined for purposes of this Agreement as a process wherein the parties negotiate differences they have, under the direction and guidance of the mediator. Said mediator shall not be appointed as an arbitrator. The cost of the mediation shall be borne equally by the parties. In the event that mediation fails to resolve the issue(s) in dispute, either party may petition a court of competent jurisdiction to determine such issue(s). The parties agree however that each shall negotiate in good faith before resorting to any judicial proceedings.

IN WITNESS WHEREOF, the parties have hereunto set their hands and seals on the day and year first above written.

[signature lines and notary public acknowledgment if necessary]

Index